Protection
and Industrial Policy
in Europe

Protection and Industrial Policy in Europe

Joan Pearce and John Sutton
with Roy Batchelor

The Royal Institute of International Affairs

Routledge & Kegan Paul
London, Boston and Henley

First published 1985
by Routledge & Kegan Paul Ltd,
14 Leicester Square, London WC2H 7PH,
9 Park Street, Boston, Mass. 02108, USA
and Broadway House, Newtown Road,
Henley-on-Thames, Oxon RG9 1EN
Set by Hope Services, Abingdon
and printed in Great Britain

Library of Congress Cataloging in Publication Data

Sutton, John, 1948–   Pearce, Joan, 1944–
  Protection and industrial policy in Europe.
  Bibliography: p.
  Includes index.
1. Europe—Commercial policy.   2. Tariff—Europe.   3. Free trade and
  protection—Protection.   4. Industry and state—Europe.
  I. Sutton, John.   II. Bachelor, R.A.   III. Title.
HF1531.S86 1985   382.7'3'094   85-10835

ISBN 0-7102-0733-6

Contents

Acknowledgments

This book was commissioned by the Department of Trade and Industry from the Royal Institute of International Affairs. Neither the Department nor the Institute is responsible for the opinions expressed in this book, which are attributable solely to the authors. Chapters 1 and 3–6 were written by Joan Pearce, Chapters 7–12 by John Sutton, Chapter 13 by Roy Batchelor and Chapters 2 and 14 by Joan Pearce and John Sutton.

The Institute and the authors are grateful for the opportunity to conduct and present their research. Most of the chapters were discussed by a study group which met at the Institute during 1983 and 1984. The authors wish to thank the members of that group for their comments, for indicating further lines of inquiry and for assistance with sources and data. All or parts of the manuscript were read in draft by Willem Buiter, David Currie, Peter Neary, Alasdair Smith and William Wallace. We are indebted to them for commenting so expeditiously and so thoroughly. Particular thanks are due to Richard Portes, whose unstinted and unerring advice throughout the project contributed greatly to its successful outcome. Susan Walker's diligent and painstaking assistance in preparing the final manuscript was much appreciated.

Joan Pearce is most grateful to all those in government departments and in the private sector in France, Germany and the United Kingdom, the Commission of the European Communities and the British Embassy in Bonn who took time and trouble to explain and discuss policy issues. The knowledgeable, efficient and cheerful response of the RIIA's Press Library to a wide range of requests was also invaluable.

John Sutton would like to thank Louise Orrock for her excellent research assistance; the librarians in the Chatham House Press Library for providing such invaluable service; David de Meza, Brian Hindley, Elhanan Helpman and Tony Venables for a series of enlightening discussions; and Alasdair Smith and Peter Neary for their penetrating comments on an early draft.

J.P., J.S. and R.B.

1 Introduction

At the end of 1982 the Department of Trade (now the Department of Trade and Industry) asked the Royal Institute of International Affairs, together with the National Institute of Economic and Social Research, to undertake a study of the idea that the European Community should shift towards a more strongly protectionist external-trade policy. This book is the RIIA's contribution to that study.[1] In it we seek to explain why this shift is advocated and to examine the case that can be made for it. We also consider what form such a policy might take, the prospects for member governments agreeing to adopt it, and what is actually most likely to materialize. We approach these questions in terms of both policy-making and economic analysis.

The growing support from the late 1970s for a more protectionist external-trade policy was in part the European expression of the new protectionism which was a feature of the trade policies of most developed countries. But it also reflected a specifically European debate about the future of the Community as a manufacturing and trading entity. In this chapter we discuss new protectionism and the European debate, indicating the main themes that are developed in the rest of the book.

It may be helpful to say something at the outset about terminology. We mean by protection those measures directly applied to trade: export subsidies, import tariffs and levies, quotas and other quantitative restrictions, and so forth. But, as is shown, trade can be equally affected by policy measures which operate through other parts of the external economy, such as the exchange rate, or through the domestic economy, such as subsidies and taxes. Intervention means all government measures which influence the economy, so it includes both protection and other measures. All these terms – protection, intervention and the individual measures which they encompass – are used in a neutral technical sense. We set out the advantages and disadvantages which policy-makers see in them and which economic analysis indicates. Protectionism we take to mean advocating systematic adoption of measures of protection.

The fact that some domestic measures can be equated with protection, in that they have comparable effects on international competitiveness, is not as widely appreciated as it should be. It was acknowledged in the original articles of the General Agreement on Tariffs and Trade (GATT), though the sporadic references to domestic subsidies gave no clear guidance for dealing with them. To draw the line between measures which have an impact on trade and those which do not is difficult. It is still surprising that in 1984 the OECD, for example, could publish a document entitled *Competition and Trade Policies: Their Interaction*, which suggests that these are two separate areas of policy between which there is some overlap. The bureaucracies of some countries also perpetuate the idea that policies can be compartmentalized, and that only the one actually labelled 'trade policy' is relevant to consideration of trade issues. This book adopts a comprehensive approach, taking account of all aspects of policy which determine a country's international trading position.

New protectionism

The new protectionism is variously attributed to economic recession, intensified by two oil shocks; to the emergence of new economic powers (notably Japan, but also the newly industrializing countries – NICs); to technological change; and to the advent of floating exchange rates. It should more accurately be described as renewed protectionism. During the 1950s and 1960s protectionism subsided, but by no means disappeared, and the past decade has witnessed a reversal of this trend. For the most part this has meant an intensification of existing measures of protection. Tariffs have remained at the low levels achieved by the successive rounds of GATT negotiations, however, so resort to non-tariff barriers (NTBs) has been greater. There have been some new departures in the form of voluntary export-restraint agreements and in aspects of industrial policy.

Just as some of the instruments of the new protectionism have been in existence for a long time, so too have some of the arguments that are advanced to support it. They can be divided into two broad categories. The first recognizes the relevance of free trade as an organizing principle but points out certain shortcomings. Sometimes the consequences of free trade may be thought unacceptable for income distribution or for employment in a particular sector, and protection is seen as a way of easing adjustment. Or the industry may be considered a strategic one which must be retained even if it is not competitive. If an industry suffers a temporary loss of competitive advantage, perhaps as the result of 'dumping' by foreign competitors, protection may enable it to hold on to its market share until competitive conditions are restored. Some believe that trade with countries of different socio-economic systems is undesirable and hence should be subject to protection. There is also a view that because developed economies have lost their technological monopoly in some goods they should restrict imports of those goods from those countries which have only recently begun to produce them. Moreover, it is argued that the case for free trade assumes that there are no distortions in the economy, but if in fact there are distortions in product markets, protection may be able to bring about a better allocation of resources, and if there are distortions in labour markets, protection may result in a higher level of employment.

This first set of arguments has cropped up in one guise or another over many years. The second set of arguments can more appropriately be described as new. It rests on the neglect, in the traditional defence of free trade, of certain key features of international trade as it has developed in recent decades. Economies of scale and the related phenomenon of intra-industry trade in differentiated products are frequently cited examples. In certain industries there are significant economies of scale; it is then argued that protection may ensure that a domestic producer has a market large enough for production to be viable. Another area which trade theorists are accused of ignoring, at least until recently, is industrial policy, in particular the special problems posed by 'research and development' (R&D) activities. In R&D-intensive sectors a firm which invests in developing a product often does not fully capture the benefits. Some suggest that this can be dealt with by subsidizing R&D activities; others propose that new products be protected until they are established. Some industries are natural oligopolies, that is, there is room for only a handful of firms in the world market. It is argued that public-procurement policies can be used to ensure that one firm rather than another, and hence one country rather than another, retains a place in the market. During the past few years trade theory has been developing rapidly in the areas highlighted by imperfect competition and industrial policy. We explain how the progress in theory elucidates the trade and industrial policy issues.

We examine both sets of arguments and show that whereas some are spurious others are valid, though usually they need to be carefully qualified. There is an important practical qualification: most arguments are for temporary protection – to tide an industry over while it adjusts to a change in competitiveness, suffers a short-lived loss of competitiveness, or develops a new product – but measures of protection once introduced are often difficult to remove and tend to become permanent. We conclude that protection is often detrimental and sometimes beneficial. In some instances there is a case for intervention but not for protection; in others, protection could yield benefits but a better practicable alternative exists. In our conclusions we differ not only from many proponents of protection but also from its more entrenched opponents, who argue against any intervention, even under imperfect competition.

The European debate

The debate in Europe about trade and industrial policy during the past few years has been fuelled by two parallel concerns. There has been growing disquiet at Europe's loss of competitiveness in world markets, and there has been anxiety that the integration process in the Community has reached a stalemate. These concerns have prompted consideration of how the Community might pursue what are often seen as interdependent objectives: to re-establish its international competitive position, and to move towards a more unified market and structure of industrial production. Various proposals have been made over a number of years: to open up public purchasing, to set up a much wider system of European standards, to increase cooperation in research, and to promote joint projects. None of these was intrinsically protectionist. But more recently a comprehensive approach has been proposed entailing liberalization of the internal market, industrial policy and external-trade protection. The argument for this is that lowering internal barriers would create a single market in Europe, comparable to that of the United States, thus achieving one of the basic objectives of the Treaty of Rome. But European firms have fallen badly behind, and the benefits of this large domestic market, notably economies of scale, might be lost to their US and Japanese competitors. Industrial-policy measures should be devised to enable them to catch up. To ensure that while this is happening they and not their competitors reap the benefits of the internal market, they should be afforded external protection. Lowering internal barriers is an objective common to both 'Europrotectionists' and 'liberals'. What divides them is whether this should be accompanied by industrial policy and greater external protection.

A package of proposals was presented by the European Commission at the meeting of the European Council in Copenhagen in December 1982. The aim was to establish Europe as an industrial power able to take a leading role in the world. This would require the removal of barriers to trade within the Community coupled with what the President of the Commission, M. Thorn, called an active external-trade policy. A spokesman defined this as meaning that any industrial sector in the Community whose existence was threatened must be better protected by trade restrictions. M. Thorn himself said that Europe would need external protection for its advanced-technology industries for at least five years to enable them to reach international levels of competitiveness. As a result of their discussions the Community heads of state and government agreed to make a serious effort to strengthen the internal market; to speed up research related to industry, energy and technology; and to channel substantial funds into investment loans for energy and industry. They also paved the way for the Commission to negotiate with Japan voluntary restraints on several of the products which it exported to the Community.

The link between lowering internal and raising external trade barriers was very much in line with French views. President Mitterrand stressed that this dual strategy was necessary if the Community was to reconquer its own domestic market. British thinking was less structured but went along with the practical implications of this strategy. Mrs Thatcher was reported to favour export-restraint agreements with Japan and perhaps with the NICs. West Germany, in company with Denmark and the Netherlands, showed some apprehension at the turn of events. But Herr Kohl, who was attending his first European Council meeting, seemed to be chiefly concerned with the political implications of a confrontation with the United States. He distinguished protection aimed at the USA from protection aimed at Japan and the NICs by observing that there were no Japanese, South Korean or Latin American forces manning Checkpoint Charlie. By the end of the Council meeting the Community was embarking, at least with regard to Japan, on a more systematic use of protection in its external-trade policy. A Commission official explained, 'What we are witnessing is the emergence of something new, which could be called managed protection, European-style.'

In September 1983 the French government submitted a memorandum to the European Council on a common industrial and research area. It too argues for a comprehensive approach incorporating the development of Community-wide industrial policies, a reduction in trade barriers within the Community and more effective external protection. Its thesis is that in most advanced-technology sectors Europe is not competitive with the United States and Japan. To rectify this will require the pooling of research efforts and a domestic market larger than that of any single member state. Hence industrial cooperation at the European level is essential, internal barriers should be brought down and temporary external protection may be necessary. The memorandum proposes advances along these three tracks. First, there should be more cooperation in funding and conducting research, more Community infrastructure projects, and new forms of aid for Community firms. Alliances and cooperation between European firms should be encouraged by adapting national competition policies, revising Community company law and affording preferential treatment in the form of Community aid and public purchasing. Second, the fragmentation of the European market should be reduced by greatly extending common standards and revising national public-procurement policies. Third, sectors which are in difficulty and emerging industries should be given external protection, the Community should equip itself with stronger trade-policy instruments, apply strict criteria to direct investment coming into the Community and tighten the definitions of a Community product and a Community firm.

The memorandum's main argument for linking industrial policy to lowering internal barriers and reinforcing external protection to that the emergence of new products requires industrial subsidies to stimulate their development and protectionist policies to guarantee the producer a secure domestic market over some initial period. There is a further rationale for linking internal liberalization with external protection which is not very explicit in the memorandum. In the view of the French government there are gaps in the Community's external protection. If barriers within the Community are lowered, France will be exposed through these gaps. Hence more robust external protection is a necessary pre-condition for the relaxation of internal barriers. A more controversial line is taken by some proponents of stronger external protection, notably Wolfgang Hager (1981), who insist that this will suffice to bring about liberalization within the Community. On this view, external protection is merely the price to be paid for liberalization of the internal market.

This is different from the French memorandum, which offers several quite separate reasons for moving to a more protectionist stance towards the rest of the world. These are much the same as some arguments underlying the new protectionism. With some the European dimension is not very important. For example, the case for intervention to ease adjustment problems by reducing sectoral unemployment in the clothing and textile industry is much the same whether posed in a UK framework or with respect to the Community as a whole. The additional consideration which arises at the Community level is that of policy coordination, aimed at avoiding beggar-my-neighbour policies by individual member states. In other contexts the European dimension is more central. For example, the presence of significant economies of large-scale production is vital to the argument that a unified and protected European market could achieve the cost reductions essential for export success.

The most distinctive characteristic of the Europrotectionist case is its insistence on treating industrial policy, internal-market policy and external-trade policy as integral parts of a strategy for tackling the Community's problems. This is consistent with the observation made earlier in this chapter that policies cannot be compartmentalized, though concurrence in that point does not imply endorsement of the prescriptions of Europrotectionism.

From a British perspective there may seem to be something lacking in these arguments, for there is a widespread view that protection is basically about 'reducing aggregate unemployment'. As we note later, in the presence of aggregate unemployment associated with rigid (real) wages, it is true – under some quite strong assumptions, whose plausibility is open to question – that a particular form of generalized tariff protection can lead to a reduction in aggregate unemployment. Within the UK, this line of argument (associated with the Cambridge school) has dominated the public debate on protectionism in recent years. Arguments of a similar kind were also relevant to recent French policy, in that they could be used to suggest a rationale for protectionist measures as a part of the reflationary policies of the Mitterrand government.[2] By and large, however, the kind of generalized protectionism which is motivated by these arguments has been receiving less attention within the European context recently. The emphasis has shifted towards consideration of specific protectionist measures, motivated by a wish either to ease the problems of declining sectors or to promote certain industries which offer a strong potential for expansion. The questions posed by the 'macroeconomic' analyses of protection remain important, whether we are discussing specific or general measures. None the less, advocates of the specific protectionist measures which have received particular attention recently have usually chosen to put their case on the basis of quite different arguments. The change of emphasis rests partly on the belief that, as the world recession continues, any move to generalized protection is almost certain to provoke retaliation by major trading partners. The fear of a vicious circle of retaliatory moves leading to a highly protectionist global economy, in the manner of the 1930s, has been an important restraining influence.

Advocacy of protectionism rests in practice on the hope that retaliation is unlikely. In the current European debate, it is more or less explicitly assumed that increased protection is likely to evoke a strong response from the United States, and this is a major bar to Europrotectionist shifts. It is partly for this reason that so much attention has been placed on competition with Japan and the NICs; there appears to be a widely held view that retaliation is less likely from a trading partner with whom one has a negative trade balance. How seriously policy-makers fear retaliation also depends on their assessment of the size of the gains from trade. A policy-maker considering protection who believes these gains to be small, and hence that there is relatively little to lose from retaliation by a trade partner, will be more likely to take that risk. This point underlies claims that the European market is sufficiently large to allow economies of scale to be exploited fully across manufacturing industry.

For those who would like to see an itinerary before embarking on detailed exploration, the next chapter provides a synopsis of the rest of the book. Other readers should omit this chapter. In Chapter 3 we sketch some of the background by summarizing the evolution of the GATT. A catalogue of the principal measures of protection currently applied by the Community and its member states is set out in Chapter 4. Chapters 5 and 6 analyse the stances on trade and industrial policy of the Commission and member states, particularly France, Germany and the UK.

In Chapter 7 we present the classical argument for free trade. We note that the presence of wage inflexibility generates sectoral unemployment, as the pattern of world trade changes over time. We then develop the rationale for policy intervention aimed at slowing down the rate of job loss in declining sectors. Chapter 8 considers the experience of intervention aimed at easing 'adjustment problems' in the European clothing and textile sector.

We turn in Chapter 9 to the particular issues which arise when there are significant scale economies in production, and survey the recent literature on international trade in this setting. We attempt to develop some broad conclusions about the implications of this literature for the analysis of commercial policy. Chapter 10 pursues these issues in the context of the European car industry.

In Chapter 11 we examine the case made in the French memorandum for using commercial policy as a concomitant of industrial policies for R&D-intensive industries. Chapter 12 introduces a second element of the French memorandum: its plea for a more relaxed approach to European antitrust law. We analyse the events surrounding the failure in 1983 of the attempt to merge Grundig with Thomson-Brandt, which provided the main stimulus for this strand in the memorandum.

Chapter 13 investigates the 'macroeconomic' aspects of protection, in particular the use of the exchange rate as an active tool of macroeconomic policy. Finally, Chapter 14 provides a brief summing-up.

2 Synopsis

This synopsis is provided for readers who would like a general view of the book's arguments and conclusions before tackling them in detail. In condensing we have curtailed or omitted altogether some important points. To appreciate the reasoning properly it is essential to read the detailed explanation in the relevant chapter. Reading the synopsis is not a substitute for reading the book.

The evolution of the GATT (*Chapter 3*)

As a result of the various rounds of GATT negotiations since World War II tariffs have been reduced and held at a low level. This has made existing non-tariff barriers (NTBs) more evident. Furthermore, when policy-makers have wanted to introduce new measures of protection they have usually turned to NTBs. The Tokyo round of negotiations, which was completed in 1979, reached agreement on several codes which set out how the GATT articles were to be applied to some NTBs. These included export subsidies, domestic subsidies, government purchasing policies and technical standards. Whether the codes are being observed, or how effective they are, is so far not clear.

A number of issues have yet to be dealt with in the GATT but are likely to be on the agenda of the next round of negotiations. Trade in agriculture and in services (not covered in this book) remain outside the GATT. Textile trade is regulated through the Multi-Fibre Arrangement (MFA), which is a formal derogation from the GATT. Some comparatively new types of protectionist measure are not included in the GATT. The Tokyo round failed to agree on a code on safeguards, which would have encompassed safeguards already provided for in the GATT and voluntary export restraints (VERs). These are bilateral agreements between governments or industries to limit the quantity of exports of a product. They are a major innovation in the protectionist armoury of the past decade or so. Trade distortions resulting from governments' treatment of foreign direct investment are a recent development yet to be discussed in the GATT. So too is the extensive support given to high-technology goods because of the sizeable investment in R&D which they require.

The free-trade foundations of the GATT are being challenged. Some people take the view that the GATT should be directed towards the more realistic objective of fair trade rather than the unattainable objective of free trade. At a theoretical level it is argued that the model of trade which underlay the GATT does not easily tally with the present-day realities of world trade.

Trade and industrial policy in the European Community
(*Chapters 4, 5 and 6*)

In theory the member states of the European Community pursue a unified external-trade policy, but in practice they retain a substantial measure of autonomy. In common with other countries the Community has significantly lowered tariffs. It has, however, increased its use of other trade measures, such as anti-dumping actions, safeguards and VERs. Statistics indicate that of the major economies in the EC, France and Italy use protectionist measures more than the UK, which in turn uses them more than Germany. In recent years the Commission has sought to regularize national measures and to assume more responsibility for determining policy.

Most internal trade proceeds without much hindrance, but there are numerous barriers to trade in specific products or circumstances. Some derive from the differences among the external barriers of member states. Member states with national restrictions on imports of certain goods from outside the Community seek to prevent those goods being imported through another member state. Other barriers are national measures which affect imports originating in other member states. Many are clearly intended to be protectionist. The most common are rules concerning technical safety and public health. The Commission has argued that removing barriers to create a unified internal market is essential to regenerate Europe's industrial strength. Member states have endorsed this view, though some have insisted that elimination of internal barriers should be accompanied by reinforcement of external barriers. Although progress has been made in achieving agreement on removing barriers, member states are slow to take action.

Industrial policy is still largely a national responsibility, but the Commission has begun to intervene more. Industrial subsidies provided by member governments and aid for direct inward investment are being scrutinized more, and in some cases proscribed. At the same time, the Commission has become more active in promoting advanced technology, both through waivers from competition law and through devising Community programmes for specific sectors. Member governments and industrialists have been giving more thought to European industrial policy. In particular, the French government has circulated a memorandum on a unified European industrial and scientific area.

In general the official positions of France, Germany and the United Kingdom represent the three groups into which member governments of the Community divide on trade and industrial policy. The virtues of free trade are extolled in Germany but doubted in France. British policy aims to maintain the present degree of openness in world trade. It is accepted by member governments and by the Commission that Europe is protectionist, though no more so than the United States and Japan. There is disagreement as to whether in this situation Europe should become more or less protectionist. Commission officials would like to achieve a reduction in European protection, but believe that it would be unwise to steer a naïvely free-trade course.

The French government is keen to see internal barriers lowered but does not want to expose the economy to the gaps it sees in the Community's external protection. Hence it argues that increased external protection should accompany reduced internal protection. The German administration cautiously welcomes the French position on internal market policy but regrets the connection being made between this and the demand for a more robust external-trade policy. For successive British governments, lowering internal barriers has been a major objective. The present government has strongly endorsed the Commission's initiatives and has sought to use French insistence on linkage between external and internal trade policy to advance the opening up of the internal market.

Of the various documents which have been circulated on European industrial policy the French government's memorandum is the most detailed, the most comprehensive and the most radical. The thesis of the memorandum is that in most advanced-technology sectors Europe is not competitive with the United States and Japan. To rectify this will require a domestic market larger than that of any single member state. Hence industrial cooperation at the European level is essential, internal barriers should be brought down and temporary external protection may be necessary. The memorandum proposes that to make cooperation between European firms more attractive, member states should channel more of their R&D expenditure through the Community for the financing of joint projects. Cooperation should also be made easier by revising national company and competition legislation. National competition policies should be applied at least at the Community level. The internal barriers that the memorandum specifically recommends should be freed from national restraints are technical standards and public contracts. Because Europe is starting out later than the United States and Japan, and because these two countries have protected their advanced-technology industries, Europe should be prepared to introduce temporary protection of infant industry. Also in the context of external trade, the memorandum advocates defining criteria for direct investment in the Community from third countries. Such investment should be encouraged only if it makes a net contribution to employment in the Community as a whole or if it introduces new technology into Europe.

In Germany the contention that Europe is lagging behind the United States and Japan in advanced technology is more accepted than it was, but is not as widely acknowledged as it is in France. The French memorandum is viewed with mixed feelings. Severe criticism is directed at proposals which are seen as reducing competition, whether in the domestic market through increased government intervention or in the external market through increased protection. German officials agree that there should be more cooperation in basic research but believe that Community financial support should be confined to projects of a European dimension in which Community action would yield greater benefits than national action, and that it should be kept as far as possible from production and from the market. Cooperation between European firms is welcome if the firms take the initiative. The role of government is to provide a climate conducive to innovation and investment by firms. Similarly, the role of the Commission is not to initiate projects but to construct a real common market and to promote free cooperation and competition that is not distorted by subsidies. From a German perspective, cooperation among European firms is complicated by some elements in the existing structure of European industry, notably the French nationalized companies.

German competition policy gives priority to maintaining a competitive situation in the German market; the suggestion that the Community is the relevant market is resisted. The German administration favours liberalization in technical standards and public procurement. It dismisses the case for protecting infant industry. This might seem useful in the short run, but temporary protection tends to become permanent, and in the long run it would be very damaging. Attitudes towards inward investment are generally more positive than in France.

The British government has for some time been perturbed by the failure of its high-technology industry to keep pace with those of the United States and Japan. It attaches importance to making Community action in research innovation and new technologies more effective, particularly in facilitating cooperation between firms, though it emphasizes the need to control costs. It favours joint European ventures and has pressed for the removal of impediments to them, and it advocates directing competition policy towards promoting industrial development as well as preventing distortion of competition. Proposals to open up the internal market are received warmly in the British administration, though there are reservations about measures designed to benefit other member states but not third countries. As in Germany, temporary strengthening of external protection is rejected. British officials also object to the suggestion that the Community should establish criteria for direct inward investment from outside the Community, on the grounds that such a system would be unjustified and difficult to apply.

Views of the French memorandum vary between different parts of the Commission. Those responsible for trade policy are unenthusiastic, but those responsible for industrial policy are keen to promote new technology in Europe and are inclined to favour infant-industry protection.

The classical argument for free trade, and the clothing and textiles industry (*Chapters 7 and 8*)

The central idea underlying the classical view is comparative advantage. This is explained by taking a situation where there are a number of countries which differ from one another in their relative endowments of the various factors of production – land, raw materials, labour of various skill categories, and so on. In the absence of trade, these differences will be reflected in differences in the *relative* prices of various products between one country and another. This difference in the relative prices of products provides an opportunity for mutually beneficial trade. By exchanging a good which is less costly to produce in terms of domestic resources for one which is more so, each country can enlarge its range of consumption possibilities. In other words, trade allows each country to specialize in the production of those goods in which it has a *comparative* advantage relative to its trading partners. Hence the advantage of a free-trade regime is that it permits an optimal allocation of resources throughout the global economy. It follows that any restriction on trade alters the pattern of resource allocation away from that optimum and thus imposes a 'dead-weight loss' on the global economy. The classical argument also presupposes that, under a free-trade regime, domestic resources are allocated optimally, so that for the domestic economy, too, any restriction on trade imposes a 'dead-weight loss'.

But there are qualifications. First, the argument applies to countries not large enough to influence world prices. For a country whose purchases and sales are large enough to influence world prices, the imposition of a (sufficiently small) tariff will be superior for it in welfare terms. This qualification does not, however, figure significantly in the policy debate.

Second, the global pattern of comparative advantage is constantly changing and, though free trade remains optimal for the domestic economy as a whole, there are changes in employment and income distribution from which some individuals gain while others lose. If those who suffer a 'permanent' loss in real earnings are to be compensated, it is better to do this directly by payments out of general taxation while maintaining free trade, than to adopt measures of protection which result in a loss of efficiency for the domestic economy as a whole.

Third, changes in the pattern of employment and output across domestic industries, resulting from shifts in comparative advantage, may impose costs both on firms and on workers. The adjustment cost which most concerns policy-makers is that associated with frictional unemployment, which arises as workers displaced from one industry take time to find jobs elsewhere. Substantial falls in wage rates and rapid job loss in the contracting sector may be unacceptable. But if workers and firms are fully compensated they will have no incentive to migrate to other industries and the economy will be deprived of the efficiency gain that could be achieved if resources were reallocated. In practice a compromise must be struck. There is a further complication: the trend of import penetration varies over time and is very difficult to forecast. This makes it hard to calculate the optimal employment subsidy. It may be possible that some form of quantitative restriction is desirable, which becomes operative when imports surge above the anticipated level.

Fourth, the classical argument presupposes that under free trade resources are allocated optimally. If this is not the case, restrictions on trade might possibly be justified on welfare grounds, in so far as they affect the original misallocation of resources. A standard reply to this argument is that a policy aimed directly at eliminating the misallocation of resources is superior to trade restrictions in welfare terms.

Fifth, the assumption of 'no distortions' in the labour market implies that wages adjust rapidly to eliminate any 'involuntary' unemployment. But if wages adjust slowly there may be sectoral unemployment in declining industries. This we have already considered. Another possibility is that, because of a fall in aggregate demand, the economy is operating below the 'full employment' ceiling. This suggests the question: can protection raise aggregate employment? In recent years interest has focused on this question in the case where there is 'real-wage inflexibility', i.e. unemployment stems from the fact that real wages are inflexible downwards. The imposition of a tariff on imports raises consumer prices relative to wages, but if the tariff revenue is used to subsidize domestic products (thus lowering their price relative to wages) the value of the real wage can be maintained. The switch in expenditure from imports to domestic goods brings about an expansion of domestic activity and hence a rise in aggregate employment. A necessary assumption, however, is that productivity does not fall as output expands.

A serious shortcoming of the models which have been offered to justify this view is that they assume that real wages are rigid but do not explain why. Without knowing, we cannot judge whether an alternative policy instrument might offer a superior option. Quite apart from this, however, a general argument can be advanced against the assumption – vital to this view – that protection will not affect domestic price–cost margins. For protected firms are likely to raise price–cost margins in response to the relaxation of competition from imports, and to the extent that they do, the scope for expanding aggregate employment is reduced.

Given some rationale for protection, how do the various instruments compare? A quota can be set so as to achieve the same level of imports as a particular tariff level. The disadvantage of the quota is that the revenue which the authorities would derive from the tariff is instead given away to foreign suppliers in assigning quota rights. Thus a quota is inferior to a tariff, though to what degree depends on how the quota is allocated. VERs are the least desirable instrument for the domestic economy because the optimal response of foreign suppliers is to raise their price until domestic demand falls to the level of agreed sales. None the less, policy-makers rely more on quantitative restraints than on tariffs, because they are easier to negotiate: they embody some concession to the trading partner; and they avoid going through the GATT procedures for raising tariffs.

Clothing and textiles illustrate some of the points made in the discussion of the classical argument for free trade and some of the problems confronting Community trade policy. Clothing is a highly labour-intensive sector in which Europe is unlikely to enjoy a comparative advantage. There is a strong case for running down much of it. By contrast, in textiles there has been a shift to more capital-intensive techniques, which make it possible that the sector could survive in Europe under a liberal trading regime.

Bilateral arrangements made by the United States with Japan

and some NICs in the early 1970s caused European fears that exports from those countries might be diverted to the Community. Consequently the Community joined the United States in negotiating the first MFA in 1978. This aimed to control the growth of imports from a number of low-cost producers by setting a series of quotas. Further fears then emerged that curbing imports from these countries would result in an increase in imports from elsewhere, notably the Mediterranean countries, so separate restrictions on imports were negotiated with them.

Policy in this area has generated tensions within the Community. In some member states (Germany, the Netherlands) the industry has adjusted successfully while in others (France, Italy, United Kingdom) it has not. Those which have not adjusted continue to press for protection while those which have are opposed to it. Furthermore, after negotiating quotas for the Community as a whole the Commission partitions them among member states. Hence the level of external protection is not uniform across the Community. This has led some member states to restrict the movement of imported textiles within the Community, thus undermining the unity of the internal market.

Whereas the MFA mainly affects imports from low-cost producers, most of the Community's imports come from other industrialized countries. The Community has not acted to stem these imports, probably from fear of retaliation.

The present situation represents the worst of all worlds. The Community has neither a common external policy nor a unified internal market in clothing and textiles. Furthermore, it has chosen the most easily negotiable instrument, quantitative restrictions, which are a relatively disadvantageous device for the Community. There was a case for temporary protectionist measures to slow down the speed at which the industry had to adjust to the changing pattern of comparative advantage. Adjustment was achieved in some member states but not in others. Those which have adjusted now have little to gain from protection, and there is no convincing economic case for increasing it.

Scale economies and the protectionist case, and the car industry (*Chapters 9 and 10*)

We next turn to the role of economies of scale, and so to the implications of departures from perfect competition. Imperfect competition comes in a variety of forms, which makes things much more complicated. It opens up the possibility that intervention could be welfare-improving, but the desirable form of intervention may be a subsidy rather than protection; indeed, protection may still be inferior to *laissez-faire*. Each type of imperfect competition needs to be considered individually.

Several important features of international trade, especially trade between developed countries, cannot be analysed within the confines of the classical model. In many industries the fixed costs of setting up production are substantial. The more a firm produces, the lower its average cost per unit because these fixed costs are spread over a larger volume of output; in other words, they enjoy economies of scale. Such markets necessarily depart from perfect competition. In these cases, price must exceed marginal cost at equilibrium – otherwise profit would be negative and some firms would leave the industry. Under perfect competition, by contrast, price is driven down to the level of marginal cost. For the equilibrium price to lie above marginal cost, either the number of firms must be small (oligopoly), or the various firms must offer differentiated products. Either of these situations permits a reduction in the degree of price competition, and so allows price to exceed marginal cost.

The concept of comparative advantage suggests that a country exports the products of one set of industries while importing others. Trade between industrialized economies, however, is characterized by a two-way flow of similar products (intra-industry trade). This can be accounted for if the products of the various firms in each industry are differentiated. Differences in taste among consumers provide an incentive to firms to differentiate their products. On the other hand, the presence of economies of scale ensures that each country will not produce all possible varieties.

If a market is not perfectly competitive the possibility opens up that there may be some form of intervention which is welfare-improving. Can protection improve welfare? Its effects depend on the particular characteristics of each industry, but two features often recur. First, a relaxation in the degree of international competition may cause domestic price–cost margins to rise. Second, if protection leads to an increase in the profitability of domestic firms, new firms may eventually enter the domestic market and some foreign firms may exit from it or migrate into the domestic economy. In the case of a domestic monopolist facing imports from a competitive world industry, protection is particularly harmful. For example, suppose his product is identical to that offered on world markets: if a tariff is imposed his optimal response is to raise his price to just below the post-tariff price of imports. Protection raises the monopolist's profits at the expense of a fall in output and employment in his industry and higher prices for consumers. If there is no tariff the monopolist's optimal response is to lower his price to just below the price of imports. He then captures all domestic sales, but the adverse effects of protection on the economy are avoided.

What of a situation in which there are increasing returns to scale, and a domestic producer finds that at low levels of output his unit costs are higher than the world price but that if he could 'capture the domestic market' his unit costs would be at or below the world price? There may be a case for intervention here in the form of a subsidy to the domestic producer: protection would only make matters worse.

In cases where the world market is oligopolistic, matters become much more complex. In certain circumstances it is possible that protection may be welfare-increasing, relative to *laissez-faire*, for the domestic economy so long as there is no retaliation. But there may be a practicable alternative instrument which is superior in welfare terms to protection. In other circumstances, protection may make things worse, relative to *laissez-faire*.

Another case is that of an industry in which a large number of firms produce differentiated products. It is often assumed that free entry will drive (pure) profits to zero. The effect of a tariff is to reduce the profits of foreign firms and increase those of home firms. This causes exit abroad and entry at home, a process which may be achieved by the migration of foreign firms to the domestic economy. If so, there is a welfare gain which derives from more varieties being available more cheaply to domestic consumers, in that they do not carry a price premium to cover costs of transport. Other advantages may also result: profits of migrant firms add to the domestic tax base; and some of the profits may accrue to workers in the form of higher wage rates. A vital assumption is that the tariff does not lead to a rise in domestic prices relative to costs.

In the discussion both of the classical argument and of increasing returns to scale, protection is assumed not to invite retaliation. Yet policy-makers are deterred by the prospect of retaliation, so it is worth investigating what might be lost by a slide into protectionism, or alternatively, what is gained by engaging in trade. Empirical studies based on the classical model have suggested gains of 1 per cent of GNP or less for a wide range of economies. Estimates which encompass the contribution of enhanced economies of scale emanating from intra-industry trade have so far been undertaken only for the Canadian economy. These found that unilateral elimination of current Canadian tariffs would yield gains of 2–5 per cent of GNP and multilateral free trade 8–10 per cent of GNP. No similar study has yet been done for the EEC. It is possible that the percentage gains for the (larger) European economy might be smaller than for Canada, in so far as an integrated European market might be large enough to exhaust economies of scale in some industries.

The car industry offers an example of sizeable economies of scale: eight firms share 70 per cent of the world market. The main European producers are France, Germany, Italy and the UK. Of these only the German industry seems confident of its ability to survive under free trade. The EEC and EFTA together account for about three-quarters of the exports from France, Germany and Italy but less than half of those from the UK. The main source of imports is Japan, which has about 10 per cent of the total EEC market, though its share differs widely among member states. Italy in effect excludes imports from Japan almost totally; France imposes quotas limiting imports to 3 per cent; imports to the UK are subject to a VER agreed at industry level and currently account for about 11 per cent of the UK market; imports to Germany were for a time subject to a government understanding limiting their annual growth to 10 per cent and currently account for about 10 per cent of the market. Japan's share in the markets of the six other member states, which produce few or no cars, is 20 per cent or more. When Japanese manufacturers increase their sales in Europe those who lose most are French and Italian manufacturers, partly because they produce similar models. Consequently France and Italy have most to gain from a shift towards EEC-level protection.

Would it be desirable or feasible to replace the existing

situation, in which trade is restricted at the national level by bilateral agreements involving quotas or VERs, with a higher external tariff (currently 11 per cent) accompanied by a freeing of the internal market, either within the EEC or in conjunction with EFTA? Italy would almost certainly keep its prohibition on Japanese imports, and unless the tariff were very high France would probably keep its quota. The main impact of introducing a high external tariff would be a fall in Japan's share of the market of the six smaller member states. The main losers would be consumers in those countries, and the main gainers would be France and Italy. The UK and Germany are intermediate cases. Because only about 40 per cent of the UK's exports go to other West European countries it would be particularly vulnerable to retaliation in the form of a diversion of Japanese exports to third-country markets.

The current Europrotectionist case relies substantially on the assertion that a strengthening of external barriers will permit increasing liberalization of the Community's internal trade. This is unlikely to happen in the car industry because even within a unified Community market, isolated from outside competition, the present number of firms probably could not survive under free competition. The absence of free trade within the Community has little to do with outside competition, and the claim that increased external protection would bring about liberalization of internal trade is without substance.

Another important strand in the Europrotectionist argument is that the European market, extended to include EFTA, is large enough to allow the economies of scale necessary to achieve efficiency. The case for protection when there are economies of scale is highly qualified, even if there is no retaliation. It depends on, among other things, particular assumptions as to the likely impact on price competition in the protected European market. If, as is probable, reduced competition prompts European producers to raise prices, the net effect of protection, even with no retaliation, is likely to be detrimental. Furthermore, it is by no means clear that if the present number of European producers remains unchanged efficient levels of operation can be achieved.

It is unlikely that member governments could agree on replacing existing barriers with a higher common external tariff. France and Italy would probably veto such a move unless the tariff were very high, in which case Germany would not want to accept it. Nor would the smaller, non-producer countries. The main trend now is towards collaborative ventures, particularly with Japanese companies, partly with the aim of enhancing productivity levels. European governments have begun to compete with each other to attract foreign firms. If such a firm intends anyway to set up somewhere in the Community, then competitive bidding for investment by member governments only results in redistribution to the firm of the putative gains. It is imperative that a 'cooperative' solution to this problem be achieved, by setting a practicable and enforceable standard.

The French memorandum: R&D-intensive sectors and competition policy (*Chapters 11 and 12*)

So far the range of goods produced by each country has been taken as given. But commercial or industrial policy instruments can be used to affect the range of products, through stimulating R&D activities. Is there a role in this area for commercial policies beyond those already discussed? The French government's memorandum has been the focus of much of the current debate in Europe on this issue. A major theme of the memorandum is the role of subsidies and of related commercial policies in R&D-intensive sectors.

A convincing economic rationale exists for some form of intervention in support of R&D activity. A firm's R&D efforts produce benefits which are not wholly captured by the innovating firm itself: some spill over to other firms in the industry; and some accrue to consumers. There may be some tendency for the social gains (to the economy as a whole) from R&D to exceed the private gains (to the individual firm), and hence for the market economy to generate 'too little' R&D, relative to the social optimum. This creates a case for intervention aimed at subsidizing R&D activity. The level of the subsidy should then be determined on the basis of some view as to the size of the likely benefits relative to costs incurred. None of the Community and national schemes for R&D subsidies seems to offer such calculations.

The memorandum notes that the combined spending of member states on research is high relative to that of their competitors, and is not reflected in performance. It asserts that the inefficiency of European spending derives from the fragmentation and duplication of research effort among member states. There is a strong a priori case for joint endeavours in R&D aimed at exploiting economies of scale. In practice, however, governments are reluctant to rely on cooperative ventures to the exclusion of national programmes, chiefly because they fear that their country will benefit less than others.

The use of commercial policy to complement a new European industrial policy is a central idea of the French memorandum. The most controversial instance is its advocacy of protection for newly developed European products, on 'infant industry' grounds. There is little economic substance in this. Infant-industry arguments are valid only in situations where the firm which invests in developing a product is unable fully to capture the benefits. And though a case can then be made for intervention, protection is inferior to subsidies.

Another aspect of commercial policy addressed by the memorandum is public procurement. Noting that the practice of reserving public contracts for national suppliers is a major form of protectionism, it proposes an opening-up process but, more questionably, would confine access to Community suppliers. Public procurement is closely complementary in two respects to the kind of industrial policies advanced in the memorandum, though this is not made explicit. First, public procurement may be used indirectly to subsidize R&D. Government support for the US micro-electronics industry through military procurement is cited as an important example. Some commentators, however, doubt that US military procurement played a significant part, and even if it did this does not provide a basis for a general policy.

A second way in which public-procurement practices may contribute to industrial policy is illustrated by the success of the Airbus project. The fixed costs incurred in product development in this industry are sufficiently great to ensure that no more than two or three producers will choose to operate in any particular submarket. For example, in the market for the next generation of 100–175-seat aircraft, of the three initial contenders (Airbus, Boeing, McDonnell Douglas), one, McDonnell Douglas, opted out in 1983. It seems that the decision was to an important extent based on what McDonnell Douglas saw as clear indications that, come what might, Airbus would remain in the market. These indications were the large amount of subsidy enjoyed by the Airbus project, and the sizeable orders secured by Airbus, in part as a result of French procurement policy.

It may be possible to reach a formal agreement on removing public-procurement barriers within Europe, i.e. replacing a bias towards national suppliers with a bias towards Community-based suppliers. Whether this would change the practice of public procurement is open to question, unless there is more progress towards common standards and unless national officials can be persuaded not to plump for the 'safe' alternative of choosing a domestic supplier.

As well as the role of subsidies and related commercial policies in R&D-intensive sectors, another major theme of the memorandum is the need for cooperative ventures among European firms if they are to achieve the appropriate scale to compete effectively on world markets. This raises two important issues, both addressed explicitly in the memorandum. The first is the possibility that cooperation may run foul of the antitrust legislation of member states. The memorandum wants member states to treat the Community market and not their individual domestic markets as the relevant context for assessing whether there is a risk of excessive concentration in an industry. This is particularly directed at German antitrust law, the strictest in the Community. Many companies, of their nature, must face a world market, and it is worth emphasizing that if a case is to be made for an open and liberal trading environment, there must also be a willingness not to allow inappropriate 'domestic' criteria to bar European firms from effectively competing in world markets.

Second, European firms often favour cooperation with non-European firms, especially from the United States and Japan. The memorandum advocates European alliances, seemingly in the belief that in an external alliance the European partner is likely to be in an inferior position and hence liable to gain little.

Both issues were central to the abortive merger between Grundig of Germany and Thomson-Brandt of France, which motivated much of this part of the memorandum. By the 1980s Japanese competition in electronics had prompted various attempts at cooperation among European firms and also cooperation between European and Japanese firms, including Thorn-EMI and

JVC, and AEG-Telefunken and JVC. Soon after it came to office the Mitterrand government received for its approval a plan for a joint venture between Thomson-Brandt and JVC. The new French government, in line with its views on promoting European industrial cooperation, asked Thomson-Brandt not to sign the agreement but to explore the possibility of a European alternative. After some months Thomson-Brandt proposed a link with Grundig. The result would be a group of similar scale to Philips, which with Philips would dominate the European consumer-electronics sector. The French government could be expected to favour this plan, but the approval of the German cartel office was also needed. In Germany there were doubts stemming from two sources. First, in Germany Grundig/Thomson-Brandt would have 55 per cent of the market. Moreover, Philips held a 24½ per cent share in Grundig, so the two dominant European producers which would emerge would not be independent. Second, public opinion came to see the plan as a takeover of Grundig by Thomson-Brandt. This led to fears, partly based on past experience, that Thomson-Brandt, now a nationalized company, would if pressed preserve employment in its French plants at the expense of its German plants.

There was a fundamental difference between official attitudes in the two countries. In France, where industrial policy and protectionism were seen as going hand in hand, the prospect of creating a major new group in the European market comparable with Philips, and indeed linked with Philips, was extremely attractive. But in Germany this was precisely what was likely to convince the cartel office that international competition was being unacceptably stifled and hence that it should rule against the merger.

Early in March 1983 the cartel office made it known that it would not approve the merger. Thomson-Brandt immediately agreed with AEG-Telefunken to buy 75 per cent of its consumer electronics business, thus obtaining a stake in the AEG-Telefunken/JVC joint venture. Later it concluded a licensing agreement with JVC. The balance of opinion within Thomson-Brandt seems throughout to have favoured a Japanese link. There appears to be an inconsistency between the firm's assessment and the view taken in the memorandum that in an external alliance the European partner would tend to be in a relatively disadvantaged position. If this view is correct, the choices made by Thomson-Brandt and a number of other European firms can be rationalized only by positing some kind of dynamic effect whereby a large European unit will catch up on its international rivals, despite the fact that the short-run pay-offs favour an external alliance. This amounts to claiming that firms are more short-sighted than governments, which seems unconvincing.

The German position on antitrust is also open to criticism. To insist, as the cartel office did, that the two major European groups must remain completely independent would be reasonable within an isolated European economy or if the European industry were heavily protected. But the German government advocates a quite open trading environment, in which case competition must be seen in the setting of the world market, and any constraints on European firms must be imposed with great caution.

The French memorandum takes exactly the opposite line to the German cartel office, calling for a more relaxed approach to antitrust law coupled with increased reliance on protection. Both approaches fall between two stools. If commercial policy is to become tougher, then a relaxation of competitive pressures among European firms presents a serious danger; but if the trading environment is to become more open, then a more relaxed approach to competition law is essential. This is an area in which a clear policy lead is wanting in the Community. Britain, with its traditionally pragmatic approach to antitrust issues, may be unusually well qualified to provide such a lead.

Macroeconomic aspects of protection (*Chapter 13*)

All of the foregoing analysis has treated protection as a microeconomic issue. Although it has taken account of the repercussions throughout the economy, it has emphasized the effects on consumers and producers of the output of the protected industry. But there are also macroeconomic aspects, concerning the functioning of the economy as a whole. Two subjects in particular are worth investigating: the use of a macroeconomic policy, in the form of exchange-rate devaluation, for protectionist purposes; and the use of a tariff as an instrument of macroeconomic policy.

For any economy there is some real effective exchange rate between its currency and those of its trade partners which will bring about current-account balance (the fundamental equilibrium rate). Theoretical analysis suggests and empirical observation demonstrates that in a regime of floating exchange rates a currency's actual market rate takes time to adjust to changes in price competitiveness, and hence remains for prolonged periods above or below its fundamental equilibrium rate. A situation analogous to dumping may arise in which firms whose long-run competitive position is sound are forced to contract or leave the industry because of a temporary phenomenon. There is then a case for government to intervene to bring the market rate back to the fundamental equilibrium rate. Such intervention is temporary exchange-rate protection or exchange-rate stabilization.

Governments may also seek to apply permanent exchange-rate protection, i.e. intervene to keep the market rate below the fundamental equilibrium rate. This has a similar effect to generalized protection, amounting to a subsidy to all exports and a tariff on all imports. Permanent exchange-rate protection, however, has important consequences which generally offset its beneficial effects. It requires either forcing the capital account into permanent deficit, which will lead to an unjustified shift of resources away from relatively (foreign-)capital-intensive sectors and towards relatively labour-intensive, tradable-goods industries; or continuous foreign-exchange intervention, which is likely to bring about a permanent contraction in aggregate demand. Like exchange-rate protection, tariffs and quotas have macroeconomic effects which tend to neutralize their impact. At the microeconomic level a subsidy is more efficient than exchange-rate protection. In terms of acceptability to trade partners, a quota probably ranks above exchange-rate protection, which ranks above a tariff.

In practical terms the overwhelming drawback of exchange-rate protection as a policy for Europe as a whole is that the Community does not operate as a single economy. The Community has, in the ECU (the European Currency Unit), a common currency unit, but unless problems of policy coordination are solved the network of bilateral rates within the European Monetary System (EMS) is unlikely to be optimal, and the burden of intervention necessary to achieve a given target for the effective rate of the ECU will not be equitably shared.

A joint programme of exchange-rate management would entail protecting the entire tradable-goods sectors of all member states to the same extent and at the same time. Whether this is desirable is open to question: parts of the tradables sector have been very successful and they would be promoted unnecessarily. Moreover, a uniform devaluation of all EMS currencies would have non-uniform effects, since it would benefit countries whose tradables sectors are dominated by problem industries or which trade intensively with aggressive foreign exporters far more than it would benefit other countries. This would probably make it hard to sustain for long. A further point is that at any given time some EMS currencies are liable to be above and some below their fundamental equilibrium rates, so a uniform devaluation would bring some currencies closer to their equilibrium rates but would move others further below them.

The second issue investigated in this chapter is the use of a tariff as an instrument of macroeconomic policy. The main academic proponents of this form of protectionism are the Cambridge Economic Policy Group (CEPG). They take a non-classical view of the macroeconomy, arguing that because markets do not function well there is a pool of idle resources and unexploited economies of scale. Protectionism can enable these to be activated, so generating employment and growth. The CEPG starts from two premises. First, prices of goods are flexible, but instead of responding to excess demands for or supplies of goods, they are simply calculated as a fixed mark-up over costs. Second, money wages are similarly flexible, but instead of responding to excess demands for or supplies of goods, they are simply tied to the general price level, i.e. real wages are inflexible. These premises alone do not establish a situation in which a tariff can lead to increased employment. Rather, under flexible exchange rates, a tariff would lead to an appreciation of the exchange rate and matching rises in prices and wages. The real economy would be left undisturbed except for a switch of resources which would create employment only if the protected sector used labour relatively intensively.

The tariff, under CEPG assumptions, can raise activity but only if two circumstances both occur. First, to ensure that there is no upward pressure on money wages, the aggregate price level must remain unchanged. This means that the tariff revenues must be used either to subsidize domestic producers of import substitutes or to reduce indirect taxation across the board. Second, economies of scale must exist in the protected sector. Then the natural tendency of costs to rise as domestic production of import substitutes is stepped up will be offset by increased productivity at the new higher level of output.

A major difficulty with this argument is that there are serious doubts as to whether firms and workers would behave in the way posited in the CEPG's two premises. The tariff, together with the production subsidy and the economies of scale, would allow firms and workers in the protected industries to raise prices and to negotiate higher wage rates, but the CEPG assumes that they would not do so. This might be plausible if there were a small or temporary change in the competitive position of the protected industry. But in the case of a tariff which is large, visible and expected to be fairly long-lived, it is unrealistic to expect that producers and workers in the protected sector would not seek to raise their standard of living. Even if the premises are valid, the effect of the tariff may not be desirable, since it will tend to retain workers in sectors which in the long run are not viable and to inhibit them from moving into sectors with better prospects.

3   The evolution of the GATT

In the aftermath of World War II memories of the protectionism – tariff and non-tariff – of the 1930s were fresh, and determination to create a world order in which it would not recur was strong. After protracted negotiations the Havana Charter was signed in 1948. The charter was an ambitious attempt to establish a comprehensive set of global economic rules which were to be implemented by an International Trade Organization (ITO). During 1947, while these deliberations were proceeding, negotiations aimed specifically at reducing tariffs took place. The result was the General Agreement on Tariffs and Trade (GATT), which was intended to become a self-administered commission of the ITO. In the event, the US Congress failed to ratify the Havana Charter, and the ITO never came into being. The GATT alone was left to ensure that an open trading system was instituted and maintained.[1]

An important feature of the GATT is the principle of non-discrimination. The 'most-favoured nation (MFN)' clause requires all the contracting parties to grant each other treatment as favourable as they give to any country. The GATT prohibits quantitative restrictions and seeks to confine protection to tariff measures. It also endeavours to minimize tariff protection by 'binding' the tariff levels that have been agreed among the contracting parties. Bound tariffs may be renegotiated but any increases must be compensated for. Various exceptions are permitted, including exceptions from the most-favoured nation rule for regional trading groups and developing countries, and from the quantitative restrictions prohibition for countries in balance-of-payments difficulties. In addition, in certain defined circumstances, a country may seek a derogation from a particular GATT obligation or may take emergency action. There is also provision for a country to retaliate, for example, in the case of dumping.

Following the first round of GATT negotiations in 1947, four more rounds were completed in the period up to 1961. All five negotiations were virtually confined to cutting tariffs. At the same time many countries dismantled quantitative restrictions, though substantial numbers remained, protected by the GATT clause allowing governments not to comply with GATT rules if these were inconsistent with existing legislation. The sixth round (the Kennedy round) lasted from 1964 to 1967 and agreed across-the-board tariff reductions. It also sought to tackle non-tariff barriers, but except for the drawing up of an anti-dumping code little progress was made.

The lowering of tariffs made non-tariff barriers more prominent. Moreover, when policy took a more protectionist turn in the early 1970s governments found it easier to use non-tariff barriers than to increase tariffs which had been bound in GATT negotiations. By 1974, when the Tokyo round began, tariffs were relatively low while non-tariff barriers were arousing growing concern. In the course of these negotiations, which continued until 1979, agreement was reached on a further reduction in tariffs, which by 1987 were to decline to an average level of 4·7 per cent for industrial products imported into the main OECD countries. The negotiators also agreed on a small measure of differential treatment for developing countries. The main achievement of the Tokyo round, however, was the drawing up of a comprehensive set of interpretative codes which spelled out how the articles of the GATT were to be applied to various types of non-tariff barrier.[2] The codes need not be signed by all GATT members and could be signed by non-members. In some cases special arrangements were provided for developing countries.

One code deals with subsidies and countervailing measures. The code identifies and proscribes various types of export subsidy. Countervailing duties may be imposed multilaterally against users of export subsidies, even though the injury to other parties may be small, and the onus is then on the exporting country to disprove that there have been any adverse effects. Domestic subsidies were less easily dealt with. The sporadic references to them in the articles of the GATT gave no clear guidance. Yet the use of domestic subsidies had increased since the GATT had been signed. The code sets out those objectives and methods which are acceptable in the context of domestic subsidies, but it also recognizes that they may harm other parties. For this eventuality it provides a dispute settlement procedure, conducted by a committee of signatories of the code, which may permit countervailing duties to be imposed if the subsidy is causing, or threatening to cause, material injury. Although the position is clearer than it was, problems of defining and measuring subsidies remain.

The anti-dumping code which had been agreed in the Kennedy round was revised to bring it into line with the code on subsidies and countervailing measures. Dumped goods are broadly defined as imports which are sold at prices below those charged by the producer in his domestic market. In the revised anti-dumping code the criteria for determining the impact of dumping on the importing country's industry are comparable with those in the subsidies code. Similarly, the powers of the committee on anti-dumping practices were extended to encompass dispute settlement.

The GATT originally excluded government-purchasing policies from its rule of non-discrimination. The code on government procurement states that in their purchasing policies governments should not discriminate against foreign products or suppliers.To ensure that they do not, the code lays down detailed rules for inviting and awarding tenders for government purchasing contracts. An annex lists the government agencies which signatories have agreed will adhere to the code. Many signatories have excluded certain sectors, particularly telecommunications, from the code.

Two other codes aim at making administrative practices neutral and fair. The code on import-licensing procedures recognizes that while these are appropriate in some circumstances (for example, in a developing country where foreign exchange is in short supply), they may be applied in a manner which hampers trade. To minimize such interference, the code furnishes rules to make the process open, straightforward and non-discriminatory. Likewise, the customs valuation code, by expanding and making more precise the existing provisions of the GATT, establishes a system of uniform, realistic and equitable treatment. The code on technical barriers to trade (also known as the standards code) attempts to prevent technical regulations or standards stipulated for reasons such as health, safety, consumer or environmental protection from being used to create obstacles to trade. Signatories

are expected to provide adequate information about their requirements, to apply them genuinely and to give ample notice and
opportunity for consultation when they plan to introduce new
regulations.

The most contentious issue in the Tokyo round was the proposal
for a safeguards code. Article XIX of the GATT provides
safeguards against an unforeseen increase in imports which causes
or threatens serious injury to domestic producers. The importing
country may withdraw or modify, on an MFN basis, concessions
previously granted, though equivalent concessions on other
products must then be agreed with the exporting countries. Failing
this, the exporting countries may retaliate. In recent years Article
XIX has been used relatively little; instead, orderly marketing
agreements and voluntary export restraints (VERs) have been
preferred. These are bilateral agreements between the governments
or the industries of the two countries directly concerned to limit
the quantity of exports, without offsetting concessions or retaliation.
Japan was the exporting country most often involved in such
agreements, though they were beginning to affect the NICs. The
proposed safeguards code sought to bring within the GATT
framework the various safeguards negotiated outside it and to
specify the procedure for applying them. The sticking-point came
on the question of selectivity. The EEC insisted that an importing
country should be able to act against a single supplier, and the
United States was prepared to consider some form of compromise
on this. There was, however, vehement opposition from the
developing countries, which saw selectivity as being chiefly
directed against them. This conflict could not be resolved, so no
safeguards code was adopted.

Other issues have yet to be dealt with in the GATT.[3]
Agriculture is a sector characterized by widespread government
intervention and a high level of protection, which has generated
severe trade tensions. Textile trade between developed and
developing countries is regulated through the Multi-Fibre Arrangement (MFA), which is in effect a collection of VERs. The MFA is
a formal derogation from the GATT, but has been negotiated
under its auspices. Trade in services has greatly expanded as older
branches, such as banking and insurance, have increased their
international activities, and as new branches, such as data
transmission, have come into existence, but services for the most

part remain outside the GATT. Another area not so far tackled in the GATT is the trade distortions resulting from the constraints or incentives which governments apply to foreign direct investment. High-technology goods, because they require substantial investment in R&D, are extensively supported through domestic subsidies and trade protection. There has not to date been any discussion in the GATT of what kind of practices should be deemed permissible in this sector.

Most of these issues were raised at the ministerial meeting – the GATT's highest level – held in November 1982. A bitter dispute between the European Community and the United States about export subsidies for agriculture came close to causing the meeting to break down, and little was accomplished under other headings. In July 1984, trade officials from the United States, Japan, Canada and the EC met and agreed (subject to national approval procedures) to bring forward by one year the tariff cuts set in the Tokyo round. They also undertook to proceed with plans for a new round of multilateral trade negotiations. These are expected to begin in 1986. Safeguards, agriculture, services and high-technology goods are all likely to be items on the agenda.

The achievements of the GATT have been substantial, particularly in view of its originally provisional nature and the fact that it has never acquired the legal status of the IMF. Precise evaluations of the effects of the GATT on economic activity are debatable. There is no doubt, however, that in the 1950s and 1960s high growth rates and rapid expansion of trade stimulated each other, and that the expansion of international trade was made possible by the removal of obstacles, chiefly the lowering of tariffs, in which the GATT was instrumental. None the less, the reach of the GATT is limited. It is not yet clear whether the codes agreed in the Tokyo round are being observed and to what effect, and some major areas remain beyond the GATT's scope.

In several respects views differ as to how the GATT should now proceed. Some think that before the GATT can be extended into new areas, the recent agreements, notably the codes, need to be consolidated, whereas others think that the two processes can and should advance in parallel. A more fundamental and long-standing difference exists between those who see the guiding principle of the GATT as being free trade, and those who believe that, since there will always be distortions in trade, the GATT should be directed at ensuring a system of fair trade, in which nobody will be unduly favoured or penalized.[4]

Until recently the free-trade foundations of the GATT had remained relatively intact. But they are now being challenged at both a practical and a theoretical level. Practices have come into use, particularly VERs, which are inconsistent with the GATT's underlying principle of free trade. Those who are committed to this principle are faced with the dilemma of either leaving these practices outside the GATT, in which case there is a threat of erosion from without, or bringing them in so as to impose some control on them, at the risk of diluting, if not polluting, the fount of free trade. At the theoretical level it is argued that the model of trade which underlay the GATT does not easily tally with the present-day realities of world trade. These arguments will be analysed in the European context in later chapters. First we shall examine the current practice and politics of the Community's trade and industrial policies.

4 Principal measures of protection in the European Community

This study uses a broad approach to protection, which embraces all measures that have a substantive impact on the trade of member states. Besides trade policy towards third countries the study examines internal barriers, industrial policy and exchange-rate policy. There are several reasons for adopting a broad definition. First, it is unsatisfactory to consider only measures explicitly directed at external trade and to ignore those which, though differently conceived and implemented, have similar effects. Second, in many cases the different types of measure stem from a single set of objectives, namely, to alter the international competitiveness of the Community or one of its member states in a particular sector. Third, the links between them frequently appear in the policy debate, as the Copenhagen summit and the French memorandum demonstrated.

This study is confined to trade in manufactured goods, therefore excluding agricultural products and services. Agriculture cannot, however, be eliminated from the discussion. This is partly because the Common Agricultural Policy (CAP) is a major Community policy and so is often used as a standard of comparison and as an element in trade-offs among member states. Moreover, in agricultural trade the Community is at its most protectionist and consequently has in recent years been in almost constant conflict with the United States – conflict which has sometimes spilled over into trade in manufactures.

The barriers to trade in services differ from those found in goods. They include denial of the right of establishment, and restrictions and requirements which discriminate between foreign and domestic firms. Almost without exception they are applied at the national rather than the Community level. Progress towards liberalizing services within the Community has been very limited. In these discussions the alignment of member states favouring and those resisting liberalization is different from the usual alignment on trade in goods. For instance, the UK is keen to liberalize insurance services and air transport, whereas Germany is unenthusiastic. If services are to be negotiated in the next round of GATT negotiations, the member states will have to agree on a joint stance on this issue.

Nor will this paper consider protection of exports. A major type of export subsidy permitted by the GATT is export credit. This has been regulated in the OECD, and the GATT subsidies code implicitly adopts the limitations imposed by the OECD Arrangement on export credit. All member states provide insurance for export credit for a wide range of manufactures. This represents a subsidy in the case of those risks for which the private sector either would ask a higher premium or would not provide insurance at all. In addition, many governments directly subsidize the interest rate on export credit of two years or more, which chiefly benefits capital goods. They also enable export credit to be combined with aid funds in so-called 'mixed credits', which make export finance cheaper still. Aid funds are used in other ways as well, through direct allocations, such as the Aid and Trade Provision in Britain, and through the tying of aid programmes. There is, too, official support for exports of the 'batting for Britain' variety, which may include political as well as economic or financial inducements. Export protection applies almost entirely to external trade. Export-credit subsidies for trade within the Community are severely restricted, and obviously only trade with developing countries is eligible for aid funds.

Three groups of measures will be discussed in this chapter:

1. *Measures directed explicitly and exclusively at external trade.* Some of these are common to the Community as a whole whereas others are applied by individual member governments either with the approval (albeit sometimes reluctant) of the Community or in defiance of the Community. The fact that external trade is treated differently by different member states is one reason for the barriers to trade within the Community.
2. *Obstacles affecting internal trade.* These are national measures, or in some cases lack of measures. Some are clearly aimed at restricting imports. Many are formulated with other objectives but, intentionally or unintentionally, impede imports. They

affect the movement between member states both of goods produced within the Community and of goods imported from outside the Community.
3. *Industrial-policy measures at the Community and national levels*. These measures aim to ease the decline of old industries or promote the emergence of new ones which have or could have significant implications for external or internal trade.

Measures directed at external trade

Article 9 of the Treaty of Rome states that 'the Community shall be based upon a customs union'. Hence the Community was intended not only to be a free-trade area, with no restrictions on trade among its members, but also to apply a common external customs tariff to third countries. The six founder members aligned their external duties in 1968, and the power to enact binding tariff regulations then passed from them to the Community. The creation of the Common Commercial Policy implied in theory that the member states would pursue a unified external trade policy. In practice they have retained a large measure of autonomy. Nevertheless, in international organizations the Commission speaks for the Community as a whole, so that, for example, before GATT meetings the member states and the Commission have to agree on a common negotiating position.

The average level of duties when the Common Customs Tariff was introduced was about 11 per cent. Subsequently, in the Tokyo round, the Community accepted reductions which by 1987 would bring the average level to 7½ per cent. After Britain, Denmark and Ireland joined the Community in 1973 tariffs on industrial trade between the Community and EFTA were progressively dismantled, and a free-trade zone came fully into operation at the beginning of 1984. The Community also has free-trade agreements with most Mediterranean countries, though these exclude some manufactured products. In addition, the Lomé Convention grants duty-free access to the Community for many manufactured exports from 63 African, Caribbean and Pacific countries. Furthermore, under the Generalized System of Preferences the Community each year offers duty-free access to given quantities of manufactured exports from all developing countries. These concessions are designed to favour the least developed countries rather than the newly industrializing countries. As a result of the Community's various preferential arrangements the Common Customs Tariff now applies in full only to trade with North America, Japan, Australia, New Zealand, South Africa and the state-trading countries.

Although the Community has lowered its tariffs and reduced the extent of their application, it retains a variety of instruments for curbing imports which it regards as being traded on unfair terms or as being harmful to its domestic producers. These include anti-dumping and anti-subsidy measures, safeguard and surveillance procedures, and voluntary export restraints.

The Community's anti-dumping procedure was changed in 1980 to conform with the GATT's new anti-dumping code. Firms or industries, as well as governments, can make a direct request for an investigation to the Commission, which is empowered to take decisions, though in principle these can subsequently be reversed by the Council. A report submitted by the Commission to the Council and the Parliament in 1983 showed that there had been a steady increase over the previous three years in the number of investigations.[1] In 19809, 25 were initiated; in 1981, 48; and in 1982, 58. These investigations involved suppliers in 32 countries, of which the most important were the United States (21), Czechoslovakia (13), East Germany (12) and Brazil (9). The chemical industry was the chief source of investigations (60); the mechanical engineering (26) and iron and steel (17) industries accounted for most of the rest. Of the 149 investigations terminated during the three years, 25 resulted in the imposition of a definitive duty, and 88 in the acceptance of a price undertaking.

Numerous safeguard measures are applied in the Community, often on a national basis. Many of them are quantitative restrictions of long standing, indeed, pre-dating the GATT. These mostly relate to quite specific items, which are chiefly imported from Japan, the newly industrializing countries and Eastern Europe.[2] The Commission clarified the situation somewhat in 1979 by establishing a common set of import rules and compiling a list of items restricted by member states. In 1982, France and Italy had quantitative restrictions on 121 items, Britain on 65 and Germany on 31. Most were for textiles and clothing, cars and steel.

In adopting new safeguard measures the Community has tended

to avoid using Article XIX of the GATT. It has also supplemented safeguard measures by surveillance of specified 'sensitive' imports which can be applied at Community or national level. Surveillance does not restrict imports but may precede measures which do. Some indication of the extent to which the Community has used safeguards outside Article XIX is given by data compiled for a restricted GATT document circulated in 1982.[3] They showed that of the safeguard measures notified to the GATT since 1978 or in force before 1978, there were 30 under Article XIX, 37 voluntary-restraint or orderly-marketing arrangements and 47 other safeguard measures, ranging from quotas to price monitoring. Whereas Australia was the principal user of Article XIX, of the total of 84 measures not under Article XIX the Community was the importer in 56 cases. Some of these were national rather than Community measures.

In recent years the Commission has sought to regularize national measures and to assume greater responsibility for determining policy in this area. A regulation which came into force in February 1982 gave the Commission power to carry out an investigation before safeguard or surveillance measures were adopted; set out more precise criteria for determining whether the actual or potential harm from imports was serious enough to warrant safeguard measures; and assigned to the Commission the competence to adopt safeguard measures. Member states can impose national measures but these must be lifted after one month unless they have by then been included in the Community's list. It has been proposed that from 1985 member states must obtain the Commission's agreement before they institute safeguard measures.[4]

In a few sectors the Commission has for some time been responsible for negotiating safeguards on behalf of the member states, notably in textiles and steel. Textile and clothing imports are controlled through the Multi-Fibre Arrangement, which now covers twenty-seven low-cost exporting countries.[5] There are similar agreements with countries which are not signatories to the MFA, notably Taiwan, China and Mediterranean associated countries. The MFA was negotiated under the auspices of GATT in 1973 and began to operate in 1974.[6] It was renegotiated in 1977 and again in 1981. Within the framework of the MFA the Commission, on behalf of all member states, negotiates with each of the exporting countries bilateral agreements which fix annual quotas for a detailed list of products (130 in all). The Community import quotas are then divided into national import quotas. Although originally intended to regulate the growth of imports, the MFA has increasingly been used to slow down their growth. As a result of the bilateral agreements concluded by the Community under MFA 3, the global import ceilings were slightly lower in 1983 than in 1982, and the 'growth rate' for quotas in future was reduced by 1½ per cent.[7] Probably, a successor to MFA 3 will be negotiated to take effect from July 1986, but in return Third World exporting countries will press for a commitment to dismantle the MFA within the next six to ten years.

The Community's first experience of voluntary export restraints on steel was as a supplier. In 1968 the United States obtained assurances from exporters in Japan and the European Community that they would limit shipments of steel to the USA for the next three years. This led Community producers to seek similar agreements with Japan, and at the end of 1971 the Japanese Iron and Steel Federation announced a 'voluntary' limit on exports to the Community and Britain. The first VER agreement between the Commission and Japanese producers was reached in 1975. The deteriorating situation of the steel industry and the introduction by the United States of a trigger-price mechanism prompted the Community to introduce at the end of 1977 a similar instrument, the basic-price system. At the same time the Commission offered, as an alternative to the basic-price system and its associated anti-dumping investigations, to negotiate VERs with suppliers. The offer was taken up, with varying degrees of enthusiasm, by the EFTA countries, four East European countries, Australia, Japan, South Africa, South Korea and Spain. The agreements fixed quantity limits by weight for each category of product and also stipulated minimum prices.

Following the demise of the trigger-price mechanism, in January 1982 US steel-makers filed a number of suits alleging dumping and subsidization against Community producers. Under this threat the Community negotiated an agreement to limit steel exports to the United States until December 1985, the deadline for removing member states' subsidies to the industry. Immediately afterwards the Commission announced further curbs on imports to be effected by tightening the existing VERs and by extending them to additional countries, particularly Brazil.[8] As of 1984 there were agreements with the EFTA countries and eleven others whereby they observed certain conditions regarding price and volume for pig iron, and in return were exempted from anti-dumping action.

The bulk of the nationally negotiated (by government or by industry) VERs apply to exports from Japan, including cars, fork-lift trucks, colour television sets and tubes, video-cassette recorders, motor cycles, audio-cassette recorders, quartz watches, machining centres and lathes. Also affected are exports of footwear, television sets and parts, radios, cutlery and ceramics from developing countries such as Taiwan, South Korea and Brazil, and exports of footwear from Eastern Europe.

In 1982 some members of the high-level working party on Japan (which reports to the Council on trade-policy issues related to the Community's industrial competitiveness with regard to Japan), notably the French delegation, suggested that the Community should define and implement a common policy of export restraint on sensitive products for which national measures did not already exist. This idea was supported by the European Council at the Copenhagen summit in December 1982 and shortly afterwards the Commission presented Japan with a list, consisting mainly of items for which national VERs already existed, on which Japan was asked to show restraint. It also for the first time negotiated an export restraint agreement with Japan. This set quantitative limits on Japanese exports of videotape recorders for three years beginning in 1983, required the prices of Japanese VTRs sold in the Community to be aligned with those of comparable European products and guaranteed minimum sales within the Community for European firms.

A recent case in which the Commission has acted under GATT Article XXVIII and introduced a temporary increase in duty, rather than quantitative restrictions, is that of compact-disc players.[9] The Philips company, which had developed the technology for these players and had licensed a Japanese manufacturer to produce them, considered that imports from Japan were causing serious harm. Consequently, in February 1983, following a request from the Netherlands government, the Commission informed the GATT Secretariat and the Japanese government of its intention temporarily to raise the duty on compact-disc players from 9½ per cent to 19 per cent. The Commission expected that there would then be talks with Japan (and, in principle, with any other country concerned) to explore what compensation the Community would offer on other goods. Japan was reluctant to pursue these discussions, however, so in December 1983 the Community decided autonomously to impose the increase in duty from 1984 to 1986 and then to phase the increase out in 1987 and 1988. As compensation the Community offered over the same period to suspend and then progressively reintroduce the 7 per cent duty on reel videotape recorders (excluding video-cassette recorders).

Anti-dumping and safeguard measures do not encompass all 'unfair trading practices'. In the first half of 1982, France prepared a memorandum which called for a strengthening of the Common Commercial Policy. The European Council, at its meeting in June 1982, underlined this call, saying that the Community in conducting trade policy should act 'with as much speed and efficiency as its trading partners'. Consequently, in March 1983 the Commission put a proposal to the Council for a new commercial policy instrument. This comprised several elements. It furnished a specific instrument for dealing with a broad range of prejudicial practices, including injury suffered by Community producers in third-country markets, and it indicated a comprehensive set of countermeasures to penalize such practices. The most contentious aspect proved to be innovations aimed at improving and speeding up procedure. The Commission would be empowered to conduct its own investigation, subject to consultation with the appropriate parties, and to take a decision which would be considered adopted unless a qualified majority of the Council decided otherwise. Precise deadlines were laid down for each stage of the procedure.

Three member states (Denmark, Germany and the Netherlands) expressed reservations about the need for such an instrument, pointing out that adequate provision already existed for dealing with the practices concerned. Other member states responded that the Community could not at present respond as quickly or as effectively as its main trading partners. A comparison was drawn with Section 301 of the 1974 US Trade Act, which enables the President, acting 'on his own . . . or on a petition filed with the US trade representative', to suspend or withdraw trade-agreement concessions or impose duties and other restrictions on an offending country's imports.[10] Hence the debate about the instrument focused on the powers to be given to the Commission. The three member states with reservations, together with Britain, insisted that the Commission should be empowered to act only if a qualified majority of the Council approved of its decision. In the spring of 1984 a compromise was reached. The procedure for acting under the new instrument will comprise two stages. In the first, consultative, stage the Commission may act unless it is opposed by a qualified majority of the Council. In the second, active, stage the Commission may not act unless it is supported by a qualified majority of the Council. The new instrument was adopted by the Council in September 1984 and came into effect almost immediately.

Obstacles affecting internal trade

The Treaty of Rome provided for free movement within the Community of all goods, both those produced in the Community and those imported from outside it. Very few departures from this provision were permitted. Article 36 makes an exception for restrictions 'justified on grounds of public morality, public policy or public security' and for health and safety reasons; Article 109 allows for protective measures to be adopted in balance-of-payments crises; and Article 115 seeks to curtail trade deflection by authorizing member states which have restrictions on particular goods imported from outside the Community to prevent these goods from being imported from another member state.

Although for the most part trade proceeds without much hindrance, there are numerous barriers to trade in specific products or specific situations. One set of internal barriers derives from the differences among the external barriers of member states. These are authorizations under Article 115, whereby the Commission authorizes a member state to exclude imports from another member state of goods from outside the Community on which it has imposed national import restrictions. As would be expected, the member states which use Article 115 most frequently are on the whole those which have the most external restrictions. During the period 1975–80, for example, France made 404 applications, of which 360 were authorized, the UK made 261 (86), Italy made 178 (95), and Germany 23 (23). Similarly, the products most subject to Article 115 authorizations are those most subject to external restrictions, namely, textiles.

Other barriers affect imports originating in other member states, though they may also affect imports from outside the Community. Some of these arise from the fact that member states still have different legal, tax and administrative systems. In other cases, Community law may exist but is not properly applied. Most barriers, however, are the result of specific policies or measures, often justified under Article 36. Many of them are clearly intended to be protectionist.

On the initiative of the French government, which perhaps was attempting to belie its protectionist reputation, the Commission began late in 1982 to compile an inventory of barriers on the basis of information supplied by member governments.[11] The resulting catalogue was rather unsystematic, ranging from very general points ('the plethora of rules and regulations and the lack of transparency') to very specific ones ('provisions which require that meat products must have been cooked at 70°C'). Furthermore, some governments were more assiduous than others in drawing up their lists. The relatively large number of complaints relating to processed food may reflect French concerns.[12] The Commission classified the items under four major headings:

1. *General barriers and constraints,* notably national preference and legal uncertainty. National preference takes various forms, such as 'Buy British' or 'Buy French' campaigns aimed at encouraging consumers to purchase national products, tax concessions or financial assistance for domestic producers and discrimination by public purchasing agencies in favour of national products. Legal uncertainty results from rules and regulations that are too numerous, complicated or obscure, or are altered without adequate notice; and from deficient application of Community law.
2. *Frontier barriers.* Trade is impeded by complex formalities and by unwarranted requests for certificates and licences. Imports are restricted by being subjected to a timetable or to examination by a committee including representatives of the domestic industry. There are also administrative shortcomings, such as too few customs posts, often in inappropriate places or short-staffed. In addition, customs procedures and methods of calculation can place imports at a disadvantage.
3. *Rules concerning technical safety and public health.* This is the

commonest type of barrier. A general complaint is that there are too many rules and that they are obscure, complex and changed too often. In many cases the standards which they stipulate are considered to be too much influenced by domestic industry and to take too little account of the standards of other member states. Some rules are excessively stringent with regard both to the product itself and to aspects such as packaging. Furthermore, procedures for inspecting and approving goods are sometimes lengthy, elaborate and expensive, and the rules may be applied in an intransigent or unreasonable manner.

4. *Other barriers and constraints.* These include items such as transport requirements, tax schemes, price regulations and so forth which discriminate against imports.

In the report accompanying this list the Commission argued that the creation of a unified internal market was essential to the regeneration of Europe's industrial strength both because it would make possible economies of scale and because it would establish a more secure business environment. The Commission acknowledged that, despite some progress, many impediments still existed.

At the Copenhagen summit the European Council agreed that priority should be given to renewing efforts to dismantle internal barriers. An explicit formal link between these efforts and the introduction of a new commercialpolicy instrument was established at the Stuttgart summit in June 1983. France laid great stress on this link and for some time stalled internal-market proposals, insisting that there should also be progress on the new instrument.

None the less, some advance was made in measures to make the internal market more open. Member states agreed to facilitate crossing of frontiers by ensuring that customs posts were open at more appropriate hours and that freight lorries were cleared more quickly. They also revised the list of data which could be required in connection with internal trade. The new list was shorter and uniform for all member states. It was decided to adopt fifteen directives which set common technical standards for a range of industrial products, as well as several other directives, of which the most important set up an 'early warning' system for standards. This aimed to prevent overnight changes in national standards by requiring member states to give notice of new standards in advance of implementing them.

Little was achieved during the French presidency of the Council in the first six months of 1984, partly because efforts were being concentrated on agriculture and the budget. During this period the Internal Market Council met only once, though some internal-market issues were dealt with in other councils, notably transport. Officials in the Commission and in the Netherlands and the UK harboured hopes that the delays on the French–Italian border and subsequent blockade by French lorry drivers in February would provide a fillip to action on the internal market. When the Council met in Brussels in March it agreed to give priority to 'strengthening of the internal market so that European undertakings derive more benefit from the Community dimension', but this prompted no immediate activity.

The Commission was anxious to revive interest and in June drew up an eighteen-month programme of action. This included some specific measures which were already being considered, such as the introduction of a common customs document to cover all movement of goods within the Community, a further easing of frontier controls, and the adoption of a uniform method of collecting VAT on imported goods. There were also more general proposals for harmonizing the company law and tax systems of member states. To expedite decisions the Commission suggested that the Internal Market Council should meet more frequently and that there should be a binding timetable for carrying out its work. When the Irish government assumed the presidency in July, it indicated that strengthening the internal market would be a priority. The Irish presidency began inauspiciously for the internal market, however, with the Finance Council rejecting the proposal that VAT on imports from within the Community should be levied not when they crossed the frontier but when they reached their final destination.

The new Commission which took office in January 1985 rapidly showed that it intended actively to pursue internal market problems. Early in February the new Commissioner responsible for the internal market, Lord Cockfield, recommended to the Community's trade ministers that a new approach should be adopted to harmonizing industrial standards. Instead of continuing to seek agreement on detailed technical standards for the Community as a whole, he proposed that member states should each set their own national technical standards. The Commission would set only safety standards, and any product which conformed to these would be allowed to circulate freely in the Community. Trade ministers generally supported this proposal, and there were hopes that it could come into effect in the second half of 1985.

The Commission's annual programme, presented to the European Parliament in mid-March, gave prominence to the internal market. It announced that the Commission would put forward a programme for all member states to introduce common rates of VAT and excise duties by 1992. There was also a call for common standards for telecommunications and information technology to be implemented in the course of 1985. Furthermore, the Commission intended to insist that all public tenders for telecommunications contracts in the Community should be open to all EC manufacturers.

The main difficulty in tackling internal barriers, as the Commission recognizes, is less to get new ideas accepted than to convince member states to implement measures which have been under discussion, or even agreed in principle, for some time. Furthermore, implementation often involves detailed technical preparation and consequently tends to proceed in a piecemeal fashion.

Industrial-policy measures

Unlike the Common Commercial Policy and the internal market, industrial policy is not explicitly mentioned in the Treaty of Rome. The assumption appears to have been that the establishment of a customs union would in itself lead to the emergence of a European industrial structure. There are several genuinely multinational companies in the EEC, various examples of industrial collaboration at company level and a few at government level, notably the Joint European Torus (JET) and Ariane (which include some non-EEC participants). Perhaps the best-known cooperative venture is the Airbus, which is something of a hybrid in that it involves companies backed by substantial support from their national governments. The creation of a European industrial base, however, in the sense of the Community rather than the individual member state being treated as the domestic market and hence as the level at which firms deploy resources and organize production, has not happened. Given that the Community is still far from being a unified market, this is not surprising. The omission of industrial policy from the Treaty of Rome and the continued segmentation of European industry have meant that industrial policy has remained largely a national responsibility, on which the Community impinges through its competition and internal-market policies.

National industrial policies include a number of subsidies which can have repercussions on trade, such as adjustment assistance for declining industries, support for new technologies and aid for direct investment. Article 92 of the Treaty of Rome prohibits subsidies which distort or threaten to distort competition. Certain aids, however, are considered compatible with the common market, and the Commission may authorize other aids if it considers that any distortions of competition are offset by advantages to the Community. In November 1983 the Commission signalled a stricter approach to subsidies granted without its approval, warning that it would require not only that they be dismantled but that assistance paid be recovered. The Commission's power to do this without recourse to the Council had been confirmed in 1973 but was not being used. Recently, however, the Commission has ordered that several illegal subsidies be reclaimed, repaid or their distortive effects removed.

The Commission has also become more vigilant with regard to aid for direct inward investment. It has adopted a more stringent attitude towards cases of assistance which amounts to finance for replacement investment, impinges on sectors already suffering from capacity problems, or is unlikely to contribute to improving Europe's technological base. A recent example is that of Yamazaki, a Japanese company which decided to build a plant in the EEC possibly to obviate curbs on imports of Japanese machine tools. The company decided to locate the plant in Britain and was offered a government grant of £5 million. Following objections from the German government the Commission withheld approval and asked the British government to provide more information to demonstrate that the investment would serve the overall Community interest. In particular, the Commission wished to know whether the plant would simply perform an assembly operation or would involve a real transfer of technology.[13]

By contrast, in the area of research and development in high-technology industry the Commission has relaxed its application of the competition rules to state aids. It has also permitted exemption from the rules relating to company agreements in the case of companies wishing to engage in joint research projects. In

December 1983, for example, a ruling allowed three German companies to set up a joint subsidiary to develop a combined pressure coal-gasification process, despite the fact that the companies had agreed not to compete with the subsidiary, and hence among themselves. Subsequently the Commission announced two general exemptions. One extended the scope for joint production agreements among small and medium-sized companies, with the aim of making them more competitive on world markets and increasing their potential for technological innovation. The other, also intended to encourage the development of new technology, relieves patent-holders and their licensees of the obligation to compete among themselves for five years from when a new product comes onto the market.

Endeavours by the Commission in the early 1970s to develop a Community industrial policy came to naught.[14] For the most part its role has been confined to the 'crisis' sectors, notably shipbuilding and steel. In the past few years, however, it has fostered initiatives relating to new industries, in particular the European Strategic Programme for Research and Development in Information Technology – Esprit. This is a joint Community/private-sector programme to promote cooperation across national boundaries in research programmes. It emphasizes pre-competitive research with potential industrial applications. Within a framework drawn up by the Commission and the Council, private-sector enterprises undertake projects, half of whose cost is met by the Community. The total cost of the five-year programme will be ECU 1½ billion. Viscount Davignon, the then Commissioner, persuaded twelve large European companies to back Esprit by initiating a number of pilot projects. Later they were joined by others, and in the first full year of activity (announced in January 1985) support was given to 104 projects involving 270 concerns. Each project had an average of five participants, often combining universities, large companies and small specialist firms.

The Commission is also involved in planning the framework for Community-wide telecommunications and biotechnology industries. Proposals were presented to the European Council meeting in Stuttgart in June 1983, and the heads of government expressed their determination 'to develop and make more effective Community action in research, innovation and the new technologies with a view to facilitating cooperation between firms'. The Commission's efforts to secure agreement on a telecommunications programme, which date from 1980, have recently made some headway. In May 1984, following consultations with governments, industry and telecommunications authorities in the member states, it adopted a programme aimed at establishing a Community-wide market for telecommunications. An essential feature was the acceptance of common standards, which would facilitate, in the first instance, open tendering for terminals, followed by the gradual opening up of national markets for other equipment. The Commission also proposed a research programme for telecommunications which, like Esprit, would receive half its funds (ECU 25–30 million a year for five years) from the Community. Some steps have also been taken within the industry by four of the largest European telecommunications companies. At the beginning of 1985 CIT Alcatel, Italtel, Siemens and Plessey reached agreement on technical cooperation with the aim of reducing duplication of R&D activity and making Europe more competitive.

Similar initiatives were made for biotechnology. In this case the Commission suggested that over five years the Community would contribute ECU 88.5 million to the total cost of ECU 153.8 million, with national governments contributing the balance. Emulating the pattern of Esprit, Viscount Davignon in December 1984 brought together the chairmen of the major European companies involved in biotechnology. Europe is thought to be relatively strong in this area, and companies have been mainly concerned with obstacles such as pricing policy and differences among member states regarding patents. There is anxiety, however, about the scale of R&D efforts in the United States and Japan.

These developments reflect in part the increasing attention which several member governments have been paying to European industrial policy, particularly in the context of relaunching the Community. The French government's memorandum on a unified European industrial and scientific area was followed by documents from the British, German and Belgian governments.

Besides government proposals from France, Britain, Germany and Belgium, a programme was put forward by some twenty leading industrialists who in 1983 formed the Round Table of European Industrialists, also known as the Gyllenhammar group after its chairman, Per Gyllenhammar.[15] The group identified three main obstacles to reinvigorating European industry: excessive official subsidies; barriers in the internal market; and fragmentation of major industries and of R&D efforts. As well as seeking to remove these obstacles, the group proposed to set up an institution to provide venture capital; to arrange for large firms to give technological assistance to smaller firms; to establish a professional centre to train European businessmen and a postgraduate institute of technology; and to initiate major industrial and infrastructure schemes which would contribute to the unity of the market, for example, motorways, railways, bridges and a Channel tunnel. A number of these proposals are being elaborated, and a few are beginning to be put into effect. At the end of June 1984, ten companies from five European countries announced that they had committed at least $30 million to a venture-capital fund which will channel investment into high-technology enterprises with good growth and export potential.

This chapter has presented a largely descriptive survey and, though some indications have been given, it has not attempted specifically to assess the level or trend of protection in Europe. This has been discussed most systematically in Olechowski and Sampson (1980) and Page (1981), and also in Henderson (1983), Holmes and Shepherd (1983) and Wolf (1983). The general consensus is that protectionism is on the increase, both in Europe and elsewhere. Opinions differ as to how much of the increase is truly new, as against renewed, protectionism. One undisputed innovation is VERs. These have emerged partly because successive rounds of GATT negotiations have reduced the scope for protection through tariffs and partly because VERs are a means by which governments can circumvent the GATT – indeed, when agreements are negotiated at industry level, government need not be involved at all.

As well as the rise in protectionism, two other themes emerge from this survey. First is the interconnection between external-trade, internal-market and industrial policies. In all of these, concern about Europe's competitiveness influences attitudes. There is widespread agreement in principle on the desirability of creating a truly common market and hence of removing internal barriers, though action to achieve this is less forthcoming. Views differ on how far intervention, by governments or by the

Community, will help to make European industry better able to compete either with the NICs in less sophisticated products or with Japan and the United States in high technology. Still more dissension exists on the issue of whether European industry requires increased external protection. This explains some of the reluctance to lower internal barriers, since member states with a relatively high level of national protection are loath to relinquish that unless it is replaced by an equivalent level of protection at the Community frontier.

The second theme is related to the first: the extent to which protection is applied at the national level, despite the Common Commercial Policy, the internal-market policy and competition policy. The Commission is assuming a greater role. In external-trade policy it has established common import rules, acquired greater powers in the adoption of safeguard measures and, with the new commercial policy instrument, expanded its competence to respond to unfair trading practices. The programme of action drawn up by the Commission for the internal market is intended to set in motion a comprehensive and concerted effort. To remove internal barriers, however, necessitates for the most part initiatives from member governments. The Commission's scope for action in this area is largely confined to exhortation and coordination. The increase in the subsidies channelled into industry by member governments has prompted the Commission to be more rigorous in applying Community competition rules. It has also become more active in promoting advanced technology, both through waivers from competition law and through devising Community programmes for specific sectors.

Although the Commission is asserting greater authority, especially in the implementation of policy, the substance of policy is very much a matter for negotiation among the member governments. They hold disparate views on the state of European competitiveness and on the appropriate measures to deal with it. The debate among them and its likely influence on policy will be analysed in the next two chapters.

5   The policy debate: trade

Proposals for Community policy are drawn up by the Commission, though they may be initiated by a member government, as in the case of the new commercial policy instrument. On most issues the Commission's proposals are moulded into policy measures through negotiation among officials and ministers of the member governments in the relevant committees and councils. On external trade policy the Community usually acts by unanimity, the main exception being matters related to Article 113. Interest groups such as companies, trade associations, industrial federations, trade unions and consumers' organizations, can attempt to influence their government's policy by lobbying parliamentarians and officials. They can also seek direct access to the Commission, though the Commission is unlikely to pay much attention to individual companies and more likely to heed the concerns of Community-wide organizations. The influence of interest groups at the Community level is greatest in relation to specific items, like packaging requirements, and much less for broad policy issues.

A thorough study of the policy debate would examine the views of all the relevant interest groups in the Community; the impact they have on member governments and the Commission; and the way in which the positions of governments and the Commission interact to produce policy. Such a study would be well beyond the scope of two chapters, and consequently this and the next chapter are much less ambitious. They concentrate on analysing official views of policy in France, Germany and the UK. Although we shall not deal directly with interest groups, their views are channelled into those of their administrations. We try to indicate where an important strand of opinion is not represented in an official position. Official opinion is not invariably monolithic, so we also point out divergences among departments. Member states have different divisions of responsibility among departments. In

Germany the economics ministry encompasses the functions of macroeconomic policy (shared with the finance ministry), trade and industry. In France, the trade department was part of the ministry of finance and the economy until July 1984 when it was merged with the industry ministry. The British Treasury has always had a separate existence, but since 1983 the departments of trade and industry have been combined in one department.

The decision to focus here on France, Germany and the United Kingdom is based on two grounds. First, on trade and industrial policy member governments usually align in groups, with Germany, Denmark and the Netherlands leaning towards a liberal stance; France, Greece, Ireland and Italy an interventionist stance; and the United Kingdom, Belgium and Luxembourg an intermediate stance. There are deviations from this alignment. On the specific question of compact-disc players the Netherlands has been protectionist; in general, the United Kingdom is relatively liberal on internal market policy. Nor is the precise line of argument used by, say, Ireland in support of interventionism necessarily the same as that used by France. None the less, these three member governments broadly represent the different currents of thought in the Community. Second, as the three largest countries in the Community they carry the most political and economic weight. It would, however, be misleading to suggest that they are between them decisive. Smaller member states are able to tip the balance, and German officials state that they have sometimes been obliged to concur in a more protectionist policy than they wanted because of the combined pressure of several other member governments.

This chapter concentrates on those aspects of the policy debate which relate to external trade and the internal market. The next chapter deals with industry issues, particularly in the light of the French memorandum. It concludes by examining the Commission's position, seeking to assess the balance of forces among member governments and the Commission; and considering the implications for future policy developments.

External-trade policy

Views on the basic tenets of international trade differ distinctly. In the German economics ministry there is a firm belief that the survival of the economy is possible only if an export-oriented liberal trade policy is pursued. Elsewhere in the administration there is more willingness to admit that deviation from free-market principles may sometimes be desirable to achieve social objectives. The position widely held in France is that free trade is a system which benefits countries or sectors that are economically strong. They naturally favour it, much as first-born sons might favour primogeniture, but it is not a system which universally confers good. British officials eschew doctrine and emphasize realism and pragmatism. They acknowledge that in principle a world of free trade would be beneficial but point out that we live in a world in which everyone protects some part of their trade in some way. Furthermore, there is probably little prospect of significantly curbing protection in the foreseeable future, so policy should aim to maintain the present degree of openness in world trade.

French officials point out that the Community, not member states, is competent to act in external-trade policy. In addition, member states are obliged to comply with GATT rules. Hence a government seeking to pursue a markedly protectionist policy would come up against severe constraints. They aver that the effective level of protection is similar among all the member states, but each uses different mechanisms. Whereas France is frank about its problems, other countries are more discreet or more subtle in controlling their imports. Because France's form of protection is particularly apparent, it is thought to be more protectionist than others. That this is false is, they say, demonstrated by France's large trade deficit.

In the German administration, however, there is little doubt that some member governments are more interventionist than others and that Germany is the chief defender of free trade. This can be an uphill struggle, since it is often under pressure from domestic interest groups and from other member states. Sometimes one interest group can be played off against another; for example, the farm lobby against the steel lobby when the United States threatens to limit imports of wine in response to exports of subsidized steel. German officials also reckon it a great success that in the Community's early years France was persuaded more or less to accept the principle of free trade. They acknowledge, however, that this was made possible by favourable economic circumstances and that with the recession their own country has in general become less free-trade-minded than it was some years ago.

Their British counterparts tend to see themselves as striking a balance between the economic ideal of free trade and the political imperative of preserving employment. At the close of the Copenhagen summit, when the Council had endorsed the idea of the Commission negotiating VERs, a British official declared that members of the Cabinet were 'free traders to the last man and woman' but the government lived in the real world. When whole industries were threatened with destruction ministers had to be concerned about the political consequences. The British government and most others would have to walk a narrow road between defence of the open trading system and defence of vital industrial interests. This concept of balance, however, can lapse into a prescription of free trade for everyone else. The British document on the future development of the Community states that the Community 'must avoid the temptation to solve its internal problems by increased protectionism' but then lists actions all of which are directed at reducing protection in the rest of the world, including 'to deal effectively with unfair practices in the rest of the world and to defend Community industries in transition (e.g. steel, textiles and shipbuilding)'.[1]

Perceptions of the Community's two main competitors, the United States and Japan, are similar throughout the Community. The USA is seen as adopting a protectionist stance in many respects, and sometimes showing scant regard for GATT obligations and others. Japan, too, is considered protectionist and more of a problem in that its protectionism is less a matter of tariffs or regulations than a cultural and social phenomenon. On the question of how to deal with protectionism in these two countries, however, views differ. The French inclination is to respond in kind: to stretch or circumvent the rules of GATT (though not to breach them) and to introduce a more potent weapon of trade policy, namely, the new commercial policy instrument. Most German officials do not regard protectionism as a weapon (except of self-destruction) and would prefer to persuade Japan to abandon its policy of industrial targeting and to encourage those elements in the United States which are more outward-looking to take account of the interests of the country's trading partners. The British approach is similar, emphasizing the need to ensure that more is exported to, rather than less imported from, Japan. In parts of both the British and the German administrations there is concern about the implications of trade tensions for other aspects of relations with the United States, notably the Atlantic alliance. British officials also point out that the Community's agricultural export policy is a major irritant (to the United States) which has repercussions on trade in manufactured goods.

Policy measures

One respect in which France, together with Italy and Greece, is more protectionist than other countries is the number of quantitative restrictions it applies. Most of these protect declining industries and they chiefly affect imports from East European and newly industrializing countries, amounting in all to less than 5 per cent of French imports. There is a view in the administration that, given the disproportionate amount of bad publicity that France and the Community receive because of numerous quantitative restrictions on relatively unimportant items, these restrictions should be abolished.

France, like Britain, however, is willing to use quantitative restrictions when products come under threat from new competitors. British officials recognize that in terms of the overall impact on the economy tariffs would in principle be preferable, but a tariff increase would first have to be negotiated in the Community and then in the GATT, and would entail offering a compensating concession. Moreover, both domestic manufacturers and exporters in other countries prefer quantitative restrictions because they reduce uncertainty. The size of the market and the amount of revenue are known in advance. By contrast, the effect of a tariff on price can be more than outweighed by exchange-rate variations, so the outcome is much less clear.

The German government has resisted pressure for safeguard measures in several sectors, including watches, shoes and ceramics. In the case of watches it took the view that, since restructuring had already proceeded to the point where most of the industry had disappeared, even if safeguard measures were applied the industry would afterwards be in no better position to withstand international competition. Usually the smaller the industry, the less political support it can mobilize and the easier it is to resist. German officials feel, however, that they face a problem of 'bad examples' in other parts of the Community. For instance, the situation of ceramics is similar to that of watches, but the French and British governments, under the appropriate EEC regulation, adopted safeguard measures on imports from South Korea, which subsequently offered VERs. As a result the pressure from the ceramics industry in Germany has increased.

Similar discrepancies exist with regard to the MFA. In France, the approach adopted towards textiles through the MFA is deemed preferable to the Commission's handling of steel, which is considered too brutal. Officials responsible for trade policy regard the MFA as a good system for France because it permits the textile industry to be run down in an orderly fashion. Without it, they note, the reduction in employment would have been greater and more rapid. The MFA is also good for developing countries because it guarantees them access for a known and increasing amount of their exports. Eventually, except for a few limited branches, the textile industry will disappear and the MFA can be dismantled. There is a difference of emphasis in the Ministry of Industry, where the purpose of the MFA is seen as defending the French market by stabilizing import penetration, though not attacking exporters in developing countries.

British officials justify the MFA on the grounds that it is enabling the textile industry to be restructured systematically so that it will in the future be healthier and more competitive. Quantitative limitations are necessary because no conceivable level of tariff would affect the price of imports from the developing countries sufficiently to have a significant impact on their volume. None the less it is acknowledged that the imports which in the absence of the MFA would be supplied by developing countries have been replaced not so much by domestically produced goods as by imports from other developed countries, both inside and outside the Community.

In the German administration the MFA is disliked because it reduces competition, and it is even said that had Germany not been a member of the Community it would not have entered into the MFA. Comparisons are made between the continuing distress in the French textile industry and the experience of the relatively unprotected German industry, which was compelled by an upsurge in imports to undertake major restructuring. It became more capital-intensive, shifted into higher-quality products and was able to increase its exports, so that the increased imports of lower-quality products ceased to matter. German officials point out that the MFA was intended to be temporary but has twice been prolonged and looks likely to remain for some time yet. German industry believes that the MFA continues to be necessary though it could be dismantled by the mid-1990s. Industry leaders have criticized the government and the Commission for failing to demand that the developing countries remove the high tariffs and large subsidies with which they protect their textile industries.[2]

When MFA 3 was negotiated Germany, supported by Denmark, tried to persuade other member states to make it more liberal. It was unsuccessful, partly because of resistance from other governments and partly because of pressure from its own industry, perhaps influenced by interest groups in other member states. Notwithstanding the official strictures on the MFA, outside observers point out that the German textile industry has gained more than any other from external protection. It is one of the largest industries in the world and, as the strongest international supplier in the Community, gains most from Community preference.

Textiles is a sector for which there is an influential producers' organization at the Community level. Comitextil argues strongly for retaining the MFA as long as developing countries extensively protect their own textile sectors. The MFA, it claims, has brought about an expansion of trade, and its abolition would result in disorder in international trade in textiles.[3]

Some dissatisfaction with voluntary export restraints on imports from Japan is discernible in France. Trade officials still tend to favour them. They consider that there are some advantages to this grey area outside the GATT: because VERs are negotiated between the supplier and the purchaser they do not invite retaliation, as the imposition of a tariff does. French trade policy-makers say that their drawback is that Japanese exporters often fail to respect them. They have tried to tackle this by proposing that the Commission should take more responsibility in this area, as it did in the case of videotape recorders in February 1983. Elsewhere in the administration, and outside it, some reservations are expressed about VERs. In part these stem from the fact that VERs are becoming internationally less respectable. More important, it is recognized that arrangements of the sort agreed with

Japan for videotape recorders, in which quantitative restrictions are combined with a guaranteed minimum price, are disadvantageous because the economic rent accrues to Japan.[4] Furthermore, large firms which operate in the world market are said to be beginning to appreciate the adverse effects of quantitative restrictions and the relative advantages of tariff measures.

The British position on VERs is somewhat evasive. No VERs have been negotiated by the government, but industry has negotiated various agreements at least with official acquiescence, if not approval. A number of the agreements relate to imports of consumer electronics from Japan. As a result of these and other limitations, about one-third of the UK's imports from Japan are 'restrained'. There are also VERs on imports of footwear from South Korea and Taiwan. The situation in this sector is comparable to that in textiles: curbs on imports from NICs have benefited imports from other developed countries, notably Italy and Spain, more than they have benefited domestic production.

Germany also maintains that it has no VERs. In 1981 Japan offered a 'firm forecast' to the Commission and later to Count Lambsdorff, the economics minister, when he visited Tokyo, that Japanese car exports to Germany would not grow by more than 10 per cent in 1981. The Japanese trade ministry issued a corresponding administrative guidance. In the event, new registrations of Japanese cars declined by 7·5 per cent in 1981, and their share of the market stood at 10 per cent, against 10·4 per cent in 1980. Despite official denials, it is widely believed, in Germany as well as elsewhere, that Japan was prompted to act by Germany. The understanding was not, however, extended, because German car manufacturers rose to the challenge. For the most part, German actions have been consistent with the government's view that competition from Japanese imports benefits German industry, and that restricting Japanese access to the European market will thwart the main aim in trade with Japan, which should be to export more to the Japanese market. Germany opposed unsuccessfully the Commission's agreement with Japan on videotape recorders, and derives mild satisfaction from the fact that it had some adverse repercussions in causing a shortage of components for European manufacturers. There is, however, little enthusiasm for the tariff alternative. The action taken on compact-disc players is seen at best as a lesser evil.

The sharpest division in the Community on external-trade policy in the past few years has been over the new commercial policy instrument. The case put by France to the Commission was that the Community should respond to the highly effective instruments of trade policy which the United States had at its disposal. If the US laws were contrary to the GATT, the Community must take the United States to the GATT; if not, the Community should avail itself of similar instruments. The Commission did not deal directly with the question of whether the US laws contravened the GATT, but said that there were gaps in the Community's external trade regulations which it should fill, in conformity with the GATT, to prevent its situation from deteriorating. The French criticism of existing arrangements was that they did not enable the Community to react quickly enough. It could take months for the ten member governments to go through their decision-making processes and then to reach agreement in the Council, and meanwhile the imports concerned continued to flood in. France accepted objections to a process which would allow the Commission to decide in cases where there was inadequate support from the Council but pointed out that the Commission would not, under the proposal it had put forward, be able to implement a decision which was opposed by a majority. Furthermore, the new instrument was intended to be used not to make the Community more protectionist but as a deterrent to pre-empt unfair trading practices.

The German government considers the new commercial policy instrument to be unnecessary. The Community already has, under Article 113, a procedure which served well, for example, in 1983 when the United States imposed quotas and tariffs on imports of special steels and the Community replied by introducing, with the approval of the GATT, restrictions on a number of imports of chemicals and other products from the USA.[5] Germany was willing to compromise by accepting the setting up of the new instrument but would not agree that decision-making powers should go to the Commission while the Council had only a right to review. If the Commission was to have these powers then there must be a requirement that unless a qualified majority of the Council supported a Commission decision it could not be implemented. In this way the onus of mustering a majority would be on those who supported the decision, not on those who opposed it. Underlying the strong German reservations about the new instrument was the conviction that the stance of the Commission was more protectionist than that of the German government and consequently that the proposed procedure would be a further step away from free trade.

British trade officials were not convinced of the usefulness of the new commercial policy instrument, but they were prepared to accept any procedure based on majority approval, though not one based on majority disapproval. Consequently, Britain suggested the compromise on which agreement was finally reached, and also sought, with some success, to use the linkage which had been established between the new instrument and internal-market policy to achieve some progress in that area. The French portrayal of the new instrument as being the equivalent of Section 301 of the US Trade Act is discounted in Britain where it is pointed out that the Commission will use the instrument only to respond more quickly in actions which comply with the GATT, whereas Section 301 specifically authorizes the President to take actions which contravene the GATT.

Internal-market policy

French policy on the internal market has shifted over the past year or more and is now characterized less by national protectionism and more by Europrotectionism. In its first eighteen months in office the socialist administration, in its effort to reflate the French economy and to reconquer the domestic market, resorted to Article 115 and to less legal means of protection. The most notorious example was the measures requiring that import documents be exclusively in French and nominating Poitiers as the sole customs post for all imports of video recorders. But these measures, introduced in 1982, seem to have been the high-water mark of this type of behaviour.[6] The French government has become convinced of the importance of being able to operate at the European level, and is willing to bring down barriers in Europe provided that an adequate level of external protection is assured around Europe. Hence it insisted on linking acquiescence in opening up the internal market to progress on the new commercial policy instrument. If lowering barriers within Europe means exposing France to what it sees as gaps in the Community's external protection, then it will be reluctant. The German administration was perturbed by France's increased use of protectionist measures. It cautiously welcomes the shift on internal-market policy but regrets the connection being made between this and the demand for a more robust external-trade policy.

France has drawn attention to a particular barrier to trade with Germany. This is the various series of standards, through which a form of protection operates.[7] Some goods are required by German law to comply with safety standards specified in the German norms for industrial products (DIN), while further safety standards are laid down by the relevant professional association. Other standards, which are regarded as a seal of approval by German customers, are set by manufacturers' associations. More generally, whereas French industrialists are not concerned about whether products they import correspond to their national norms, German industrialists are. German officials point out that the system was set up and is organized by private industry with no government involvement. They acknowledge that the norms, because they are well conceived and compatible with one another, do assist the competitiveness of German goods on the domestic and international markets.[8] The norms are not protectionist in intent, and they are difficult to abandon partly because they are the responsibility of the private sector and partly because new products are designed to conform with them. All the same, as a result of the French complaints, Germany agreed to bilateral negotiations about norms. Except for some minor protectionist practices, the Ministry of the Economy was not persuaded that German standards were a barrier to trade. It was agreed, however, that where German law stipulated DIN safety standards the corresponding French standards would be specifically accepted.

In the context of Community trade-and-industry issues, British policy is probably at its most coherent in respect of the internal market. Lowering internal barriers to trade has been a constant preoccupation throughout Britain's membership of the Community, though this derives in part from a particular concern to accomplish the liberalization of trade in services, because it is believed that the United Kingdom is highly competitive in this sector. None the less, British governments have consistently promoted the opening up of the internal market and, though achievements have not been dramatic, officials are encouraged by the fact that there has been progress which a few years ago seemed impossible. Britain was quick to endorse the Commission's eighteen-month programme of action when it was announced in June 1984. As well as the Commission's specific initiatives, it supported the idea of adopting a comprehensive rather than a piecemeal approach to internal barriers. In July the Trade Minister, Mr Channon, announced a British programme in which over the next eighteen months efforts were to be concentrated on reducing frontier formalities, increasing common minimum product standards and liberalizing trade in services.[9] The British government hopes that now the budget problem is no longer paramount, the boost provided by the Commission's action programme, together with the prospect of a much more complicated situation if these internal-market issues are not resolved before Spain and Portugal join the Community, will result in substantial progress.

British business, in the form of the Institute of Directors, made a particularly vigorous plea to the new Commission to achieve a genuine common market in goods, services and transport by the end of 1988. It proposed 'a dramatic acceleration' towards adopting common standards, eliminating all frontier formalities and opening up public procurement, including defence procurement. At the same time the Commission should refrain from encumbering business with a common bureaucracy and from pursuing 'irrelevant proposals for social engineering and structural harmonization'.[10]

At the end of the next chapter we sum up the conclusions to be drawn from the policy stances of member governments on external trade and the internal market. Before that we consider industrial policy.

6   The policy debate: industry

The French memorandum

Although Germany and Britain have each produced a memorandum on European industrial policy, unlike the French memorandum neither has been published in full. Furthermore, the French memorandum is more detailed, more comprehensive and more radical. Consequently, this chapter focuses on the French memorandum.[1] It seems to have been prompted by two considerations. First, there was a realization that it was very difficult for France to solve alone some of the basic problems of its industry, and an awareness that this was also true of other member states. Second was the belief that even if Europe succeeded in solving its budgetary and agricultural problems and agreeing to an increase in its own resources, this alone would not be enough for the Community to progress. Ensuring the future of the Community required policies to enable Europe to participate fully in the third industrial revolution. Indeed, such policies could play a part in resolving the Community's present problems. The member states which will have to make sacrifices in the context of the CAP will find them more palatable if at the same time the Community takes initiatives to reinvigorate industry.

The thesis of the memorandum is that in most advanced-technology industries the USA and Japan have a duopoly. Europe must aim to be an industrial pole in its own right, not a subcontractor for the USA and Japan. The investment required to achieve this implies a market size larger than that of any one member state. Hence industrial cooperation at the European level is essential. Cases in which European industry is internationally competitive are often the result of such cooperation (for example, Airbus, Ariane, Euratom and various military projects). Industries which have remained fragmented have fallen behind badly. The same will happen in biotechnology and other new technologies unless the Community, member states and firms assume their respective responsibilities in developing European projects. Since Europe is starting out later than the United States and Japan, and since these two countries have protected their advanced-technology industries, Europe should be prepared to introduce temporary protection. In sum, Europe needs to draw up a plan towards the rest of the world.

The memorandum proposes that member states should channel more of their R&D expenditure through the Community for the financing of joint projects by firms, along the lines of Esprit. French officials note that where Community funds were involved it would be particularly important to ensure that the projects would be useful. The Commission would be responsible for this and for seeing that the funds were fairly distributed. The principle of *juste retour* would be pointless, but it would be bad for the Community if a member state felt hard done by. Some of the actions suggested in the memorandum would require little or no money; for example, the sharing of equipment and information and the exchange of personnel between research institutions, or the removal of red tape to promote joint research by two firms. Joint development of technology might entail divulging secrets to rival firms. Within Europe France sees no ready answer to this problem but with regard to the rest of the world steps could be taken to secure the same confidentiality for a Community project as for a national project. It is also likely that one firm would gain more than another from jointly developed technology. This is difficult to avoid in the case of any one project, and the aim should be some sort of overall balance among companies and among member states.

Other areas which the memorandum recommends freeing from national restraints are technical standards and public contracts. On specific aspects of these two areas France has tried to make progress through bilateral negotiation. Establishing common technical standards in high-technology sectors can be particularly complicated, as in the case of direct broadcasting by satellite. In May 1984, French adherence to an independent standard for direct broadcasting by satellite was at long last abandoned, but the French government then sought an option which would suit French purposes rather than the standard supported by the

European Broadcasting Union, which had been developed by the British Independent Broadcasting Authority. Thomson-Brandt, the French nationalized electronics group, and Philips, the Dutch electronics company, agreed on a variant of the IBA standard, which was attractive because it was compatible with the needs of cable television. French officials and industry representatives have proposed to their British opposite numbers that they should adopt the same variant, but in Britain there are reservations about the variant because it carries data at half the rate of the British system. The memorandum calls for a phased opening up of public procurement, but with access reserved for Community producers (despite the GATT code). French officials envisage responsibility for awarding public contracts remaining with national authorities on the basis of bilateral reciprocity. A limited agreement of this sort for telecommunications was concluded with Germany in 1983. Efforts to conclude a similar agreement with Britain have so far been unsuccessful.

The establishment of high technology in Europe requires not only the removal of internal barriers, says the memorandum, but also some temporary strengthening of external protection. A distinction is made between protection of infant industry and 'defensive' protection. The argument advanced for protection of infant industry is that if an infant industry, which already exists in a more advanced state elsewhere, is not given temporary protection in a country where it does not yet exist then it will never get off the ground.[2] It is pointed out that Japan pursued this strategy twenty years ago. One official asserted that there were no examples of a new technology being developed without state aid and some protection of the market. A further justification for protecting Europe's infant industry is that the United States is trying to prevent the development of technology in Europe: it acquired its dominant position by protectionist means (R&D subsidies from NASA and the Pentagon) and wants to preserve it, in a duopoly with Japan.[3]

Officials stress that the proposed protection would be temporary. There is a great difference between protecting an industry until it becomes internationally competitive and retaining protection beyond that point. Without temporary protection one country could get a lasting monopoly in a particular product, which would be a much greater threat to free trade. It is politically and economically undesirable that, for doctrinal reasons, a firm which is first to develop and market a product should then exercise a monopoly. The memorandum refers specifically to the increase in the duty on compact-disc players requested by the Netherlands. French officials note that Britain supported this request, and Germany, though not in favour, did not obstruct it. If there is willingness in each member state to accept some protection it would make sense to convert this into a coherent policy at the European level. Infant industry is not the only reason advanced for temporary protection; it is also needed to allow European industrial cooperation to take root.

Also in the context of external trade, the memorandum advocates defining criteria for direct investment in the Community from third countries. The view of the French administration is that member states should not invite investment which increases production capacity in industries where there is already excess capacity, since this creates jobs in one country only at the expense of jobs elsewhere in the Community. Investment should be encouraged if it makes a net contribution to employment in the Community as a whole or if it introduces new technology into Europe. Assembly plants installed by US or Japanese companies to bypass the Community's external trade policy are Trojan horses. For sensitive sectors a code of conduct is needed which would establish criteria, including the appropriate level of participation, for the granting of all Community and national aids to investment from third countries. Unless a common approach is adopted to inward investment, internal protection will increase. If Britain, for example, persists in admitting Japanese assembly plants, other member states will erect barriers against British exports with Japanese content.

The French administration notes that an alliance with a US or Japanese firm is often easier to negotiate than one with a firm from another Community country. The government would like co-operation between European firms to be more attractive and simpler to arrange and believes that this could be achieved by providing financial incentives for joint R&D and by revising national company and competition legislation. National competition policies should be applied at least at the Community level.[4]

Officials are keen to explain that, though France is suspected of wanting extensive government intervention, it in fact believes that only firms can achieve industrial development, and that the role of the government is to coordinate and to provide firms with the incentive to reach agreement among themselves, as was done with Esprit. The reason why much of the memorandum is concerned with government action is that it was written to be presented by the French government to other governments and to the Commission. At the Community level it is not possible to be *dirigiste* in industrial policy. National industrial policies are not amenable to integration because either their scope is very limited (Germany) or they are incompatible (Britain and France). The aim should be to promote a few common projects, to provide financial and other support for joint projects initiated by firms and generally to coordinate.

The Commission cannot be transformed into a super Ministry of Industry. There is no intention to parallel the CAP. More than 90 per cent of the Community's agricultural production is covered by the CAP; industrial policy would cover a much smaller percentage. No new powers would be needed for the Commission: Articles 100, 113 and 205 of the Treaty of Rome encompass all the powers that might be required for a European industrial policy. Furthermore, the Community should not always seek participation in projects by all ten (or twelve) member states but should find a suitable formula for each case. Those enterprises which have already proved their worth, such as Airbus, JET and Ariane, involve only some member states. If the most appropriate group for a project comprises firms from only two, three or four countries, a 'variable-geometry' solution should be found.

Understandably, the memorandum reflects French concerns, particularly about competitiveness. In many areas of high technology France is at a disadvantage to Germany and the UK, and all three lag behind the USA and Japan. In France the electronics industry has run into difficulties, relatively little headway has been made in biotechnology, and though the use of micro-electronics by manufacturing industry is increasing rapidly it is significantly less than in Germany and the UK.

Lately the administration has tacitly recognized the benefits that cooperation with US and Japanese firms can confer in terms of access to new technology. In the first half of 1984 there was a spate of deals between French nationalized companies and US companies in the form of direct investment, joint ventures or collaboration in marketing and research, in sectors which included computers, telecommunications, integrated circuits, biotechnology, medical equipment and energy. This was a new departure for France, whose direct investment in the United States is much less than that of other Community countries such as Britain, Germany and the Netherlands. Attitudes towards inward investment from Japan have also changed, partly because it is seen as creating employment. In 1983 new investment from Japan amounted to 604 million francs compared with 271 million francs in 1981. None the less, the government is chary of deals in which France does not have the upper hand. At the European level it takes a similar line. In the European Space Agency, for example, while agreeing to joint development of space stations with the USA, it has pressed for Europe at the same time to develop an independent capability in this area.

German perspectives

The French memorandum is regarded in Germany as something of a mixed bag. Some of its elements are commendable, about others there are reservations and others are rejected outright. The most severe criticism is directed at proposals which are seen as reducing competition, whether in the domestic market through increased government intervention or in the external market through increased protection. On two levels the German administration has some difficulty in responding to the memorandum. First, there is uncertainty as to how much of it can be accepted without opening the door to the undesirable aspects. Second, because Germany has no comparable industrial policy of its own it can counter French proposals only by the general argument that they are contrary to the basic principles of German economic policy.

The memorandum's thesis that Europe is lagging behind the United States and Japan in high-technology industry has been echoed recently in a lively debate about Germany's position in relation to the USA and Japan. Reports prepared by the Bundesbank, the five major economic research institutes, the Ministry of Research and Technology and the Battelle Institute all indicate that whereas Germany is well ahead of European countries, it is falling behind the USA and Japan.[5] The picture is not uniformly unpromising. The reports suggest that some parts of high-technology industry are doing very well, but overall it is less broadly based than it should be and its share of the world market is too low. Industry as a whole has greatly increased both the application of micro-electronics to production processes and their incorporation into products, but comparatively little of the preliminary research and development has taken place in Germany.

The explanations offered by the five economic institutes for Germany's failure to keep pace were that bureaucracy and state intervention had interfered with the free market; German financial institutions were unduly cautious; and too many resources had been channelled into bolstering declining industries at the expense of new industries. The Battelle report showed that in 1984 expenditure on R&D in Germany would total DM50·4 billion (DM30 billion from industry and the rest from federal and provincial governments), which would probably amount to 2·8 per cent of GNP compared with 2.6 per cent for both the USA and Japan. Their spending on R&D is, however, growing much faster.

Officials attribute some of the deterioration in Germany's competitive position to US defence subsidies and to targeting by Japan, but add that the solution does not lie in imitating these policies. A variety of measures are needed, and firms have to change. If industrialists cannot see what is required, nobody else can do it for them. None the less, in its report on US and Japanese competition in high technology the Ministry of Research and Technology proposed a programme to promote the development and application of micro-electronics, computing and communications technologies, which was subsequently approved by the government. Under the programme up to DM3 billion will be spent over four years on direct and indirect support for high-technology industry. It involves the ministries of defence, economics and posts and telecommunications. The German electronics industry is expected to collaborate closely on the research and to devote sizeable additional funds to develop and manufacture the products which result from the programme. The report also recommended creating a better environment for high-technology industry by expanding training schemes, encouraging venture capital, revising public-procurement policies and drawing up a long-term telecommunications strategy.

It is often acknowledged by German officials that more R&D and innovation are needed throughout the Community. They are content that the Community should promote more cooperation in basic research and suggest that the results should be published so that they are available to everyone. Joint efforts in applied R&D up to the level of Esprit are acceptable, and it makes sense to share the costs of a very expensive project such as JET. Community financial support should be confined to projects of a European dimension in which Community action would have greater benefits than national action, and it should be kept as far as possible from production and from the market. The French idea that money should be given to companies for product development because this is where it would have most effect is strongly opposed. This is likely to distort competition; moreover, the sectors selected for support may be the wrong ones. Industry ought to know where tomorrow's markets will be. The role of government is to provide a research base, not to direct research towards particular production processes.

In theory, German officials very much favour opening up public procurement. The present fragmented market in Europe means, first, inadequate economies of scale; second, a lack of competition and hence too little impulse to innovate. It is recognized that even Germany is not very liberal in this respect. The necessary legislation exists but attitudes tend to remain nationalist. Perhaps bilateral understandings between member states are the way to make a start, but there should not be discrimination against third countries. Officials argue that if, for example, a member state opened up a certain percentage of its public purchasing to other member states, it should also open up a similar percentage to third countries. In practice, however, there is little inclination on the part of the main public-purchasing bodies, such as the Bundespost, to make any move towards extensive liberalization.

The German administration dismisses the case for protecting infant industry. This might seem useful in the short run, but temporary protection tends to become permanent, and in the long run it would be very damaging. A pattern which might be acceptable for a developing country is not acceptable for Europe. If a new product is developed in a mature economy and is not competitive right from the beginning, it is doubtful that it ever will be. One official suggested that the situation might be somewhat different if there were large gains to be made in liberalization of trade in other products. Then there might be opportunities for trade-offs between these and the new candidates for protection.

The duty on compact-disc players is seen as a bad precedent. In the first place, Philips should have ensured that in its contract with the Japanese company there was a clause covering sales in the European market. If a large rich company is not clever enough to write a proper contract and then too slow to develop a product in the volume required by consumers in its home market, the Community should not be expected to help it out. Furthermore, this case was a matter of industrial policy, not trade policy, and should have been dealt with not under Article 113 but Article 28, which requires unanimous agreement. Germany considered going to the European Court about this case, but decided to withhold its opposition for political reasons, chiefly that the Netherlands usually supports the German position.

The German government welcomes cooperation between European firms and believes that it is up to the firms themselves to take the initiative. There is a more positive attitude than in France towards cooperation with firms from the United States and Japan as a means of gaining access to technology. Some parts of the administration share the British view that in sectors where Europe has fallen a long way behind, the only hope of catching up is to welcome direct investment from the United States and Japan. The German government recognizes, however, that collaboration among European firms can confer a particular benefit, because it can lead to the development of a cross-border industrial structure. From a German perspective, cooperation among European companies is complicated by some elements in the existing structure of European industry, notably the French nationalized companies. Forms of association with them are limited, since other companies can neither merge with nor buy them. Moreover, cooperation with French nationalized companies carries the risk of being subjected to French economic policy. For example, Thomson-Brandt closed down a factory which it owned in Ulm, though it had factories in France which were producing the same goods more expensively. This decision was not based on economic criteria: as a nationalized company, Thomson-Brandt had to abide by French employment policy.[6] German industrialists are also apprehensive that over the longer term shifts in French policy could cause them financial loss, for example, through nationalization or restrictions on remittances.

In the German view the role of government is to provide the right 'framework conditions', that is, a climate conducive to innovation and investment by firms. This they can do through tax relief, removing fiscal obstacles and reforming company law. Germany could do more, for example, in encouraging venture capital. But governments should not provide positive financial assistance nor attempt to pick winners. Intervention of this sort should be the exception not the rule. None the less, if other governments intervene the German government may feel obliged to follow.

Despite this deprecation of industrial policy, there is some measure of intervention in industry. Subsidies have been provided, particularly for steel and shipbuilding, and the Ministry of the Economy has not yet fulfilled its declared intention to scale them down. Large firms and trade associations concur with the government in opposing industrial policy in principle, but smaller firms concerned about their international competitiveness are inclined to favour it. Even within the administration there are some doubts about the lack of a policy. So far, however, these have resulted chiefly in closer observation of the structure and evolution of industry and have had little effect on policy. The inadequate supply of venture capital, to which the Bundesbank has drawn attention, presents the government with a dilemma.[7] It could remove the fiscal disincentives to equity ownership, but this is thought unlikely to have a significant impact. The main constraints are German investors' long-standing dislike of equities, the conservatism of the banks and the reluctance of the companies themselves to seek external finance. Hence the market is not behaving as the government believes it should, and the question arises whether, and if so how, the government should intervene to ensure that sufficient venture capital is available.

Just as the role of the government is only to ensure appropriate framework conditions for industry, so the role of the Commission is not to initiate projects but to construct a real common market and to promote free cooperation and competition which is not distorted by subsidies. Ariane and Airbus are reckoned to be worthwhile collaborative efforts involving member governments, but they are seen as exceptions. So too is Esprit. All European countries, even those which have no computer industry of their own, have an interest in more reliable hardware for European computers. There are few comparable sectors.

A specific difficulty is the question of whether Germany should regard the German market or the European market as the appropriate context for its competition law. France raised this following the Grundig/Thomson-Brandt case, and the memorandum refers to it.[8] The essence of Germany's competition law is to maintain a competitive situation in the German market. This may entail applying the law beyond its national borders, since there is a clause stating that it relates to all restraints of competition which affect the German market, even those resulting from acts performed outside Germany. If, for example, two non-German companies which are established in Germany merge, and the resulting company has a share of the German market large enough to constitute a restraint of competition, the merger may be held to contravene German law. This happened in the case of Philip Morris and Rothmans.[9]

In the Grundig/Thomson-Brandt case, the German cartel office resisted the idea that it should consider the new company's share of the European market, rather than of the German market, in determining whether the merger would result in a restraint of competition. It took the view that priority must be given to applying German law and to ensuring that the German market remained competitive. Germany has since told France that the problem of the relevant market can be resolved by taking into account the effects of imports and potential competition on the national market. Germany is not prepared, however, to accept the idea advanced by France and the Commission that competition should be considered at the Community level instead of at the national level.

British perspectives

Some of the ideas advanced in the French memorandum have been sympathetically received in Britain. The British government's own memorandum stressed the need to develop research and new technologies; to examine the impediments to joint European enterprises; to develop a competition policy geared to the positive dimension of industrial development as well as the possible distortion of competition; to follow up suggestions from the Commission and France regarding industrial cooperation within the Community framework among undertakings from a number of member states; and to encourage training for new industries.

The government is enthusiastic about developing high technology and convinced that this should involve collaboration with other countries, though not exclusively within Europe. The Foreign Office is conscious of the negative image which Britain has in the Community as a result of the long-drawn-out budget dispute, and is keen to overshadow this by assuming a constructive attitude towards Community industrial policy. There is, however, resistance to measures which would involve sizeable additional expenditure. Furthermore, though there is substantial intervention in industry, Britain has never adopted centralized planning as France has. In some respects, the industrial policies of the present French and British administrations have diverged. While the French government has carried out extensive nationalization to add to the significant portion of the economy already in public ownership, the British government has been returning a number of nationalized companies to private ownership.[10] Overall, however, the contrast has been less sharp than was to be expected from a rigorous application of free-market principles, because in practice the British government has intervened both to alleviate difficulties in declining industries and to promote new high-technology industries. Nor has it sought to break up the newly privatized companies to promote competition.

The British government has for some time been perturbed by the failure of its high-technology industry to keep pace with those of Japan and the United States. In 1981, government spending on R&D was about the same in Britain as in France, allocated in roughly the same proportions. About half went to defence procurement and some 20 per cent each to industry and to education and science. In Germany total expenditure was sub-stantially more, about the same as in Japan. Like the Japanese government, the German government spent much less than the British or the French on defence procurement and much more on industry and on education and science. In Britain the government accounts for about 30 per cent of the total spent on industrial R&D. The picture varies among sectors, but in recent years overall spending has not kept pace with increases in costs.

The Alvey committee, set up by the then Department of Industry to investigate the computer and electronics industries, reported in September 1982. It pointed to the threat posed by Japan's fifth-generation computer programme and by the corresponding effort that would be made in the United States. If Britain was not to fall irretrievably behind, the government would have to act urgently to coordinate and substantially fund a cooperative effort with industry to develop advanced technology for a new generation of 'intelligent' computers. The committee proposed a five-year programme costing £350 million, of which the government should provide £250 million. This should aim to produce research results of practical commercial benefit to British industry.

At the end of April 1983, the then Secretary of State Mr Patrick Jenkin announced that the government would spend £200 million on the programme. Of this, £50 million would be for work in academic institutions and the rest for industry projects. These would be 50 per cent publicly financed. The committee had recommended that those industrial projects which entailed long-term basic research should receive 90 per cent of their financing from government, but Mr Jenkin said that this would not 'secure a sufficient industrial commitment and could lead to the programme becoming divorced from industry's needs'.[11]

The shift towards giving more support to research which is directed at developing technology for industry has also been evident in micro-electronics. The use of microchips in industry is increasing faster in Britain than in Germany, and according to the Department of Trade and Industry, Britain is now the largest market in Europe. Officials stress, however, that expanding the application of micro-electronics will not alone make British industry internationally competitive. It also needs to become more involved in designing and manufacturing microchips. To encourage this, in March 1984, the Microelectronics Industry Support Programme, which had previously been cut back, was extended for a further six years and its funding raised from £55 million to £120 million. More than half of the money was expected to help create the capacity to produce materials and equipment for making semiconductors, an area dominated by the United States and Japan.

British R&D policy tends to be distinctly nationalist, though more in relation to the United States and Japan than to the rest of

Europe. In the Alvey committee, for example, all the industry members were from British-owned companies. Although British subsidiaries of US-owned companies are not in principle excluded from receiving funds under the programme, Mr Jenkin did state that: 'We shall require cast-iron assurances that the work does not leak overseas.'[12] The Alvey report welcomed the Esprit initiative as a supplement to, not a substitute for, a British national endeavour. British companies, however, have to date responded more enthusiastically to Esprit than to the Alvey programme.

The attitude towards European R&D policy is markedly cost-conscious. In its memorandum, the British government, quoting from the Stuttgart summit communiqué, stated that the Community must give priority to generating 'more effective Community action in research, innovation and the new technologies'. At the same time it recalled that the heads of government had stressed that such action must be developed within the bounds of financial feasibility. 'In the Government's view,' it continued, 'emphasis will need to be placed on cost-effectiveness and economy. In many cases results can be achieved, without additional Community spending, by greater co-operation between member states to cut out waste and duplication.'[13]

Quite apart from the question whether further funds should be allocated, some officials doubt that there is much scope for Community R&D initiatives. They regard the Esprit programme favourably but point out that information technology was unique in that there were a small number of companies, which had already taken some steps towards cooperating in R&D, and there were some recognized centres of excellence. The situation in robotics or biotechnology, for example, is not comparable. In telecommunications there are a few leading manufacturers who are interested in cooperation, and a common R&D effort may be feasible, though it would probably be organized differently from Esprit.

The proposal in the French memorandum on technical standards is welcomed by the British government, which would like to see more progress on lowering these and other barriers. Britain's support for opening up the internal market has been evident in the Internal Market Council, and its memorandum recommends that the Community should 'examine critically the administrative and legislative impediments to joint European ventures, risk-taking and investment'. There are some reservations about France's bilateral negotiation of common standards, to the extent that they seem to be geared more to French policy objectives than to the interests of the Community as a whole, but Britain is willing to seek mutually acceptable solutions. A more serious matter is the French idea that Europe should set common standards which differ from those in the rest of the world. Not only is this condemned as being deliberately protectionist, but officials doubt whether even in the short run it would benefit Europe.

Britain claims to operate an open public-procurement policy, or at least not to use public procurement explicitly to protect domestic suppliers. In 1980, the government launched the Public Purchasing Initiative with the purpose of encouraging the public sector actively to use its purchasing power to develop and maintain the efficiency and international competitiveness of its suppliers. The Treasury issued guidelines, which were formally cleared for EC and GATT purposes. These advised all purchasing departments that in assessing value for money they should always take account of factors such as design and reliability, as well as the effect of a procurement in helping sustain British-based suppliers who would in the long run be competitive. This, officials insist, is emphatically not protectionist because though the policy aims to increase the amount of goods bought by the public sector from British suppliers, it rejects the notion of 'buy British regardless'.

The French suggestion that the opening up of public procurement be confined to Community producers has been received unenthusiastically. Officials point out that the amount of public purchasing over which the government has control is substantially less in Britain than in France, because the treatment of nationalized industries is different. In the case of the Public Purchasing Initiative, the nationalized industries did offer support for its aims, but the government has no power over their purchasing activities. It cannot, for example, require British Airways (even while it remains a nationalized industry) to buy the Airbus in preference to an aircraft produced in the United States. There is also concern that the adoption of such a policy by the Community would engender a dispute with the United States.

Anxiety about the response of the United States is also a reason why the British administration rejects the temporary strengthening of external protection proposed in the French memorandum. More generally, the French view that the trade policies of member states interact is accepted, but a rather different lesson is drawn from this. If one member state erects trade barriers, trade is deflected to other member states, and the pressure on them to put up barriers increases. Similarly, if the Community raises its level of protection there is a greater risk of higher protection in the rest of the world. British officials share the German fear that temporary protection would prove to be permanent. Moreover, they question whether a Community insulated from the rest of the world in this way would have the capacity to develop its advanced technology industry to become internationally competitive. The British government agreed to the duty on compact-disc players as a signal to Japan of the Community's disquiet. It was not intended to be a precedent for building up Community protection.

Direct inward investment from outside the Community is an area of disagreement between France and Britain. The suggestion in the French memorandum that the Community should establish criteria for such investment is dismissed by the British administration. A system of this sort could not be applied in Britain, where the government has no general powers to prevent direct inward investment from coming to the country. The only controls are those which apply to the activities of domestic and foreign businesses alike; for example, the Monopolies and Mergers Commission might forbid a takeover of a large company.[14]

There are two French responses to this argument. First, the British government may not be able to stop direct inward investment, but it can refrain from encouraging it. Britain, like other member states, observes the Community rule which prohibits discrimination between financial assistance to domestic and to foreign investment. None the less, applying the criteria for providing assistance is complex, and inward investment sometimes appears to be treated more advantageously. Certainly the British government tries hard to promote inward investment by other means. Moreover, comments by British ministers have served to confirm French suspicion of British intent. In the House of Commons on 6 June 1984, for example, the Trade and Industry Secretary, Mr Norman Tebbit, was asked whether there was a difference in the incentive offered to British and overseas companies undertaking the same kind of investment, and if so how it was justified. Mr Tebbit replied: 'Of course there is a justification for offering particularly attractive terms to bring to the country internationally mobile projects which otherwise might go to another part of the European Community and have free access to our markets, but would not provide any jobs in this kingdom.'[15]

Second, France contends that if a foreign company sets up within the Community a manufacturing operation which uses a substantial proportion of imported parts, the goods it produces should be partly treated as imports into the Community. In August 1983 the French government indicated that, since it believed 40 per cent of the content of BL's Triumph Acclaim was Japanese, from 1984 it would count 40 per cent of the sales of the Acclaim in France against the unofficial import quota on Japanese cars. The following month France accepted that the Acclaim was a European car, but it is expected to maintain, more generally, concern about the EC content of the output of Japanese operations in the EC. It is unlikely that criteria for admitting inward investment into the Community will be introduced or that the rules of origin will be revised, partly because these changes would be difficult to implement, and partly because they would conflict with the GATT. The British government would oppose both, but might agree that no state aid should be provided to inward-investment projects in which the products have a sizeable foreign content.

Considerable attention is given in the British memorandum to cooperation between companies. The removal of impediments to joint European ventures has already been mentioned. The memorandum also states that Community action in R&D should be directed towards facilitating cooperation between companies: a competition policy should be developed 'which has the positive dimension of industrial development in mind and not solely the possible distortion of competition'; and the Community should pursue proposals from the Commission and France concerning 'the possibility of industrial cooperation between undertakings from a number of member states within the Community framework'. The British government also welcomes cooperation with US and Japanese companies, since this can advance the introduction of new technology and new management methods. Many of the larger British companies are attracted by the idea of creating a unified European industrial structure. In this context they attach great importance to the dismantling of constraints on cross-border investment and disinvestment, and much less importance to the promotion of joint R&D efforts.

In principle the British government is against intervention in industry and believes that British industry should cope with international competition, even if this means that some sectors must undertake radical adjustment and rationalization. It opposes state aids and is concerned at the escalating use of them. There is, however, extensive piecemeal intervention. Several factors, including the recession, a deterioration in competitiveness and increased protection elsewhere in the world have caused some industries to suffer a decline in their share of world markets. This and the resulting unemployment have prompted industrialists and trade unionists to put pressure on the government to assist industry in various ways, and in some cases the government has acceded.

Britain has been involved in joint European projects such as Airbus, Ariane and JET. Officials regard these positively and accept that they might have been less successful had they not been developed against the background of the Community, but they point out that these were not Community projects. The British government is unlikely to support an active industrial policy on the part of the Commission. Except with respect to lowering internal barriers there is no significant domestic constituency for a European industrial policy. The government will be wary of anything which might increase Community expenditure. It will also be reluctant to loosen its control of policy because both within the government and in the country at large there is resistance to any moves which are seen as diminishing British sovereignty.

The Commission's perspective

In its role of drawing up policy the Commission considers the Community as a whole, though often this means adopting a position which is acceptable to a majority of, or sometimes all, member governments, rather than one which is properly supranational. Hence the ability of the Commission to maintain a more detached and longer-term perspective is modified by the need to take account of the views of governments, and also interest groups, in the member states. Within the Commission there may be divergences among the different directorates, similar to those between different ministries in national governments.

Commission officials believe that, in view of Europe's relatively weak competitive position, it would be unwise to steer a naïvely free-trade course, but they note that a high level of protection may not be effective in making Europe more competitive. For the time being protectionist pressures in the Community have receded, chiefly because of the firm US recovery and the recent strength of the dollar, but this situation could alter quite quickly. There has been no significant decline in European protection. The Commission would like to achieve this, and will certainly strive to avoid any increase, because of the importance it attaches to maintaining its credibility in trade relations with other countries. The new Commission is keen to strengthen the impact of the Community's commercial diplomacy and has stressed that this will necessitate the member governments acting together.

The Community's level of protection is thought to be higher than it should be, but no higher than in the United States and Japan. The Commission believes that the Community can cope with all its competitors except Japan, though some of the NICs may present serious difficulties in the future. With Japan the problem is that whereas formal protection is low, the distribution and marketing systems are extremely effective barriers to trade. In the long run, obstructing Japanese exports is not a solution, and so the Commission is trying to persuade Japan to open up its market. It is not expected that there will be further agreements like that on VTRs. This was pursued at a high political level, under pressure from Grundig, Philips and Thomson-Brandt. The Commission's policy is to revert when necessary to traditional instruments of trade policy. Even so, the duty on compact-disc players should not be seen as setting a new pattern.

Views of the French memorandum vary between different parts of the Commission. Those who are responsible for trade policy are unenthusiastic. They consider that the increased intervention in industry of recent years has complicated the conduct of trade policy because it has blurred the line between essentially domestic policy measures and those which aim to give an industry a competitive advantage in international trade.

Among those concerned with industrial policy, there has been greater support for the memorandum. They are keen to promote new technology in Europe, and though they do not regard a general pooling of research activities as feasible they would like there to be more collaboration in specific fields. They are also disposed to favour infant-industry protection. However, whereas the French government argues that internal trade barriers cannot be lowered unless external protection is strengthened, Commissioner Davignon said shortly before the Copenhagen summit, 'to reinforce the Community's trade defences would be ridiculous, unless it were done as part of a common industrial strategy'.[16]

Prospects

For the foreseeable future the present tendencies of European trade policy are likely to persist. Even if the European economies revive, and there is no upsurge in protectionism elsewhere in the world, lack of international competitiveness will continue to generate pressure to protect some sectors in some or all member states. The inclination of governments to yield to these pressures will probably not change much. Germany, Denmark and the Netherlands, and to a lesser extent the UK and Belgium–Luxembourg, will resist successfully in some cases. Measures of protection which have been in place for some time, such as the MFA, are unlikely to disappear for the time being, and some further items may be added to the list of 'sensitive' products to be subject to quantitative restrictions or export restraint. The overall trend of protection may fluctuate but probably will not diverge greatly from its present path.

This leaves the broader issue of how far the Community will move in the direction mapped out in the French memorandum. There is moderate optimism in the French administration about the prospect of persuading other governments to concur with its proposals. It is felt that the French position is beginning to be better understood. The British, German and Belgian governments have shown by preparing their own memoranda that they also recognize the need to develop European industrial policy. The responsibility for building up a European industrial structure will lie chiefly with France, Germany and Britain, and perhaps Italy and Spain. French officials believe that even in Germany awareness is growing that no member state's economy is large enough to nurture within its borders internationally competitive high-technology industries. Not that the German government is expected to declare general support for the French proposals, but it is thought likely to accept them on a case-by-case basis.

The French government is aware that its suggestion that Community industrial projects should be organized on the basis of 'variable geometry', that is, with only those member states participating which wish to, could create difficulties. It believes that in the long run those which did not participate (for the most part, the smaller countries) would benefit in any case, but in the short run there would be a problem of persuading them to acquiesce in a policy which would bring them no immediate advantage and, because of infant-industry protection, would oblige them to buy European products at higher prices than they would pay for Japanese products if these were allowed to circulate freely. To tackle this several things could be done. In some degree they could be compensated through other common policies, such as regional and social policy. European infrastructure projects could help spread the benefits of a European industrial policy. France should also try to convince others by example, for instance by setting up a European data bank.

For its part, the German government is keen on the ends set out in the memorandum but anxious about some of the means it proposes. Most of all, Germany dislikes the degree of interventionism, particularly since it expects it to be pushed by the Commission, whose role in industrial policy would be enhanced by increased intervention at Community level. Since there is no provision in the Treaty of Rome for an active industrial policy, Germany feels justified in resisting this. It will also resist, by going to the European Court, persistent use of Article 113 for the purpose of industrial protection, especially if this is done on as broad a basis as the memorandum proposes. There are also doubts about a 'variable-geometry' approach, which it is thought might weaken the structure of the Community. The path preferred by Germany is cooperation between firms. The more firms from different member states find they have interests in common, the greater will be the pressure on governments to develop harmonious policies.

The British administration has particular reservations about infant-industry protection for high-technology sectors. Officials believe that even attempting to negotiate such measures would be deeply divisive because they would be seen as benefiting some member states to the detriment of others. It would probably be impossible to negotiate watertight measures, so they would be unlikely to be effective. They also note that the United States is already pressing for liberalization of trade in high technology. If the Community were to adopt an industrial policy along French lines, this would result in conflict with the United States. There is a risk that if France fails to convince the rest of the Community, it may proceed to apply infant-industry protection at the national level. This is thought unlikely, however, since France would not want repetitions of the Poitiers episode.

Evidently other member states are not as amenable to the ideas in the memorandum as the French government would hope. There is broad support for establishing common technical standards, opening up public procurement and removing other internal barriers. It is also generally agreed that cooperation between European firms should be encouraged. Some worth is seen in extending joint R&D in high technology, but only in a few sectors. There is reluctance to permit any significant increase in Community spending on this. Similarly, the launching of major European infrastructure projects is welcome provided they do not impose a further burden on the Community budget. Additional financial resources should be made available for new industries not from public funds but by providing the right incentives for the private sector. The proposal which meets with least favour is external protection for new industries. This raises the question of how far France will be willing to proceed with lowering internal barriers if external protection is denied. France has now obtained agreement on the new commercial policy instrument and, depending on how much the Commission and other member governments are prepared for it to be used, this may suffice.

Industrial policy is clearly going to remain high on the Community agenda for some time. France can be expected to continue promoting its ideas, and so too can other member states. Industrial subsidies will be an increasingly important issue in trade policy. Most important, protectionism in Europe will subside only if a way can be found to establish a firm place for European industry in the world market.

The rest of this book presents an economic analysis of the debate about protection. We begin by examining the classical case for free trade, in the next chapter.

7 The classical argument for free trade

In this chapter, we set out very briefly the main ideas which comprise the traditional view of international trade and commercial policy. We also note some grounds on which this analysis has been argued to be unconvincing; these issues we take up at length in later chapters. The main aim of this chapter, however, is to spell out both the strengths and the limitations of the traditional argument for free trade.

Comparative advantage

We begin with the central idea underlying the classical view.

Consider a number of countries, which differ from one another in their relative endowments of the various factors of production – land, raw materials, labour of various skill categories, and so on. Reflecting those differences, we will observe, in the absence of trade, differences in the relative prices of various products, between one country and another. It is this difference in the relative prices of products which provides an opportunity for mutually beneficial trade. For, by exchanging a good which is less costly to produce in terms of domestic resources for one which is more so, each country can enlarge its range of consumption possibilities. In other words, trade allows each country to specialize in the production of those goods in which it has a *comparative*[1] advantage relative to its trading partners.

The advantage of a free-trade regime, then, is that it permits an optimal allocation of resources within the global economy.

Protection

It is easy to defend the proposition that global free trade is good for the world economy as a whole; indeed, neither liberals nor protectionists dispute that view. It is, moreover, the fear of initiating a sequence of 'retaliatory' measures, in the manner of the 1930s, which has provided the most potent argument against protectionist shifts by the major trading nations during the course of the present recession. Advocacy of protection, then, presupposes that effective retaliation is unlikely for one reason or another. The question is whether, retaliation apart, protectionist measures might be desirable.

In discussing the effects of protection, it is helpful to begin by examining the case of some particular 'small' country whose impact on world trade flows is so slight that its actions will have no influence on world prices, nor will its choice influence the trading regimes of other countries. Should such a country adopt a free-trade stance? The classical answer to this question is a carefully qualified 'yes'; and the argument runs as follows: free trade allows the country in question to allocate its domestic resources optimally, and thus benefit from comparative advantage. (An 'optimal allocation of resources' implies, *inter alia*, that the last unit of labour utilized in textile manufacture produces the same addition to the value of total textile production as the last unit of labour employed in the clothing industry adds to the total value of clothing production. Otherwise, it would be beneficial to shift some labour from that activity in which it was less productive to that in which it was more productive.)

The classical argument presupposes that, under the free-trade regime, domestic resources are indeed allocated optimally. Let us suppose for the moment that this is so. Then, any restriction to trade imposes a 'dead-weight loss' on the economy by altering the pattern of resource allocation away from that optimum. For instance, protecting the textile industry will cause a rise in output and employment in textiles, together with an associated loss in output and employment in other industries. So, protection shifts resources to the protected industry and away from other industries. But if, as we suppose, the pattern of resource allocation was optimal to begin with, this involves a 'dead-weight loss' on the economy in that we are using our domestic resources less efficiently. There will, of course, be gainers (workers and firms in the protected industry) and losers (workers and firms in other industries); but the fact that the economy as a whole has suffered this allocational loss, implies that the losses involved in this change must outweigh the gains.

One important feature of this argument is that it holds quite independently of any considerations as to *why* world relative prices happen to be at one level or another. Thus, it is unaffected by any considerations as to whether the differences between other countries' relative prices and ours might reflect differences in their institutional arrangements. It is important to emphasize this point, given the reappearance in the recent literature of the idea that European firms cannot reasonably be expected to compete with foreign rivals who have access to 'cheap labour' by virtue of their relatively ungenerous social-security systems, the absence of trade unions or some other aspect of their economic system which differs from ours. Indeed, it is precisely by trading with economies whose relative prices are widely different from ours – the target of the 'cheap labour' reference – that the scope for gains from trade is greatest.

Now, we will have occasion below to argue that the classical case is limited in certain respects. The point to be emphasized here, however, is that the kinds of consideration embodied in appeals to the 'pauper labour' argument just cited do not in themselves constitute any *separate* grounds for protectionist measures.

Some popular misunderstandings

Having stated the classical argument, however, it may be helpful first to clarify a couple of misunderstandings concerning this argument which are currently popular.

It is perhaps a measure of the growing wave of protectionist feeling that the crudest of these misunderstandings should have come to the fore in the past couple of years (it reached the pages of the *New York Times* in early 1983); in its most succinct form, this states that 'we have (or soon will have) no comparative advantage in anything'. This simply misses the point that it is differences in the *relative* prices of products which provide the opportunity for mutually advantageous trade – and it is the movement of exchange rates, in response to the balance of payments, which serves to determine the dividing line between those products which are net exports, and those which are net imports. Thus this claim either reduces to the statement that the exchange rate is overvalued (see Chapter 13 below), or else it is meaningless.

A different line of argument which has become current in recent years runs as follows: in the early postwar period, the Western world enjoyed very favourable terms of trade, by virtue of its comparative advantage, over a broad range of industrial activities. It is argued that:

1. The entry of products from the newly industrializing countries onto the world market is eroding these favourable terms of trade (sometimes this is couched in terms of an erosion of monopoly rents associated with superior 'know-how' in production technology).
2. Only protectionism can stop this decline.

This is a slightly more subtle and extremely popular fallacy. (For a discussion of the view, see Samuelson, 1981.) Its appeal derives from the fact that the first step of the argument is perfectly correct – and can be effectively put in highly emotive terms. For, a change in factor proportions abroad can indeed reduce domestic welfare; those gains from trade with which the classical model was concerned will indeed be diminished as our trading partners become more similar to us in their factor endowments – it is by virtue of trading with dissimilar economies that we achieve these gains.

The second step of the argument, however, is a non sequitur. Within the framework of the classical model (subject to the qualifications we note below), the imposition of protective barriers *can only further reduce* welfare. What the argument misses, of course, is that the gains which are being eroded were derived from exporting to those economies (and others) goods similar to those which they are now producing domestically (and exporting); and these gains cannot now be recaptured by a flight into autarky.

Some qualifications

We remarked, in setting out the classical case, that its defence of free trade was a carefully qualified one. It is now time to explore the qualifications. They concern (1) the 'optimum tariff' argument, (2) income distribution, (3) adjustment costs, (4) a series of problems which fall under the general heading of 'domestic distortion', and finally, (5) unemployment.

We first consider a point which, though it may be of importance, plays little part in the policy debate. In setting out the classical argument, we assumed that the national economy in question was sufficiently small that its purchases and sales on world markets were not so large as to influence world prices. What if the domestic economy is so large that its purchases or sales do exert a perceptible effect on world prices? Under these circumstances, there will be some (sufficiently small) tariff whose imposition is superior in welfare terms, from the point of view of the domestic economy – its role being to manipulate world prices in such a direction as to improve the terms of trade of the domestic economy (i.e. raising the price of the goods which it exports, relative to the price of its imports). This is the standard 'optimum tariff' argument, and it forms a standard proviso which must be attached to the classical argument for free trade.

How important a qualification is this? Its scope depends on the degree to which the country's purchases and sales do in fact alter world prices. Given the difficulty of accurate measurement here,[2] there is room for some disagreement. Some 'liberals' dismiss the importance of the qualification (Greenaway and Milner, 1979, p. 25), while others heavily emphasize its role (Hindley, 1978, p. 280). Among advocates of protection, however, the focus is not normally directed towards this kind of argument, but is based, even within the classical framework, on quite different grounds, to which we now turn.

Protection and income distribution

The classical argument against protection, which we outlined above, was based on an appeal to the idea that free trade was optimal for the domestic economy as a whole. But the constantly changing global pattern of comparative advantage will, under free trade, induce associated changes in the pattern of domestic employment and income distribution. For example, workers in some skill category may suffer a 'permanent' loss in real earnings, as the demand for their skills declines. This raises two questions:

(1) Should the losers from such changes be compensated? (2) If so, through what means should the compensation occur?

It is important to note that the classical argument against protectionism is neutral in respect of the first question; it focuses rather on the second. What it points out is that, if any such redistributions are to be made, then it is better to carry them out directly, by making compensatory payments out of general taxation, while maintaining free trade.

Were we in fact to aim at compensating losers, how could this be achieved? Textbook treatments usually cite the 'ideal' case, in which the 'omniscient' planner can calculate the precise lump-sum payment which suffices to compensate each particular individual; in practice, however, the informational requirements for such a scheme render it unfeasible. An alternative route is to use indirect taxation, placing suitable taxes or subsidies on both commodities and factor services (wage rates, etc.). It can be shown that any scheme of tariffs[3] can be replaced by a suitable tax scheme of this kind, so as to leave everyone better off. (Tax rates may need to be either positive or negative, here; the latter case corresponding to the payment of a subsidy.)

The simplest illustration of this idea is obtained by taking the example of an economy which is initially isolated (autarky). Opening the economy to free trade will change relative prices and wage rates, and so the distribution of income. If taxes are fixed at levels which ensure that the new *post-tax* relative prices (including wages) are equal to those which had prevailed in the isolated economy, then it follows that all individuals enjoy the same net income and consumption possibilities as before. Now, a tax scheme of this kind can be shown to raise positive net revenue; and so, by redistributing this revenue to individuals, *all* can be better off than before in the new 'open' economy. So this tax scheme leaves everyone better off. It will not normally be the optimal scheme to use, of course; but it suffices to establish the point that some scheme, together with free trade, offers an improvement in welfare, even on the strict criterion that no one must be made worse off (the 'Pareto' criterion). The reason for spelling out this particular example[4] is that it provides an illustration of a type of argument which will recur repeatedly in what follows. This line of argument asserts that protection may indeed allow the policy-maker to achieve certain income-distributional goals; but it constitutes an inefficient way of doing so. For those goals can instead be achieved using an alternative policy which is superior, in that it avoids incurring the efficiency loss to the economy as a whole which is associated with protection. Thus protection is said to be a 'second best' policy, in regard to offsetting these 'permanent' changes in income distribution.

Now in practice, however, it is not usual to aim at compensating individuals in respect of such losses. The case for free trade, as with other arguments for promoting allocational efficiency, is usually made by appealing to the idea that adhering to institutional arrangements which promote efficiency will in some average sense be beneficial to all, though in particular instances there will be losers as well as winners. (This point is elaborated in Samuelson, 1981.) With the notorious exception of agriculture, this argument underlies the European Community's official stance on matters of trade policy. Such attempts as have actually been made to pay compensation to losers do not refer to these 'permanent' shifts of income distribution. Rather, it is in respect of the 'adjustment' costs incurred in shifting to new occupations that compensatory schemes have been attempted.

Adjustment costs, labour mobility and frictional unemployment

This brings us to the central point of the present chapter. It is by reference to arguments concerning 'adjustment costs' that the Community's rationale on protection in the clothing and textiles sector is most easily stated. Since this issue is the subject of the next chapter, the arguments involved here will be elaborated in some detail.

We have already remarked that the changing global pattern of comparative advantage will induce associated changes in the pattern of output and employment across domestic industries. These adjustments in the domestic economy may impose costs both on firms and on workers in these industries. The 'adjustment' cost with which policy-makers are primarily concerned, in practice, is that associated with the 'frictional' unemployment which arises as workers displaced from one industry take time to find jobs elsewhere. (Thus it is changes in the *composition* of demand which are in question here. This case should be distinguished from that of unemployment associated with a deficiency of *aggregate* demand; this raises quite separate issues, which we consider presently.)

In introducing the possibility of unemployment, we have gone beyond the strict confines of the classical model (in which wages would immediately fall in the declining sector, and eliminate any 'involuntary' unemployment). Within the classical model, the failure of wages to adjust rapidly to shifts in the demand for labour is labelled a 'distortion' in the labour market. We will consider further such limitations of the classical model in the next section.

Now one possible response to the appearance of unemployment would be to use a system of indirect taxes and sectoral subsidies to offset the impact on relative prices in the domestic economy, in the manner described earlier. This might be appropriate if labour, and other factors, were completely immobile. Clearly, factors are not completely immobile, however, and this would not be a desirable policy in the long run. Substantial falls in wage rates and rapid job losses in the contracting sector may be quite unacceptable to the policy-maker. But to completely insulate wages and employment in the industry by paying fully compensating subsidies to firms and workers will prevent the economy achieving the efficiency gains attainable from a reallocation of resources; for workers and firms will then have no incentive to migrate to other industries.

In practice, then, a compromise must be struck. The 'optimum' level of subsidy will less than fully compensate losers, and its level will depend on the weight assigned by the policy-maker to reducing the hardships suffered by these workers through job loss relative to the economy-wide benefits attainable in the long run as a result of the reallocation of resources (Lapan, 1976). Thus, interventions can indeed be justified on these grounds. As to the form which intervention should take, however, the basic point is the one made earlier: if the policy-maker's aim is to slow down the rate of job loss, then it is better to do this by means of an employment subsidy – a measure directly 'targeted' to the problem in question – rather than attempt indirectly to achieve the same end by means of protectionist measures, which will impose a dead-weight loss on the economy.

It is important to note that the use of such employment subsidies may have 'beggar-my-neighbour' consequences for trading partners who are attempting to cope with similar 'adjustment problems'. Thus, the problem of policy coordination among Community members is of central importance here.[5] All this, however, leaves one important question unanswered. Under conditions of perfect certainty, we could indeed calculate the optimal employment subsidy, and so fix the rates of import penetration, and of job loss, over time. But in fact the trend of import penetration varies over time and is extremely difficult to forecast. In fact, its fluctuation from one month to another, in response to exchange-rate movements – a particular problem for the UK textile industry of late – is intrinsically unpredictable. Moreover, it may be administratively unfeasible to vary the level of employment subsidy from one month to the next to offset these changes.

Under these circumstances, it may be desirable to supplement the optimum-subsidy scheme (calculated on the basis of forecasts of import penetration trends) with some form of quantitative restriction. It is important to stress, however, that this would be set at such a level as to become operative only in response to surges of imports above the anticipated level. Thus, a very carefully qualified role may exist for certain protectionist measures, as part of an 'adjustment' policy package. This appears to be the most plausible rationalization, consistent with the pursuit of general welfare, that can be offered for the Community's formal position on protection of the clothing and textiles industry.

More plausible, perhaps, is the alternative view: that such protection as exists cannot be justified on the basis of any calculation of the general interest, but represents, quite simply, the outcome of effective political lobbying by industry interests. This more jaundiced view of things represents the conventional wisdom on protectionist practices generally, among 'liberal' commentators.

In the next chapter, we shall argue that the actual history of events supports an interpretation according to which temporary protection was initially (and not unreasonably) justified on the grounds of ameliorating the costs of adjustment – but that, over the years, this policy has gradually hardened into a semi-permanent stance which is difficult to justify as being in the general interest. Before proceeding to develop this argument, however, we shall devote the remainder of the present chapter to a consideration of two further qualifications which must be made to the classical defence of free trade, and which will be developed further in later chapters.

Other domestic 'distortions': imperfect competition

In the preceding section, we introduced the notion of a domestic 'distortion'; we may now look at the general idea involved here.

The trouble with protection, in the classical model, is that it brings about a distortion of world prices from their competitive level; and this distortion of prices in turn causes a misallocation of resources as factors are diverted from more productive uses to less. This is the source of the welfare loss which is central to the classical case. This presupposes, then, that under free trade resources are indeed allocated optimally. Accordingly it is standard, in stating the classical propositions, to qualify their scope by referring to the requirement that there be 'no distortions' in the domestic economy. This restriction plays an important role – both in product markets and in labour markets.

Let us look first at product markets. Up to this point, we have tacitly assumed that all product markets were perfectly competitive. This serves to ensure that the price of each product coincides with its marginal cost of production.[6] Now under 'imperfect competition', this will not be the case; price will in general exceed marginal cost. Then the possibility arises that some form of intervention might increase economic welfare – for the price consumers are willing to pay for additional output exceeds the cost of producing it.

By this stage, a standard line of argument will immediately suggest itself; this is that we should look to some form of tax or subsidy which is directly targeted to the problem, rather than introduce trade restrictions. But, in this particular context, the 'first best' solution involves tailor-made production subsidies paid to each producer, the level of which would depend *inter alia* on the firm's cost structure. Such a scheme would pose insuperable difficulties in practice (if only from the incentive each firm would have to bias its estimates of its level of costs). Thus, we are necessarily forced to look for 'second best' solutions here. Whether some justification for protection might be found along these lines is a complex issue; and will form the subject of Chapter 9 below.

Protection and unemployment

We now turn to the most serious criticism made against the

classical model: the fact that its assumption of 'no distortions', in the context of the labour market, implies that wages rapidly adjust to eliminate any 'involuntary' unemployment. Suppose that, for one reason or another, wages are slow to adjust. This raises two kinds of issue. One is the appearance of sectoral unemployment in declining industries, which we have already considered. The second issue concerns the possibility that, because of a fall in aggregate demand, the economy is operating below the 'full employment' ceiling. This suggests the question: can protection raise *aggregate* employment?

At first glance, this poses the most serious challenge to the adequacy of the classical argument. For, if resources are unemployed, then the welfare gains which are achievable if employment can be raised will be likely far to outweigh any allocative inefficiency caused by protectionist measures. In discussing this issue, it is important to distinguish two cases, which we may label 'money-wage inflexibility' and 'real-wage inflexibility' respectively. The first corresponds to the traditional 'Keynesian' analysis of protection; the second corresponds to the 'Cambridge' view. In recent years, the focus of interest has shifted away from the first of these, in favour of the second.

There are a number of reasons for this shift of emphasis. They are most easily seen by reviewing the traditional 'Keynesian' argument, which runs as follows: suppose money wages are inflexible downwards, and suppose further that exchange rates are fixed. Then protection can increase aggregate employment. The mechanism involved is straightforward: protection shifts demand in favour of domestically produced goods; the employment gains which follow from this in turn generate a further round of expenditure, which accrues in part to domestic production; and so on, via the familiar 'multiplier' mechanism.

It follows, then, that protection can increase aggregate employment. (The traditional counter-argument offered was that a superior policy tool was available. Devaluation could achieve the same employment gains, while avoiding the allocative inefficiency associated with protection.) All this hinges crucially, however, on the notion that exchange rates are fixed. If we turn to the opposite extreme, and assume exchange rates to be freely floating, the prospects for protection are much less appealing. For protection will, by improving the balance of payments, raise the exchange rate – and the secondary repercussions of this on employment may (partially or fully) offset the primary gain (see Krugman, 1982).

This has prompted interest, more recently, in the notion that *real* wages might be rigid. (The motivation must usually cited for such rigidity lies in some assumption concerning the aims and actions of trade unions in wage bargaining; but it might also reflect, for example, the provision of unemployment pay at some level, which then formed a 'floor' for real-wage rates.) The question here is whether protection can allow an expansion in employment at a constant real wage. This possibility can only arise if we further introduce the assumption of increasing returns to scale. This pair of assumptions (real-wage rigidity and increasing returns) constitutes the key elements in the 'Cambridge' case for protection.

The argument runs as follows: suppose the source of unemployment lies in the fact that real wages are inflexible downwards. Then a devaluation will not reduce unemployment. It will merely generate domestic inflation, in that it reduces the purchasing power of domestic wages, which by assumption are renegotiated upwards until their real value is restored.

Suppose, on the other hand, that we impose a tariff on imports. Then the price of imports will rise, relative to wages, but if we use the tariff revenue to subsidize domestic production (thus *lowering* the price of domestic products, relative to wages), we can maintain the value of the real wage. Moreover, the expansionary effect on domestic activity, occasioned by the switch in expenditure from imports to domestic goods, generates a rise in aggregate employment. Finally, to achieve this, we need to suppose that productivity does not fall as output expands. This is the role of the 'increasing returns to scale' assumption.

There are, however, two serious questions concerning this mechanism. The first relates to the notion that real wages are rigid. This is not motivated within the theory, but is simply introduced as an assumption. This is not merely a theoretical nicety; for, unless we know *why* real wages are inflexible, we cannot specify whether any alternative policy instrument, 'targeted' to the distortion in question, might not offer a superior policy option. The difficulty is a serious one, moreover, for if we take the obvious route, which is to let real wages be determined by a firm–worker bargaining process, then certain results of the Cambridge model no longer follow. (For example, real wages will not be unaffected by a devaluation.) Hence the Cambridge model raises a serious question in this respect.

The second important question arises in regard to the assumption that domestic price–cost margins will not be affected by the introduction of protection. In Chapter 9 below, we discuss the effect of protection in sectors in which there are increasing returns to scale (where markets are necessarily characterized by some form of imperfect competition). We note that, in general, it is to be expected that protection will lead to a rise in domestic price–cost margins, as firms in the protected industry respond to the relaxation in the degree of competition from imports. The extent to which this occurs is an empirical issue; but the 'Cambridge' case rests on the most optimistic assumption, that price–cost margins will be unresponsive to changes in the level of protection.[7] In so far as price–cost margins do rise, as protection is introduced, the scope for expanding aggregate employment is correspondingly reduced.

For a fuller discussion of these issues, the reader is referred to Krugman (1982), and to Chapter 13 below (Krugman, for example, points to the very large employment losses which result in this 'increasing returns' setting, if retaliation ensues).

A final remark: the choice of instruments

We consider, finally, the question of the choice of instruments.

Given some rationale for protection, what are the merits of tariffs, as against various kinds of quantitative limit on imports? Under 'perfect competition' we can define the quota which is 'equivalent' to any particular tariff level, in the sense that it achieves the same reduction in imports. Such a quota has the disadvantage that the revenue which would accrue to the authorities under the tariff is simply given away to foreign producers in assigning them quota rights. Thus a quota is inferior to a tariff. The degree to which it is inferior, moreover, depends on the question of how quotas are allocated: are they rights sold by the home government at the going market price, or are they distributed free of charge under some more or less arbitrary rationing scheme? The second, and less desirable, option is the more usual in practice.[8]

The use of voluntary export restraints, agreed with a specific group of foreign producers, has been a notable feature of the 'new protectionism' of the past few years.[9] This corresponds to the least desirable case, from the point of view of the domestic economy, for here the optimal response of the foreign suppliers is to raise their price until domestic demand falls to the level of agreed sales.[10] As noted in Chapter 5 above, this point now appears to be increasingly accepted in EEC policy circles.

If a tariff is always to be preferred to an equivalent quantitative restraint, then why has the 'new protectionism' been characterized by a growing reliance on these measures? A commonly held explanation for this trend runs as follows: such arrangements are more readily negotiated precisely because they embody some concession to the trading partner (in that they are less damaging to the foreign country in welfare terms than the equivalent tariff). This point has been heavily emphasized in the recent literature on the 'political economy of protection', which views the introduction of protectionist measures as the outcome of lobbying activities by particular industries (Baldwin, 1982). The underlying view here is one noted earlier: that protectionist measures will typically be damaging overall, but the potential gainers are likely to be more vocal, and more effective, in lobbying, than the losers (the general public, each of whom individually stands to lose only a small amount). This tendency is greatly strengthened, moreover, by the fact that VERs may in practice offer a way of stepping round GATT agreements on tariff protection.

A second line of argument for quantitative restrictions has been noted above, however. In an environment in which import penetration can fluctuate rapidly, compared to the speed at which tariff rates or employment subsidies can be altered by the policy-maker, the use of quantitative limits may be desirable in practice, as a supplementary measure. While this is a reasonable rationalization of quantitative restrictions, it probably plays a minor part in accounting for the recent growth of such measures.

A summing-up

Our focus in the next chapter will be on the issue of specific protection within the clothing and textiles sector. Here, it is probably fair to say that Community partners share a common view as to the rationale which in principle underlies their stance – though they differ dramatically in the extent to which they match practice to principle. The rationale is a standard one, which we noted above: the case for allowing the fortunes of the industry to be determined by comparative advantage is admitted – but rapid shifts in the international pattern of comparative advantage are held to entail heavy adjustment costs, as labour and capital shift from one activity to another. Now this cannot, in itself, provide an argument against the classical prescription, which holds good even if adjustment is costly. But the process of adjustment will involve income losses for those workers displaced by the change; and it is implicit in the classical model that we can offset any such changes by means of suitable compensatory schemes.

We have argued above that an efficient scheme might take the form of a gradually falling level of employment subsidy, designed to reduce the outflow of labour from the declining sector. We have further noted that some form of quantitative restrictions might be justified as part of such an adjustment-policy package, in order to limit the impact of unpredictable import surges during the transitional period. This appears to be in accord with the position which the Community aims, in principle, to follow. Practice, however, lags behind. In the next chapter, we follow the history of protection under successive multi-fibre agreements. What started out as a 'transitional' arrangement has, in some member countries at least, hardened into a semi-permanent stance. While the rationale offered for protection remains the same, it has come to appear increasingly implausible as a basis for the policies actually followed.

8 The case of clothing and textiles[1]

Up to 1976, the European Community enjoyed a net surplus in textiles, sufficient to outweigh its deficit on clothing. From that year, however, it ran a net deficit on clothing and textiles. While the main focus of discussion in this area surrounds the role of imports from low-cost producers, it is worth bearing in mind that the largest single source of Community imports is the United States. Among 'low cost' sources, Hong Kong, Taiwan and South Korea play a dominant role. The poorer developing countries account for less than 2 per cent of Community imports.

The clothing sector is extremely labour-intensive, and it is unlikely that Europe would enjoy a comparative advantage in such a sector. But while it might seem that this would lead to a strong case for running down much of the clothing sector within Europe, the case of textiles is less obvious. Here, the greater scope for capital-intensive techniques makes it less clear that the industry would not survive under a liberal trade regime. Shepherd (1981) has argued, for instance, that under free trade, the German and Italian industries would survive, but not those of the UK or France.

The shift to more capital-intensive techniques within the textile industry will continue irrespective of any change in the trading regime. In order to place the following discussion in perspective, it is worth stressing one point which is repeatedly emphasized by commentators: the main source of job losses in textiles is the rise in the level of labour productivity, rather than an increase in the share of imports (Woolcock, 1982a, p. 31).

Protection: early developments

The origins of trade regulations in clothing and textiles are documented in some detail by Woolcock (1982a). From the mid-1930s up to the early 1960s, the USA introduced a series of measures aimed at curbing Japanese imports. This series of *ad hoc* bilateral arrangements was in conflict with the fundamental principle of non-discrimination, which was to become a cornerstone of the GATT. Thus, in order to clear the ground for a drive towards trade liberalization in other areas, as embodied in the GATT, the United States aimed to pre-empt the issue of textiles by first of all securing an international agreement which would support bilateral arrangements in this industry. It was this which led to the Short-Term Cotton Agreement of 1961, which was succeeded by the Long-Term Agreement in the following year. Bilateral arrangements made by the United States with Japan and leading NIC exporters in the early 1970s led to European fears of a possible diversion of exports to the EEC. This, together with the offer by the United States of more liberal conditions than those embodied in the Long-Term Agreement, made possible the Multi-Fibre Arrangement of 1973. This was based on a 6 per cent growth rate for imports, with provision for bilateral arrangements to fix lower rates on sensitive products.

In 1976, the UK and France introduced unilateral measures to control imports. The Dutch and Germans, who favoured a more liberal stance, were left with a choice of accepting a more restrictive line in the 1977 MFA, or else of facing a crisis within the Community. This was a pattern which was to be repeated in the early 1980s, as we will see below. The tighter position negotiated in the MFA led in turn to new restrictions, this time aimed at Mediterranean imports. Thus, once again, the pattern of the 1960s was repeated: tightening restrictions in one area led to tightening in others, in order to anticipate the sidestepping of the original restriction through trade diversion. One further such route caused continuing concern: this was the issue of 'outward processing', whereby Community producers could have part of the processing of garments completed in 'low cost' countries: this strategy was particularly favoured by German and Dutch firms, who used it successfully both in Mediterranean countries and in Eastern Europe. French producers are also heavily involved in the development. This provoked tension with UK producers, who are themselves less active in this sphere, and who are concerned with the scope it offers for quota avoidance. In particular, the UK

refused to accept the additional quotas agreed by the Community
with Mediterranean countries under this heading.

Internal tensions

The internal tensions within the Community are particularly acute
in this sector. The tendency for Germany and the Netherlands to
take a liberal stance, in the early stages of the process, can be seen
simply as another example of the difference in their general
approach to trade issues, as compared to France, Italy and the
UK. This difference in approach, in the German case at least,
reflects a general confidence in the ability of German industry to
fare well in a free-trade environment.

But the current tensions are greatly exacerbated by the fact that
Germany and the Netherlands, quite consistently with their stated
approach to these issues, have pursued over the past decade an
active policy of retrenchment in this sector. (For example, import
penetration in clothing had reached 50 per cent for the Netherlands
by 1978 – Woolcock, 1982a, p. 31). It follows that the economic
benefits claimed for protection in this sphere will be correspondingly
weighted in favour of the other Community members.

These pressures were evident in the run-up to the renegotiation
of the MFA. This occurred against a background of unilateral
actions in various sectors, over the preceding few years. In June
1977, France introduced quantitative restrictions on textiles. Later
that year, reported threats of unilateral action by France and the
UK in relation to steel, prompted the Community to adopt a
system of minimum prices and anti-dumping duties. Thus the
MFA came to be seen, against this background, as a means of pre-
empting unilateral actions by member countries. In the event, the
Community agreed to a four-year extension of the MFA in
December 1977, only after negotiating bilateral self-limitation
agreements with over twenty countries, some of them very
marginal suppliers. The resulting quota system specified allocations
on a country-by-country basis (resulting in a complicated system of
over one thousand quotas), with a supplementary device, known
as the 'basket extractor mechanism', which allows it to introduce
restraints in certain circumstances not covered by formal agreement.

It is not surprising, then, that the new MFA negotiated at the end of that four-year extension, in 1981, was highly restrictive. Intense industry lobbying was already evident in the UK from 1979.[2] France, in particular, set out a highly conservative position from the outset: imports must not, it was stated, increase by more than internal demand.[3] By April 1981 it was already clear that the 'liberal' option of allowing the MFA to lapse was no longer a possibility. On 8 April, the European Parliament approved a resolution stating, *inter alia*, that 'under the present circumstances it is impossible to simply apply GATT rules and . . . a period of import restrictions is necessary, if the industry is to be effectively reorganized'.[4]

A common EEC policy emerged only slowly and painfully, however. In spite of having worked out a compromise negotiating position[5] in July 1981, by the following October the member states were deadlocked. France and Italy, and to an increasing degree the UK, demanded a restrictive package. Germany, Denmark and the Netherlands, however, continued to insist that the trade liberalization aims of the MFA should still be broadly respected.[6] In February 1982, the EEC Industry and Trade Ministers at last agreed to ratify the new MFA, subject to their achieving satisfactory bilateral arrangements with various Third World producers on limiting exports. It was made clear however that, failing a satisfactory agreement, the Community would withdraw from the MFA. These bilateral agreements were worked out in the course of the following eleven months; and in December 1982, the Council confirmed the EEC's participation in the new MFA. Overall, the twenty-six bilateral agreements reached were felt by most commentators to add up to an MFA more restrictive than its predecessors.[7,8]

The divergence of views, and interests, within the Community does not lead merely to a 'compromise' policy, but to one which falls short of being a truly 'common' policy. Quotas, once agreed, are partitioned by the Community on a country-by-country basis. This of course violates the pre-condition for a common internal market, that the various members adopt uniform levels of protection vis-à-vis the outside world. The effect of this discrepancy in external barriers has been to provoke continuing tensions over the movement of imported textiles within the Community, with the French demanding that 'certificates of origin' be attached to imports. This is in turn highly contentious, as the Community is pledged to the concept of a common internal market – even though political pressures have forced it into a position of differing levels of external protection across member states, which is inconsistent with this aim. (The details are described in Noelke and Taylor, 1981, vol. I, ch. 8.)

External tensions

Relations with the United States have been one of the major sources of tension in this sphere.

The tightening of controls under the MFA fell predominantly on the 'low cost' suppliers. Imports from industrial countries rose by almost 60 per cent in value terms over the three-year period 1977–80, while those from the 'low cost' countries covered by the bilateral agreements of 1977 rose by one-fifth (Noelke and Taylor, 1981, vol. I, p. 266).

Criticism by the LDCs of this tendency is usually answered by appealing to the fact that the EEC has an overall surplus vis-à-vis other 'industrial countries' as a group, and that its trading relations with these countries are relatively liberal, whereas most LDCs operate highly protectionist policies on textile imports. None the less, as Noelke and Taylor argue, the relatively open stance adopted vis-à-vis the United States, and EFTA countries, reflects the fact that the Community cannot introduce restrictive measures in these areas without detriment to its overall trading position with these countries. The fear that any restriction would provoke retaliation, whether in an overt fashion, or through a hardening in negotiations in other sectors, is a very real one. Britain dropped its import quotas on US synthetic fibres in 1980 in the face of threatened retaliation against UK exports to the USA. After talks with US Trade Representative Bill Brock, Trade Minister Cecil Parkinson said that the UK considered, and rejected, unilateral action on US textiles.[9] The ill feeling on this issue reflected in large part the advantage which the US textile industry enjoyed from artificially low energy and raw materials prices. It was further exacerbated by the US ban on the export of naphtha, an essential raw material in the manufacture of synthetics. The later deregulation of oil prices went some way towards easing these tensions.

Fears of retaliation, then, play an important part in relations with the United States. They appear to play a much lesser part in relation to LDC suppliers. This is somewhat surprising, in one way, given the importance of the LDCs as buyers of European capital equipment. The oft-cited example of Indonesia's retaliatory action, in cancelling orders for capital equipment from the UK, in 1980 (Cable, 1983), is notable for its rarity. The latest twist in the Community's relations with the outside world, in this area, relates to the growing role of China – now party to the MFA – as an exporter. In 1982, when the United States and China failed to agree on a new textile trade agreement, the USA applied unilateral export restrictions. China retaliated by halting purchase of US grain. In 1983, 51 per cent of China's exports to the USA were accounted for by clothing and textiles; this, said Mr Charles Freeman (deputy chief of mission at the US Embassy in Peking), 'could cause increased bilateral trade friction as China seeks to penetrate our most sensitive and depressed market area'. This led to fears in Europe that should the United States resort to new restrictions on Chinese imports, a diversion of its exports to the European market could ensue. As these events were occurring, the Community was already involved in preliminary negotiations with China, aimed at extending their existing agreement on textiles. The new agreement was signed in March 1984, and was described by the head of the EEC delegation as being 'acceptable to both sides'.[10] It involved a compromise whereby quotas were increased, in return for new anti-fraud and 'anti-surge' clauses.

Clothing and textiles: no way forward?

What, then, are the prospects for a unified European policy in this sphere? The prospects for any unified shift of stance, apart from a rather haphazard tightening of controls in the face of the world recession, seem remote. The distribution of gainers and losers from protectionism, across the Community, is such as to reinforce the familiar division between hawks and doves. The present policy represents, in two separate respects, the worst of all possible worlds. First, there is the failure to achieve a common external policy, with its consequences for the achievement of a unified internal market. Second, there is the choice of instrument: the most easily negotiable is quantitative restrictions, which from the Community's standpoint are a relatively unattractive device.

Could the Community as a whole follow the German and Dutch lead in actively promoting adjustment? Policies which have aimed to do this have had, in fact, a rather mixed degree of success. An overall view is provided by Woolcock (1982b). The Dutch policy was relatively successful: it aimed, realistically, both to promote relocation of production and to reduce overall capacity. In cotton-weaving, for example, alternative employment or early retirement was arranged for all those who lost their jobs.

The British Wool Textile Industry Scheme undoubtedly aided restructuring within the UK industry, where labour costs are low relative to other EEC members. The major beneficiaries were not companies competing directly with imports from developing countries, but those in market segments where the main source of competition came from better-equipped factories in high-wage countries. One criticism made of the scheme, however, was that it involved an attempt to raise productivity without reducing capacity (for details, see Woolcock, op. cit.).

Attempts to hold one's ground by simply raising productivity without reducing capacity are an expensive option. Calculations of the cost of saving jobs in the US textile industry are not encouraging in this respect; a recent study by Hartman, for example, gave an estimate of $81,000 per annum for each textile job saved (Turner *et al.*, 1980, p. 32). Thus while it may be possible to sell adjustment policies politically, this is only sensible if it is accompanied by a move to a scale of industry, as well as an achievable productivity level, which will be consistent with long-run viability.

Conclusions: clothing and textiles

The present study addresses two independent questions: (1) What are the economic arguments for and against a shift by the Community to a more concerted commercial and industrial policy (in place of the ill-assorted *ad hoc* measures currently resorted to by individual member states)? (2) What is the likelihood of the Community moving towards such a policy, given the balance of interests among member states?

In regard to the clothing and textiles sector, we have seen that:

1. A case can be made for temporary protectionist measures aimed at moderating the speed at which the industry adjusts to the changing pattern of comparative advantage. As a basis for the Community's stance over the past two decades, however, this rationale appears to be wearing thin. Some member states have been relatively successful in promoting adjustment; others have not. There does not appear to be any convincing economic case for increasing present levels of protection in the industry.

2. The balance of interests within the Community is such as to reinforce the usual division between hawks and doves – in that Germany and the Netherlands, who normally adopt a liberal stance on trade issues, are also the ones with least to gain from protection in this industry. Thus it is not likely that any major policy shift will be seen in the near future.

9 Scale economies and the protectionist case

In the present chapter we go beyond the confines of the classical model, in exploring a number of distinct but interrelated ideas: the presence of scale economies; the role of imperfect competition; and the part played by trade in differentiated products.

While scale economies and imperfect competition received a fair amount of attention in discussions of trade policy during the post-war period, it is only recently that they have begun to be fully integrated into trade theory. Much of the motivation for this lies in the fact that these considerations are now seen as being of central importance in explaining observed patterns of trade, and in particular of trade between industrialized countries. The implications of these considerations for commercial policy are complex; and at first sight they both suggest certain arguments which would appear to strengthen the 'liberal' case, and also raise possibilities favourable to protectionist measures.

For example, the presence of scale economies in an industry would seem to suggest an added disadvantage of protectionism, in so far as a small economy might not be able to support a sufficient number of firms, each operating at an efficient scale, to permit effective competition in a protected domestic industry. This suggests an additional type of difficulty associated with protection of the industry: it may exaggerate monopoly power in the domestic economy. On the other hand, firms often adduce scale economies as a rationale for seeking protection; only a 'secure domestic market', they argue, can allow them to reap the economies of large-scale production necessary for success on export markets. Can import protection, then, act as 'export promotion'?

Before proceeding to unravel the several strands in this fairly complex area, it will help first to set out the relationship between a number of basic ideas.

Some preliminary ideas

We begin by noting the link between economies of scale and the presence of imperfect competition.

Consider, for example, an industry in which each firm incurs some given level of fixed costs in setting up a plant, and can thereafter produce any volume of output at a constant level of marginal cost (the cost of labour and raw material inputs per unit produced, say). Then its average cost per unit, including an allowance for fixed costs (overheads), decreases as output rises (so that overheads are spread more thinly over a greater volume of output). The firm, in other words, enjoys economies of scale. What is pertinent to our present concern is that its average cost per unit (which includes an allowance for overheads) necessarily exceeds its marginal cost. Hence, were price to coincide with marginal cost, profit would be negative[1] – thus inducing some firms to leave the industry. So, at equilibrium, it must be the case that price *exceeds* marginal cost.

Now this is inconsistent with perfect competition: for, under perfect competition, price will be driven down to the level of marginal cost, as we noted in Chapter 7. (A detailed recapitulation of this is given in the notes.[2]) Hence, markets characterized by such scale economies must depart in one way or another from the 'perfect competition' story – in which we assume a *large number of firms*, each selling an *identical product*. Relaxing the first of these requirements brings us to models of *oligopoly* – where the number of sellers is small; relaxing the second brings us to models in which the various firms offer *differentiated products*. In practice, of course, we are likely to see both these features: a small number of sellers, offering distinct 'brands'. Both features may serve to reduce the degree of price competition in the market, allowing equilibrium price to lie above marginal cost.

Explaining intra-industry trade

The classical analysis of international trade, based on the principle of 'comparative advantage', suggests that a country should typically export the products of one set of (narrowly defined) industries, which make more intensive use of those factors of production in which it is relatively rich, while importing the products of some other industries. This is known as 'inter-industry' trade, and this picture offers useful characterization of a sizeable part of international trade flows.

On the other hand, however, if we look at trade flows between industrial economies, a large part of this trade involves a two-way flow of similar products, each country being both an importer and an exporter of goods within the same narrow industrial classification. Such trade is called 'intra-industry' trade. The bulk of trade *within* the European Community, for example, is of this kind. Indeed, Balassa's (1966) early study suggested that the main effect of the formation of the EEC on trade lay in the growth of intra-industry trade among member states.

The key to explaining these intra-industry trade flows lies in developing models in which rival firms in each industry produce *differentiated products*. The underlying rationale of these models lies in the interplay of two factors: a diversity of taste among consumers, and the presence of scale economies in production. Differences in taste between consumers provide an incentive to firms to differentiate their products. The presence of scale economies, moreover, ensures that each country will not produce all possible varieties, but will specialize in a limited number. Now this provides an impetus for intra-industry trade; as some consumers in each country will prefer a foreign variety to that offered by domestic producers.

The success of these theories in complementing the classical theory, and so offering a richer description of actual trade flows, has been very influential recently in convincing trade theorists that scale economies and related issues should be accorded a central role in discussions of commercial policy.

The implications for commercial policy

While there is only one kind of perfect competition, imperfect competition, of its nature, comes in many forms. The effects of protection will depend upon detailed characteristics of the protected industry. Two features in particular are emphasized in what follows. The first concerns the degree to which protection affects the prices of domestic producers, relative to their costs.

What is involved here is the question of whether a relaxation in the degree of international competition causes domestic price–cost margins to rise. (A valuable recent survey of the evidence on this issue is provided by Lyons (1983), who offers a critique of existing studies and sets out a methodology which avoids some of the pitfalls in earlier work. His own results, for the UK, indicate that protection leads to a significant rise in domestic price–cost margins.[3])

The second consideration concerns the possibility of the entry of new firms to the domestic industry. If protection leads to an increase in the profitability of domestic firms, we might expect that, at least in the long run, new firms enter the domestic market – and indeed, that some foreign firms, being now less profitable, exit from the market. Equivalently, this might be in part accomplished by a migration of foreign firms into the domestic economy (a phenomenon sometimes referred to as 'tariff jumping').

Analysing the effects of protection in this setting is a much more complex task than in a world of perfect competition. There is, however, a single unifying idea which underlies the various considerations involved. This is the idea, which we noted in passing in Chapter 7 above, that some kind of intervention may in principle be welfare-improving in such markets. This is so for two reasons:

1. Under imperfect competition, price will lie above marginal cost. Intervention of some kind might then be justified on the grounds that consumers are willing to pay more for additional units of output than their cost of production; output is below its optimum level.
2. Once we turn to markets in which products are differentiated, the market mechanism will not in general produce the welfare-optimal number of brands. (There is, however, no general tendency for the numbers produced by market forces to be either too high or too low – this depends on the detailed specification of consumer tastes and technology.)

It is natural to begin by asking what form of policy could bring us to a welfare optimum? (Such a policy is labelled, somewhat inelegantly, a 'first-best policy'.) The answer, in principle, is straightforward: a subsidy per unit produced would be paid to each firm in order to induce an expansion of output to the optimum level; and in so far as the number of brands on offer was suboptimal, lump-sum subsidies or taxes designed to induce entry and exit of producers – or to induce existing producers to offer more, or fewer, varieties – might be used.

But this kind of fine-tuning of microeconomic activity is quite outside the realms of practicality, as is evident in the case of point 2. Even to judge whether the current number of brands in each industry is above or below the optimal level is far beyond our powers (it would require, *inter alia*, detailed information of consumers' willingness to pay for various hypothetical products which might be offered). Even with regard to production subsidies, we would need reliable information on each firm's marginal-cost levels – which again poses major difficulties (each firm having an incentive to bias its estimate to its own advantage). Thus, no one seriously advocates a 'first-best' solution here; and it is this which motivates the search for 'second-best' remedies – devices which, though not aimed at achieving an optimal solution, might none the less be superior to *laissez-faire*.

This brings us to the central question of the present chapter: can protection be justified on the grounds that it offers a second-best instrument of this kind? If so, then such policies might be defended on the grounds of economic efficiency.

The answer, at first glance, would appear to be a clear-cut 'no'. For, in so far as protection relaxes competitive pressures in the domestic market, it might be expected to raise prices, relative to costs, thus exacerbating rather than ameliorating the original distortion. On closer examination, the answer turns out to be more complicated. We shall, however, argue that this 'obvious' response, though it needs careful qualification, probably represents the best simple generalization which can be drawn out. Let us begin, then, by looking at the way in which protection might make matters worse.

In so doing, we shall not attempt a systematic review of the literature of the past few years. (For an introduction to this, the reader is referred to Dixit, 1984; Kierzkowski, 1984; and Smith, 1983.) Rather, the focus will be on the main ideas relevant to policy issues, and particular models will be chosen which serve to illustrate these points, in a relatively straightforward manner. We shall first consider a case which was widely studied in the earlier literature (for example, Corden, 1967): that of a domestic monopolist facing a competitive world market. This affords us an extreme example, in which protection is particularly harmful. We then look at the situation which arises when the world market is highly concentrated. This 'oligopolistic' case, in which firms in the industry earn 'pure profits', has been studied in detail only quite recently.

Finally, we examine a case in which firms produce differentiated products under increasing returns to scale; price exceeds marginal cost, at equilibrium, but free entry of firms occurs up to a point at which all 'pure profits' are eroded (firms earn only 'normal' profits, i.e. sufficient to yield a normal rate of return on the investment incurred in setting up production facilities). This affords us an example of the case of 'monopolistic competition'.

A domestic monopolist

We begin, then, with the case of a local monopolist facing imports from a competitive world industry (which offers a product identical to his). The monopolist's optimal policy here is to lower his price to (just below) the price of the imported substitute. In this way, he captures *all* domestic sales. In this case, protection is particularly harmful. The effect of imposing a tariff is to raise the price of imports on the domestic market. The optimal response of the domestic producer is to raise price to (just below) the post-tariff price of imports. Thus the effect of protection is to increase the degree of monopoly in the domestic market.[4] The effect is a fall in output, and employment, in the protected industry, but a rise in industry profits, at the expense of higher prices for consumers. (Indeed, a *negative* tariff – a subsidy on imports – would provide a second-best instrument for increasing welfare in this case.) For details, the reader is referred to Corden (1967). A quota restriction is shown to be even less desirable than a tariff in these circumstances by Bhagwati (1965).

This general conclusion carries over to the case in which the domestic market is characterized by price leadership (i.e. one domestic firm sets a price, which others then 'follow', thereby avoiding mutually destructive 'price wars'). This case is of particular relevance here, as it might plausibly be argued to approximate price behaviour in the UK motor industry up to fairly recently (but see Chapter 10 below).

Our conclusion in respect of protection, here, raises an obvious question, however: with increasing returns, a local producer may find that, while its unit costs lie above world price at low levels of output, it could achieve a level of unit costs at or below the world price level if it 'captured the domestic market'. This is a theme frequently emphasized in the present debate. The answer here is that there is, indeed, a possible case for intervention. Depending on the level of world price relative to domestic costs,[5] it may be socially optimal to produce locally, but still it may not be profitable for a local firm to enter the market. In this case, it will be optimal to pay a subsidy (per unit of output) to the domestic firm, in order to achieve the optimal outcome. This is an unsurprising conclusion, given the nature of the underlying problem, and accords with our simple summary view of the matter, as stated earlier. If for any reason such subsidization is considered impracticable or undesirable, the use of protection does not offer an alternative; it can only make matters worse.[6]

We now turn, however, to a number of qualifications which arise once we go beyond this 'domestic monopolist' model.

The case of oligopoly

We assumed above that the world market was competitive. Suppose, instead, that there are only a small number of producers – the world market is oligopolistic. Then matters become much more complex. Some general ideas emerge from the literature, however, which deserve attention.

The first idea relates to the fact that, if foreign firms earn pure profit in the domestic market, then a tariff can be used as a means of extracting some of that profit – both through its revenue-raising effect and through switching industry profits in favour of the local firm. This kind of 'rent snatching' has received considerable attention in the recent literature (for an overview, see Dixit, 1984). This case is of interest in that it leads to the possibility that protection might be welfare-improving, relative to *laissez-faire*, for the domestic economy (so long as there is no retaliation).

But if it is the case that 'rent snatching' effects lead to an efficiency gain, then a practicable alternative instrument is available which is superior to protection. For, if the aim is to extract pure profits from foreign producers, then this can be achieved directly by means of price controls on imported goods. This is superior in welfare terms to protection; it is also quite different in its distributional implications – the benefits accrue to consumers through a lowering of prices, at the expense of domestic profits. (As to the practical relevance of these arguments, see page 124 below.)

It is by no means true in general, under oligopolistic conditions, that protection offers a second-best device for improving welfare (quite apart from the availability of superior instruments). The point emphasized earlier, that protection may make things worse, relative to *laissez-faire,* is emphasized by Krishna (as reported in Dixit, 1984), who considers a setting in which there is one domestic firm and one foreign rival. The two firms are supposed to be unable to sustain collusion under free trade. But now suppose the domestic government introduces an import quota. This can have the effect of raising prices by 'facilitating collusion'. This happens because, in the presence of the quota, the tendency for the foreign firm to undercut its domestic rival's price is diminished – in that the quota restriction which limits its output, at equilibrium, will prevent it from achieving any gain from price reductions. The result is that the presence of the quota allows a collusive arrangement, leading once again to the general idea that protection is likely to result in higher domestic prices, and thereby reduce welfare relative to *laissez-faire.*

One final aspect of the 'oligopoly' case is worth noting. This concerns the fact that protection might serve not only to limit imports, but to promote exports in the protected industry (albeit at the expense of export losses in other industries). This case may arise if the domestic firm's *marginal* cost falls as output expands. For now, expanding sales in the home market gives it a cost advantage relative to its rivals in export markets (Krugman, 1982).

It must be remarked, however, that (1) this result depends on some quite particular assumptions as to the firm's price behaviour[7] (it is not clear what is the most reasonable postulate to make in this context, and the results depend quite crucially on the detailed assumptions of the underlying model); and (2) there is no presumption that this policy is welfare-improving for the domestic economy.

What is of general interest here is the idea that protection might allow domestic firms to achieve lower costs by allowing them to achieve greater economies of scale. Central to such arguments is the idea that measures which enhance the profitability of domestic firms will not induce the entry of new firms (or avoid exit of existing firms). If, on the other hand, entry and exit occur in the long run, up to the point at which all firms earn a normal rate of return, then there is no longer any presumption that protection will lead to enhanced scale economies for local producers. We now examine a situation in which this latter case holds.

Product differentiation: monopolistic competition

This case has been described recently by Venables (1982), who considers an industry in which a large number of firms produce differentiated products, and in which free entry continues up to a point at which (pure) profits are zero. Thus any fall in profits will induce exit from the industry. The imposition of a tariff, in this setting, has the effect of reducing the profits of foreign firms and increasing the profits of home firms. This causes exit abroad and entry at home: a process which can at least in part be achieved by the migration of foreign firms to the domestic economy. Now the imposition of tariffs which led to such 'tariff jumping' is not specific to this particular kind of model – it is quite general. In classical trade theory, however, the use of tariffs to achieve this end would be welfare-reducing. What is of interest here is that welfare is thereby enhanced.

Where does this welfare gain come from? It flows directly from the fact that more varieties are now available more cheaply to domestic consumers, in that they do not carry a price premium to cover costs of transport. Stated in this way, the result seems to be of limited applicability; but that is to understate its interest. There might be substantial, further, advantages to engineering a switch of location of producers into the domestic market. In this regard, the model corresponds to the 'most pessimistic' case, in which only the saving of transport costs figures in this calculation. Its assumption that free entry occurs up to the point at which profits are zero excludes two further channels: (1) profits of migrant firms add to the domestic tax base; and (2) some of the profits may accrue (through wage bargaining) to workers in the favoured locality in the form of wage rates in excess of those which they otherwise could have obtained.[7]

The interest of this model lies in its pointing to the possibility that protection directed towards inducing tariff jumping might, albeit only under particularly favourable circumstances, be welfare-improving. An important qualification is in order, however; for the result that protection is welfare-improving depends crucially on the fact that the assumptions of this analysis imply that prices in the domestic economy do not rise at all relative to costs when the tariff is imposed.[8] Thus the model corresponds to an extreme 'optimistic' case in this regard. Tariffs are assumed not to make matters worse in respect of the divergence between price and marginal cost: in this regard they are supposed to be neutral.

In practice, therefore, any claims that protection aimed at inducing tariff-jumping migration by foreign firms is in the general interest would have to be argued on the basis of some rather difficult assessment of the likely implications for competition, and so for price–cost margins, in the domestic economy.

Other policies

We began our discussion of commercial policy by noting that a prima facie case for intervention existed in increasing-returns sectors. We also pointed to the fact that a subsidy, aimed at an expansion of domestic output, would be a first-best policy. It is not surprising, therefore, that it has been pointed out recently (Dixit, 1984; see also Spencer and Brander, 1983) that export subsidies can be welfare-improving, relative to *laissez-faire*, in oligopolistic industries. The welfare gain here flows through the shifting of industry profits in favour of the domestic firm – for that firm's response is to reduce its price, relative to that of its foreign rivals, thus capturing a greater share of the international market.

Of particular interest, here, is the fact that it is also welfare-improving for the foreign government, faced with such a subsidy, to impose a (less than fully offsetting) 'countervailing tariff'. This is in striking contrast to classical trade theory, where if a foreign producer offers such a subsidy to his exports, then the policy-maker would *reduce* domestic welfare by responding with a countervailing tariff.

It would be easy, however, to overstate both the attractiveness of export subsidies to the domestic economy, and the reasonableness of appeals for countervailing tariffs. While these models provide a logically coherent case for both positions, a rather serious question has been posed recently by de Meza (1984) as to whether such models really represent the arguments relevant to the current policy debate on these questions. The point at issue is this: export subsidies, like tariffs, will always be attractive to the favoured industry, the losers being workers and firms in other industries, as well as consumers generally. Likewise, the import-competing industry whose foreign competitors enjoy a subsidy will find, in this argument, convenient grounds for asking for 'counter-vailing' protection – which, whatever its merits for general welfare, will of course benefit the protected industry. What de Meza notes is that the use of export subsidies in oligopolistic industries is *less* beneficial than a simple policy of imposing a maximum price on exports. (Such a policy 'works' by influencing the foreign rival to reduce its output level. The detailed argument here is quite complex.) No one, of course, advocates such a policy. The point is, rather, that attempts to justify demands for a system of export subsidies as being in the general interest are probably suspect. Their attraction in practice lies, quite simply, in their income-redistributional effects for the favoured industry.

Retaliation

All of the above discussion is based on the notion that protection will not invite retaliation. The risk of precipitating a round of successive protectionist measures is perhaps the main deterrent for policy-makers, faced by powerful domestic lobbies. It is of interest, therefore, to ask what losses might be incurred by a slide into protectionism. This in turn raises the question: how large are the gains from trade? Empirical studies based on the classical model suggested that the elimination of existing barriers to trade could generate gains of the order of 1 per cent of GNP or less, for a wide range of economies.

Such studies, however, exclude any contribution emanating from enhanced economies of scale achieved by way of intra-industry trade. The only estimates to date which encompass this contribution are those of Harris and Cox (1984). They refer to the gains achievable by the Canadian economy from trade liberalization. They find that the welfare gains are dramatically larger than those estimated using the classical model. Unilateral elimination of current Canadian tariffs yielded gains of the order of 2 to 5 per cent of GNP, while the benefits achievable under multilateral free trade were of the order of 8 to 10 per cent of GNP. One of the most interesting features of these results, moreover, is that most of the gains would follow from rationalization within individual industries. The intersectoral reallocation of labour implied by liberalization 'was found to be minimal under both trade policies, suggesting that the adjustment costs of adopting a free-trade policy may not be large'.

These estimates underline the particular dangers inherent in a slide towards protectionism in those sectors which have been our concern in the present chapter. The claim sometimes made in Europrotectionist writings, that an integrated European market is sufficiently large to exhaust scale economies, amounts to saying that the gains from trade for the Community as a whole are not very large. If this were so, the fears of provoking successive rounds of retaliation would be correspondingly less serious. The Harris–Cox estimates cited above refer to the Canadian economy; no similar study has as yet been done for the EEC. It is at least arguable that the fractional gains for the larger European economy might be significantly smaller (though the recent study of three European industries by Owen (1983) offers some limited support for the view that gains are indeed very sizeable). This remains an important open question.

A summing-up

The presence of increasing returns to scale (which in turn implies imperfect competition) significantly alters the prescriptions of the classical theory of international trade. The main theme of the present chapter has been that protection, in this setting, is likely to lead to a relaxation of competitive pressures on domestic producers, leading to a rise in their price–cost mark-ups. This will enhance the profits of the domestic industry, and may lead to the entry of new firms. The case most favourable to protection is that in which the final result is a migration of firms to the domestic economy, with no rise in price–cost margins, and no fall in the scale at which each firm operates. Under these circumstances, protection – if it provokes no retaliation – might be welfare-improving for the domestic economy.

All of this in turn suggests the question: what determines the locational pattern of firms in each industry across countries? To answer this, we need to integrate the themes of the present chapter with the traditional comparative-advantage framework. What the classical theory tells us is that the location of industries across countries is determined by the pattern of endowments of (immobile) factors of production. These include land, capital equipment, labour of various skill categories and so on (and some of these may themselves be influenced by policy in the long run). What our above analysis lacks, then, is this kind of 'general equilibrium' perspective. The location across countries of the firms which make up a given industry will reflect the relative intensities of factor usage in that industry. To work against this pattern, by imposing protectionist measures, will lead to the same dead-weight loss in efficiency as we encountered within the classical model.

An example may help to make this clear. Consider a domestic producer whose unit costs will, even if he captures the entire domestic market, still lie above the world price. Then, protection can be used to foster a domestic industry by setting a 'made to measure' tariff which is just sufficient to cover the gap between this unit-cost level and world price. Under these circumstances, the domestic firm will just cover its costs; and it will sell to the entire domestic market. There is a very strong case for avoiding this kind of policy, on grounds of economic efficiency (for a full discussion of the costs involved, see Corden, 1979). There is a serious danger, moreover, that the pursuit of protection in increasing-returns sectors may in practice involve working against the pattern of comparative advantage in just this manner.

10   The case of the car industry[1]

The car industry offers an example of sizeable economies of scale; world-wide, a mere eight firms share 70 per cent of the market. On the scope of scale economies across various European industries, see Owen (1983). Both the degree of scale economies, and the pattern of comparative advantage across countries, vary widely between different segments of the industry.[2] Within Europe, the main producers are Germany, France, Italy and the UK. Of these, only the German industry seems confident of its ability to survive under free trade; the industry has been quite troubled in recent years both in France and in the UK, while the new-found confidence of the Italian industry follows a period of unprecedented strife. In France, the market is dominated by Renault (state-owned), and Peugeot (privately owned). In Italy, Fiat dominates the market. By contrast, the UK market supports four main producers: British Leyland, Ford, General Motors (Vauxhall, Opel) and Talbot (owned by Peugeot). Given the importance of increasing returns in this sector, the fragmentation of production in the UK is particularly striking.

Imports from outside the Community come predominantly from Japan. (The newly industrializing countries have yet to make a major impact, and East European sources, though in the news lately, account for less than 2 per cent of Community sales.) Following a major surge of exports in 1980, Japan's share of the European market became, and remains, around 10 per cent; though it varies widely across member states. Italy in effect excludes Japanese exports almost totally, under a GATT exception. France imposes quotas limiting imports to a mere 3 per cent. Imports to the UK are limited by a voluntary export restraint, agreed between the motor industries' trade association (the Society of Motor Manufacturers and Traders) and their Japanese counterparts. Japanese imports currently take about 11 per cent of the UK market. Among the four main producers, Germany has the most open policy, in that it applied the common EC tariff of 11 per cent, without further quota limits, up to October 1980, when Japanese car makers took just over 10 per cent of total registration (as compared with about 9 per cent for French imports, and about 4 per cent for Italian). Following this, Germany obtained an agreement from Japan to reduce imports in 1981, but this was not renewed, suggesting that the confidence of the industry in its international competitiveness was rapidly restored.

The West European market as a whole is currently dominated by six firms; as of the first half of 1983, the percentage shares were: Ford, 12.6; Renault, 12.4; Volkswagen/Audi, 12.2; Fiat, 12.1; Peugeot Group, 11.7; and General Motors, 11.5. (British Leyland, Mercedes and BMW have between 3 and 4 per cent each; total Japanese imports are around 10 per cent.) Ford and General Motors are currently vying with each other to increase their shares. The result of this has been particularly evident in the UK over the past two years; where two years ago GM had a 9 per cent share, it aims to reach 16 per cent in 1984. This is aided by the ending of production of the highly successful Ford Cortina, as well as the introduction of GM's Spanish-built Vauxhall Nova/Opel Corsa, which competes in the small-car sector in which GM was not previously represented. Ford, with its 30 per cent market share, is therefore in a potentially weak position. The latter half of 1983, and the first few months of 1984, saw an intermittent price-cutting war between the two. Even the Japanese firms, in spite of their 11 per cent quota limit, joined in offering discounts rather than lose market shares. (Their share, in the event, slipped by almost 1 per cent in the year ending September 1983.) British Leyland retained a fairly steady share of about 18 per cent over the period.

The UK industry has, in the past few years, achieved a marked improvement in productivity. In British Leyland, this took the form of manpower reductions, the introduction of robots and new management systems. None the less, Japan retains a clear (absolute) advantage in motor manufacture. While comparisons are difficult, Noelke and Taylor (1981) note that the number of vehicles per worker per year in Japan is about 30–40, more than double the EEC figure of 12–15. British Leyland compares well with the EEC figure at its new plant assembling the Metro

(19–20), though further improvements (to 24–25) could be achieved via scale economies if EEC sales are sufficiently favourable.

In France, the market share of domestic producers has fallen from 78 per cent in 1979 to 68 per cent in the first half of 1984; the Peugeot group actually gained 1 per cent, leaving Renault with a 4 per cent loss of share over the period. Renault, under increasing pressure abroad from the 'American Europeans', is thus particularly vulnerable to this loss in the domestic market. Its production costs have been rising, in part owing to improved non-wage benefits to workers. Its response has been to invest its way out; the French government is expected to contribute over one-tenth of the cost of its ambitious three-year programme, aimed at improving and automating its plants, and preparing to launch a new (medium-to-large) model, in 1984–5. Currently, 70 per cent of its investment is in Europe, but it is also increasing its interests abroad. In June 1983, it agreed to purchase a further 25 per cent of the second-biggest American heavy-truck producer, Mack Truck, thus raising its stake to 45 per cent. It is also extending its interests in Mexico, buying out the Mexican government's share in Renault de Mexico and Mexican Automotive Vehicles. Its target in Mexico is to achieve 15–16 per cent of car sales by 1985. Renault still faces major difficulties, however, in reducing manning levels to the extent needed to keep it competitive. Even more troubled, in this respect, is the private-sector Peugeot group, two of whose parts, Citröen and Talbot, are now fighting for survival.

The Italian market, despite the exclusion of Japan, is second to Britain among major international producers in terms of import penetration. Imports accounted for 37 per cent of the market in early 1983. Of this, the 'American Europeans' took over 8 per cent, while the Peugeot group and Volkswagen/Audi each had 6–7 per cent. Of the 63 per cent held by domestic producers, Fiat/Lancia held 55 per cent and Alfa-Romeo 6 per cent. Thus Fiat's fortunes are crucial, and these have shown a remarkable recovery over the past few years. Its 55 per cent market share in early 1983 represented a 3 per cent gain over the preceding year, and this reflects the fruits of a massive investment programme introduced in the late 1970s, when the company was at a very low ebb. The programme involved a new model range, the automation and 'robotization' of production, and a reduction in the work-force from 330,000 (in the late 1970s) to 254,000 in mid-1983. Productivity has now improved by 20–30 per cent and is at least equal to that of the company's main European rivals.

In September 1983, Alfa-Romeo launched the Arna, the fruit of a joint venture with Nissan (it is in fact a Nissan Cherry built by Alfa-Romeo and equipped with Italian mechanical components). Fiat objected to this arrangement, but failed to halt it. Most recently, Alfa-Romeo and Fiat have turned to cooperation: they will invest equal amounts in a venture which involves each company specializing in making certain components used by both; it is estimated that cost savings of 15–20 per cent can be achieved in this way.

The future fortunes of both the French and Italian industries will depend heavily on one factor: the concentration of their exports on the European market. The EEC and EFTA together account for about three-quarters of French and Italian (and in fact German) exports. This contrasts sharply with the more diversified picture for the UK, more than half of whose exports go outside Europe (Asia, Africa and the Americas each accounting for more than one-tenth). Moreover, Japanese exports to Europe are concentrated in countries other than the four leading producers. It is the French and Italian car producers who lose most when the Japanese increase sales in Europe – partly a reflection of the similarity of sizes of their respective models. Conversely, it is France and Italy who have most to gain from a shift to EEC-level protection. A second theme to emerge from the French and Italian experience is the growing acceptance of the attractiveness of joint ventures with Japanese firms. It is against this background that the tensions within the Community surrounding the recent decision by Nissan to set up an operation in the UK should be judged.

In the USA, both General Motors and Ford have been engaged in major cost-cutting programmes. Direct employment in the US industry was reduced from over 1 million in 1978 to 685,000 in 1982. By 1985, the US industry as a whole will have almost completely re-equipped its plants. Involvement with Japanese firms has also been growing in the USA. General Motors imports both from Isuzu, in which it has a 34 per cent stake, and from Suzuki, in which it holds a 5 per cent interest. Ford owns a 25 per cent stake in Toyo Kogyo, which it uses to supply its dealers in the Asia-Pacific region. This leads to a certain mixture of motives in the industry in relation to Japanese competition: any tightening of the Japanese quota is liable to affect GM's imports of small cars, which it cannot produce at similar cost in the USA.

In December 1983 the US Federal Trade Commission approved a joint production plan between GM and Toyota. The ruling permits the two companies jointly to build more than 250,000 Japanese-designed small cars at a GM plant, without violating US antitrust laws. This decision is consistent with the general loosening of US antitrust law in recent years. Ford intend to appeal the decision; if it stands, it may lead to a wave of similar deals, which in the past were avoided for fear of antitrust proceedings.[3] It was the United States which took the lead in reacting to the Japanese export surge of 1980, limiting their US sales to 1.68 million cars a year. In the wake of this agreement the EEC member states asked the Commission to negotiate a similar arrangement with Japan for the Community as a whole. But before any deal could be reached, the remaining 'unrestricted' members, Germany and the Benelux, pre-empted the issue by negotiating bilateral arrangements.[4]

Thus the present situation within the Community is one in which trade is restricted on a country-by-country basis, via bilateral arrangements involving quotas or VERs. The disadvantages of such a scheme have been noted already. The question at issue in the current protectionist debate is to what extent it might be feasible, and desirable, to replace this with a higher common external tariff (currently 11 per cent) accompanied by a freeing of the internal market, whether at the EEC level, or in conjunction with EFTA.

What would the impact of such a switch in regime be? Given the emphasis placed by French policy-makers on guarding the home market as a base for domestic producers, it seems unlikely that their present 3 per cent import quota on Japanese cars will be dismantled, unless the tariff suggested is very substantial – bearing in mind the unpredictability of their export gains to other Community members. (It is probably safe to assume that Italy would retain its prohibition on Japanese imports, under the GATT exception – the legality of which, incidentally, is disputed by Japan.)

We have already noted that Japan's share in the four main producer countries is (per cent): UK (11), Germany (10), France

(3), Italy (0). Its share in the other Community member states is much higher (up to one-fifth or more). The main impact of a shift to a high common external tariff would be a fall in Japan's share in these 'other' Community members. The main losers from such a shift would be consumers in those countries – and given the relatively small size of their industries, this would be likely to far outweigh any gain to producers. The main gainers would be France and Italy, each of whom sends over 70 per cent of its exports to other Western European countries and who compete in the same size range as Japan. Both Germany and the UK represent intermediate cases. The case of the UK stands out as an exception, in that only about 40 per cent of its exports go to other Western European countries; for the second major consequence of such a policy shift would be a diversion of Japanese exports to other markets. Clearly, the UK is notable for its greater vulnerability to such shifts.

Discussions of retaliation tend all too often to focus on direct responses in terms of access to the rival's own market; in this industry, the changing balance of sales in third countries will be far more important than any such direct retaliatory measures. Noelke and Taylor (1981) cite the case of the interesting coincidence where a number of Japanese cars denied access to the French market found their way to Algeria, where the main competitor was Renault. It appears to be generally accepted that this was a deliberate tit-for-tat move – just as it is believed that Volkswagen's half share of the (very limited) imports of cars to Japan is a reward for its liberal stance on Community decision-making.

The protectionist case

The main thrust of the current Europrotectionist case rests on the assertion that a tightening of external barriers will have the great virtue of leading to increased liberalization of intra-Community trade. This forms the centrepiece of the argument put forward by Wolfgang Hager (1982), a very influential European academic advocate of protectionism. A second, and important, strand in this argument is that the European market (extended to include EFTA) is sufficient to permit the scale economies necessary for efficiency to be achieved.

The Community market is at present seriously encumbered with a plethora of non-tariff barriers designed to protect domestic producers in their respective home markets. The British Society of Motor Manufacturers has recently objected to various technical and administrative barriers facing UK firms in the Community. The most widely noted issue is that concerning 'Type Approval Certificates'. These are issued through the car firms of the importing country, or their approved agents, and their issue may involve substantial delays. Further difficulties are posed by differences in technical standards. Currently, for example, a stalemate has been reached on the issue of agreeing common standards, for safety-glass windscreens.[5] This is an issue in which the point of difference that remains concerns the question of Community certification for non-member countries. This illustrates a general fear, that common standards help all exporters equally – but it remains a moot point whether such divergences in standards will not continue to be used to regulate the internal market, even in the absence of outside competition.

The question is, then, whether increased external protection will result in a freeing of the internal market. The issue must, to some degree, be a matter for conjecture; but one consideration which suggests that such liberalization is unlikely to be easy of achievement, let alone to follow as an automatic consequence from the removal of (Japanese) competition, is the deep-seated and persistent difficulty currently encountered by the Community in eliminating price discrimination in cars. European manufacturers typically sell at widely different prices in different member states: for example, in July 1984, British prices averaged almost 30 per cent above those in Belgium.[6] Such price discrimination can of course only be practised if UK dealers are in some way prevented from buying in Belgium. It is the associated use of various devices to inhibit the free movement of goods within the Community that brings this matter into the orbit of the Commission – which in fact sees the abolition of such barriers as a key element in its strategy. The barriers are numerous. Manufacturers can require dealers only to sell to final purchasers, and not to other dealers. Then, to prevent the final purchaser from importing the car himself, long delivery dates can be quoted – or, in the case of British buyers, who have an unusually large margin to gain, an exorbitant surcharge can be quoted for supplying right-hand drive.

The most blatant attempts are sometimes successfully foiled by the Commission. In February 1983, twenty-five German Ford dealers placed advertisements in German daily newspapers, which carried the assertion: 'We do not carry out guarantee work on new Ford cars reimported after being purchased elsewhere in the European Community.' Following a Commission ruling, a further advertisement was placed, which withdrew the earlier statement.[7] Later that year, however, a further incident arose, again involving German dealers, but this time aimed at potential exporters: dealers who had been refusing to supply right-hand drive vehicles to agents were in this instance ordered by the Commission to recommence sales.

The story is one of constant piecemeal attempts by the Commission to outlaw specific examples of such practices; but an overall solution is not likely to be forthcoming in the foreseeable future. Britain's position on the issue has been somewhat ambivalent. In May 1984, the UK government indicated that it would oppose the Commission's latest bid to reduce differentials. The following July, the Commission fined British Leyland £210,000 for trying to prevent left-hand-drive Metro cars from being reimported. But in October, the UK backed the Commission's new draft regulations, which were designed to ban discrimination. It was reported, however, that French, German and Italian civil servants were all engaged in lobbying against the new proposals. Finally, a new and separate note was published by the Commission, explaining how it would interpret the proposed regulation. This explained that Denmark, Greece and Belgium would be excluded from the terms, which will apply to all other member countries. As these countries have the lowest pre-tax manufacturers' prices in the Community, this largely vitiates the potential benefits.[8]

The erection of new external barriers is unlikely to prove a panacea in liberalizing trade within the Community. The problem, at root, is that even within a unified Community market, isolated from outside competition, the present number of firms are unlikely to survive under free competition. The fragmented state of the UK industry has already been stressed. The only industry which can count on success is the German, though given the new-found confidence of the Italian industry, it would probably rate its chances highly. The French case is less evident – there is no doubt, however, that under such a scenario, there would be no change in the French government's commitment to heavy underwriting of Renault's investment programmes, in order to ensure its survival. The absence of free trade within the Community has little to do with outside competition, and the claim that liberalization of intra-Community trade would be a major benefit of increased protection is without substance. Thus the main benefit claimed for Euro-protectionism by its adherents is not likely to materialize.[9]

The other element in the Europrotectionist argument lies in an appeal to the inadequacy of the classical defence of free trade. The main shortcoming of the classical model, in the present context, lies in its assumption of non-increasing returns to scale. This, however, as we have seen in the preceding chapter, leads at best to a highly qualified argument for protection, even in the absence of retaliation. Any case to be made along these lines must rest, *inter alia,* on particular assumptions as to the likely impact of protection on price competition in the protected European market. The most plausible scenario is one in which reduced competition is accompanied by a rise in price by European producers; and the net effect of protection, even with no retaliation, is likely to be detrimental.

Much has been made, in the present debate, of the fact that the size of the European market is adequate to permit scale economies sufficient to achieve efficient levels of operation. It must be said, in this regard, that this is by no means clear, if the present number of European producers remains unchanged. A removal of internal barriers, with or without the introduction of prohibitive tariffs on imports to the Community, would be likely to result in the exit of a number of European producers. Thus, external protection is again no panacea, in respect of the viability of an over-fragmented European industry.

So the case for protection of the European industry is at best a highly qualified one. What, then, of the question of feasibility: how likely is it that Community partners can come to some agreement as to the replacement of current barriers by a higher common external tariff? We pointed out above that such a policy would be likely to be vetoed by France and Italy, unless the external tariff was set at a (near-)prohibitive level. This in itself would make acceptance by Germany, at least, highly unlikely. Moreover, the main beneficiaries from such a shift would be France and Italy, whose gains would take the form of increased sales in other European countries (rather than domestically). The losers, therefore, would be the smaller, non-producer countries: and so the political impetus against any such common external tariff could be considerable.

Whatever its merits, then, the likelihood that this Europrotectionist route will be followed seems small. What in that case is the more likely trend? The main trend now evident is towards increasing collaborative ventures, as evidenced in the USA by both the GM-Isuzu link and the new Toyota link-up. In Europe the same trend is developing, as evidenced by the Alfa-Romeo/Nissan link. The UK approach has been different, in that it has aimed at inducing Nissan to set up independently on a green-field site. The aim of all these ventures is at least in part to enhance productivity levels, and this aspect of the Nissan deal was the one most heavily emphasized on the UK side. The new trend in itself poses problems of coordination of policies within the Community – and it is on this front that we are likely to see the most serious efforts at hammering out a common policy over the next few years.

The need for a coordinated policy in this sphere is urgent. Considerable tension has been generated within the Community by the UK-Nissan affair.[10] The French announced, in the first instance, that as 40 per cent of Nissan's product was to be imported to the UK as parts, they would count 40 per cent of the UK-based firm's French sales as part of France's 3 per cent Japanese quota.[11] This threat was later withdrawn, as a result of UK efforts to achieve an understanding.[12] More recently, however, Fiat have protested against the deal. Whether the Fiat view will be taken up by the Italian government, however, is an open question; but the tensions are evident.

The underlying problem here is a general issue surrounding all questions of inward investment. European governments now compete with each other in attracting foreign firms – especially by way of offers of tax breaks and investment subsidies. In so far as such firms are intent on locating in one or other EC country (as a means of side-stepping tariff and quota restrictions), then competition between member states in offering more attractive packages can only result in a simple redistribution of the putative gains to the incoming company. Clearly, it is imperative for the Community to agree common standards in such instances, serious though the practical difficulties in developing a coordinated approach may be. Some invidious examples have arisen in other industries of late, which indicate that the limited constraints which now exist on member countries are often breached. In April 1983 the Commission announced that it was taking legal proceedings against France and Britain over planned aid to two US companies, Timex and Hyster. A planned Hyster plant in Scotland was expected to cause job losses in the Netherlands and Belgium, while the Timex plant was scheduled to open in France at a time when the company had announced the closure of a plant in Dundee.[13]

It is in this area that a coordination of European policies is most desirable, and most urgent.

A summing-up

We have argued above along the following lines:

Desirability

1. The case for protection, in so far as it rests on the plea that a high common external tariff will lead to a freeing of the internal market, is unconvincing.
2. An appeal to the presence of increasing returns in the industry can lead at best to a highly qualified economic argument for protection. Moreover, such an argument would require unwarrantably optimistic assumptions as to the likely response of domestic car prices, in response to a relaxation of competitive pressures from imports.

Feasibility

1. The current level of protection enjoyed by France and Italy is so high that only an extremely high common external tariff would be likely to find support. This, in turn, makes German support for the scheme extremely unlikely.
2. The main winners from the shift would be France and Italy. The main losers would be the smaller, non-producer members. This further accentuates the likelihood of serious disagreement on the issue.

Other issues: inward investment

The present trend in both the European, and the American, industry, is towards collaborative ventures with foreign (largely Japanese) firms. This has led to serious tensions within the Community, as French reaction to the UK-Nissan deal indicates. It is a matter of extreme urgency that the Community coordinate its policies in agreeing a uniform scheme of incentives in respect of such inward investment. One of the main effects of current protection is that it provides an incentive for foreign firms to 'tariff jump' by setting up production facilities within the Community. The benefit accruing to recipient countries (through the creation of 'high wage' jobs, and the receipt of profit taxation *inter alia*) makes it attractive for Community members to compete among themselves in bidding for such investment, to their mutual loss. It is a matter of urgency that a 'cooperative' solution to this problem be achieved, by setting a practicable and enforceable Community standard.

Retaliation

The case for Europrotection rests *inter alia* on an assumption of 'no retaliation' by trading partners.

Direct retaliation has not been common of late, though folk memories of the vicious circle of the 1930s continue to act as a brake on unilateral moves by the major trading nations. Such cases as do occur, however, exert a profound influence. Indonesia applied sanctions against Britain in 1980, which affected UK exporters of capital equipment, in response to the UK's actions on textiles. Cable (1983) remarks: 'The threat to British exporters by a large ldc of considerable economic potential appears to have shaken the government – from the Prime Minister down – more effectively than any demonstration of the wider costs of protection.'

None the less, while this more dramatic form of direct retaliation is more effective as a political signal, it is probably much less important, in economic terms, than 'indirect' moves operating through third-country markets. We noted above the case in which a number of Japanese cars denied access to the French market found their way to Algeria, where their main competitor was Renault. It is indirect moves of this kind, operating through competition in third-country markets, which are likely to be by far the most important source of losses through 'retaliation'.

11 The case of R&D-intensive sectors: industrial policy and the French memorandum

Up to this point, we have simply taken the range of products produced by each country as given. Our focus in the present chapter is on the use of commercial- or industrial-policy instruments to affect the range of products produced, through stimulating R&D activities. The role of such industrial-policy instruments as R&D subsidies in this regard is self-evident; what is by no means clear is whether the considerations which arise in this context offer any role for commercial policies (tariffs, public procurement, etc.) beyond those which we have explored in earlier chapters. Much of the current debate within Europe on this issue has been focused around the recent 'French memorandum'.[1]

The French memorandum

In September 1983, the French government submitted a memorandum to the Council of the European Communities in which it set out a strongly argued case for a coordinated industrial policy for Europe. This document was prepared in anticipation of the ill-fated Athens meeting (December 1983), but as long as fundamental disagreement continued on budgetary matters no serious debate was possible on the merits of the French plan. It has, however, focused attention once again on the complex issues surrounding European policy.

Two main themes run through the document: the first, which is the subject of the present chapter, concerns the role of subsidies and of related commercial policies, in R&D-intensive sectors. The second theme, which we will consider in the next chapter, refers to the implications for European competition policy.

Subsidizing R&D

Article 5 of the memorandum states that Community aid must be directed towards financing technological innovation and industrial cooperation, via interest subsidies, loan guarantees, tax incentives coordinated among the member states, and participation via capital contributions and shareholdings in the undertakings concerned.

This is the least contentious strand in the memorandum. A convincing economic rationale exists for some form of intervention in support of R&D activity, and member states would be in broad agreement with the notion that a European solution makes sense in this sphere. The general rationale for such support runs along the following lines: firms' R&D efforts produce benefits which are not wholly captured ('internalized') by the innovating firm itself. Some of these benefits spill over to other firms in the industry, which profit by utilizing the enhanced knowledge spawned by the research effort. Again, some of the benefit is captured by consumers, either through reduced prices, or through their enjoying access to new products.[2] The way in which the benefits are partitioned depends *inter alia* on the efficacy of patent protection and the degree of competition in the product market. But there will be, as Arrow (1962) noted, a general tendency for social gains from R&D to exceed private gains (the profit increment enjoyed by the innovating firm). Thus, the market economy may tend to generate 'too little' R&D, relative to the social optimum. A case therefore exists for intervention, aimed at subsidizing R&D activity.[3]

One particular reason for a divergence between private and social returns is worth noting in the present context. This is that, over the duration of a lengthy product-development process, a firm may lose personnel to rival firms in the industry. The point is of particular relevance in the information-technology sector; the quite unparalleled movement of personnel, and the flow of ideas among companies, has been a widely remarked feature of the computer industry since its inception. This kind of difficulty is central to infant-industry arguments, to which we turn in the next section.

The general line of argument just cited is a familiar one; in the recent literature, however, a separate tendency has been emphasized, which runs in the opposite direction. This observes that, in so far as firms enjoy some degree of patent protection, there will be a tendency for 'patent races' to develop, in which firms compete to 'win the patent'. In so doing, they may tend to duplicate each other's efforts, with the result that the market may produce too much, rather than too little, R&D (Dasgupta and Stiglitz, 1980). In fact, the formal welfare analysis of intervention in R&D-intensive industries has only recently begun to receive attention from economists, and many important questions have not been resolved. In particular, the degree to which subsidies should be used as a (partial) substitute for (full) patent protection, and the optimal form of such subsidies, have been considered, as yet, only within the context of some special cases. (Spence [1984] presents some revealing examples of process innovation, and deduces *inter alia* the desirability of subsidizing *cooperative* R&D ventures, in situations where the degree of appropriability is high.)

Apart from the divergence between social and private returns to R&D, there is a second kind of argument which is frequently adduced to justify intervention: that many projects may entail initial costs which exceed the borrowing capacity of any one firm. The implication is that capital markets are imperfect, which leads to the notion that government should provide loan facilities of some kind (or else encourage or promote cooperative ventures – see Chapter 12 below).

The French memorandum calls for both these kinds of intervention: subsidies for R&D, as well as the provision of improved channels of financing (in fact the two may be linked in practice, via the provision of loans at interest rates below the market level). The economic rationale underlying such support, then, is a standard one. One point, however, deserves emphasis: the existence of a convincing rationale for subsidy does not of itself constitute an economic defence of the actual programmes we consider below (Alvey, Esprit), for the *level* of subsidy must still be argued on the basis of some view as to the size of the likely benefits relative to costs incurred. It is a striking feature of such schemes that no such calculation is usually offered; this reflects, doubtless, the difficulty of quantifying the likely gains – but it does prompt serious questions as to the scale of these projects.

It is interesting, in this regard, to note that the memorandum itself records the fact that the spending by the EEC countries on research is high relative to that of their competitors; in micro-processors for example, they spend, in total, twice what Japan spends ($500 million over 1977–81, as opposed to $250 million for Japan). The point which the memorandum seems to make, rather, is that this high level of spending is not reflected in performance (Japan having overtaken the USA in microprocessors, for instance, by capturing 40 per cent of the world market, relative to Europe's 10 per cent share). The lesson it draws is that the inefficiency of European spending can be attributed to the fragmentation and duplication of research effort among various member states; the problem, the argument goes, is that the economies of scale achievable by joint European programmes are not being exploited.

That this is indeed the explanation for Europe's weaker performance is asserted, rather than argued, in the memorandum. But the conclusion which is drawn is quite sound, and can stand alone: that a strong a priori case exists for joint endeavours in R&D, aimed at avoiding the duplication of effort inherent in parallel national programmes.

This argument seems compelling, at first sight, and the underlying principle would probably command strong support within the Community. None the less, the recent history of events within the information-technology sphere suggests a serious practical difficulty which makes such a goal less easy of fulfilment than might otherwise be the case. In October 1981, Japan announced its fifth-generation computer programme. At the same time, it invited a number of countries, including the UK, to discuss participation in the programme. The response of the UK, however, like that of other invitees, was to decline and to initiate instead its own national programme in this sphere (the Alvey programme). In the same vein, it is revealing that, while the French memorandum calls for stronger support by member states for the European Esprit programme, France itself is proceeding in any case to strengthen its own capability by means of a separate national programme.[4]

The pattern, then, is one of reluctance to place one's reliance on cooperative ventures to the exclusion of national programmes. The reasons for this tendency are not hard to find: there is a quite understandable fear that, in a joint plan, firms in the partner country may be quicker and more efficient in implementing the possibilities opened up by the joint development of 'enabling technologies'. Thus the benefits may accrue in a highly uneven way among participating countries. Such possibilities are not easy to judge, let alone quantify. The strength of such worries, however, is evident in the pattern of events we have just noted. Such fears probably constitute the major practical obstacle to a purely European solution in this sphere.

The implications for commercial policy

The French memorandum gives a central place to the idea that commercial policy should be used as a complement to the new European industrial policy which it envisages. It is this strand of the report which constitutes its most contentious aspect.

The memorandum makes four references to the use of commercial policy. Two of these relate to issues already discussed above (the new commercial policy instrument – Chapter 5 – and the use of protection to ease adjustment in contracting sectors – Chapters 7 and 8), while a third reference relates to the role of public procurement, an issue we discuss in the next section. The most controversial reference, however, is the following statement:

> A significant, if temporary, increase in customs duties must be possible where it can effectively encourage the emergence of a European industry, as has been already requested by one Member State in the case of the launching of a European 'compact disc' manufacturing programme; GATT provides the possibilities for this moreover.

What is being asserted here is that a special case exists for protection, on infant-industry grounds, of newly developed European products.

There is little economic substance to this view. Infant-industry arguments, as we noted above, arise only in those cases where for one reason or another a firm undertaking investment in developing some product is unable to internalize the full benefits from the project: an example would be, as we noted earlier, a case in which the mobility of personnel among rival firms over the course of a lengthy development period caused a leakage of benefits elsewhere. In such instances, a prima facie case for intervention exists; but even then, protection is inferior to subsidies as a means of coping with the problems posed by such an externality. Thus, even in the most favourable circumstances, there is little to be said for the notion that subsidies in such cases should be coupled with protectionist measures, on infant-industry grounds.

Once we turn to the illustration offered, however – the compact-disc tariff – it seems in any case quite implausible that any special difficulties arise here, in respect of a presumed inability of the firm in question (Philips) to internalize the benefits from its development expenditures. Thus the case chosen here seems particularly inappropriate. The legality of such protection, which is asserted in the memorandum, is in fact dubious. The Japanese view of the matter is that no case can be made within the GATT; but this remains an open question.[5]

Within the Community itself, views differ sharply as to the advisability of coupling industrial policies with protectionist measures. Indeed, the future of the French memorandum depends in large part on whether member states can resolve their differences on this issue. To the French, the connection is basic; to the Germans, on the other hand, the link with commercial policy is without merit.

Public procurement

On the subject of public procurement, Article 2 of the French memorandum states:

> The practice of national public contracts constitutes a major form of protectionism, in fact, if not in law. The EEC countries are far from exercising a monopoly in this area. What needs to be considered, therefore, is a phased opening-up process, the proviso being, naturally, that access be reserved for Community producers.

The view of procurement stated in the first assertion above is quite accurate. Reserving public purchasing for national suppliers is equivalent to introducing a prohibitive tariff on certain goods which applies only to buyers in the public sector. On this reading, the above proposal amounts to an appeal for the removal of such barriers *within* Europe, while leaving intact those imposed vis-à-vis outside suppliers. The merits of such a Europrotectionist solution have been discussed in earlier chapters (see also Chapter 13 below).

The French proposal makes no further claims for public procurement, and so, on the face of it, there does not appear to be any particular reason for linking up these 'commercial policies' with the industrial policies which are the focus of the memorandum. None the less, there are two ways in which public procurement is in fact closely complementary to the kind of industrial policies espoused by the memorandum; and these perhaps deserve mention here. The first relates to the use of procurement as an indirect method of subsidizing R&D; this is particularly relevant to the recent developments in information technology summarized above. The second relates to the contribution of public-procurement practices to the success of the Airbus project. Since this in turn relates closely to the central concern of the memorandum, which is that the USA and Japan may come to dominate Europe in high-technology sectors, this latter consideration is of particular interest. We now explore each of these two channels in turn.

Procurement as a subsidy to R&D. One of the important 'successes' claimed for industrial policy, outside of Japan, was the US support of microelectronics in the 1960s and 1970s (Rothwell and Zegveld, 1981, p. 92):

> The example *par excellence* of such a use of procurement to support a technological development from the stage of applied research all the way to complete specification is the American military microelectronics programme. Not only were certain manufacturers stimulated to achieve specific advances, but a whole climate was created . . . in which a branch of industry and a technological community were given a set of well-defined goals, to create (without regard to costs) electronic devices of minimal size and absolute dependability. Although it is undeniable that all stages of development were affected, it is interesting to note that commentators such as Golding . . . emphasise that the real advantages of procurement were not in influencing invention and innovation but 'in accelerating the diffusion process'. In this case the effect on the learning curve was of particular importance.

Now there are two strands involved in the above comment. The role of externalities (diffusion, and the effect on the learning curve) coincides with the avowed target of the Alvey committee. Additionally, however, there is the notion that procurement was deliberately aimed at creating an 'artificial' demand for products at the frontiers of current technology. This 'forcing' of the development of new products 'ahead of their time', on the basis of an anticipation of market demand can be seen simply as an alternative manner of subsidizing R&D, and one which incorporates a form of payment by results. What is of particular interest, as regards such a scheme, is the fact that the products which the military would buy were described in the vaguest possible terms – the nature of the undertaking resting squarely on the admission that research must take its own, necessarily unpredictable, course.

Thus, one of the successes claimed for procurement policy seems to rest, not on its use as a protectionist device – but rather on its less obvious role as an indirect channel of subsidization of R&D. It should be said, however, that other commentators have offered a more jaundiced view of the degree to which military procurement succeeded in doing this; see De Grasse (1983). In the UK, the Alvey committee has advocated procurement policies, without any recourse to (further) complementary commercial policies, which might suggest that it has in mind this last type of role.

To keep matters in perspective, however, it is worth noting that one alleged success hardly suffices to justify a general policy based on this idea. To command credence, any such strategy would need to be defended in the specific context of the industry involved.

Oligopolistic industries: a digression. Before proceeding to our second example – the Airbus case – it is necessary to set out an explicit view on the structure of the kind of industry in question, and the role within such an industry for some form of policy intervention. One reason for this is that considerable misunderstanding surrounds what is meant by the 'strategic' use of commercial-policy instruments, which arises in this context.

The framework of discussion will be that of an industry of the kind which Shaked and Sutton have recently labelled a 'natural oligopoly'.[6] In such an industry, a firm can produce a new and superior ('higher quality') product by incurring R&D expenditure.

Moreover, suppose the main burden of quality improvement is on the *fixed* costs of this kind, in the sense that unit variable costs (labour and raw materials) do not increase too steeply with quality improvement. Then, a small number of firms will dominate the market[7] (i.e. price competition precludes a market structure with a large number of firms of similar size). The mechanism through which this occurs is straightforward: the producers of the higher-quality products can sell their products at a premium over those of their rivals. If their *variable* costs are not too high, relatively, they will find it more profitable to sell at a smaller premium, and so take their profits by capturing a larger share of the market. (For a formal statement, the reader is referred to Shaked and Sutton, 1984.)

What we are likely to see, in practice, in such industries, is a small number of firms selling products of a similar 'quality' level, each of which incurs fixed costs of product development that amount to a sizeable fraction of industry sales revenue. What is crucial is that (a) such industries are *necessarily* highly concentrated, so that the 'problem' cannot simply be removed by antitrust action, and (b) free entry will not suffice to eliminate 'pure profits' (i.e. profits exceeding that level which yields a normal rate of return on investment).

What does an equilibrium configuration 'look like' here? For concreteness, say we are dealing with a situation where only *two* competing firms will be viable at equilibrium. Then an equilibrium configuration is given by a pair of product specifications which have the following property. If any two firms, or countries, plan to enter the market, and produce products 1 and 2 respectively, then it is optimal, given these plans, for all other potential entrants not to enter. Products 1 and 2 will, in general, make pure profits at equilibrium. None the less, given their presence in the market, a third firm, whatever the product specification it chooses, will make losses, i.e. in competition with products 1 and 2 it cannot cover fixed costs.

Furthermore, consider firm (or country) A, which we suppose to produce product 1 at equilibrium. Given a decision made by its rival B to produce product 2, and by all other 'potential entrants' not to complete, product 1 represents the optimal choice of product for firm A (and vice versa).[9]

All this, of course, leaves undetermined the *identity* of the firms which will enter: for every equilibrium in which A and B enter – and make (different levels of) pure profits in so doing – there is a 'mirror image' configuration in which B and C (or C and D) are the successful entrants. The role of those industrial policies which we are concerned with here lies in tilting the balance in favour of one of these potential entrants over the others. Such a policy, if it succeeds, may improve domestic welfare (the presence of 'pure profits' for entrant firms is crucial to this result).

The basic idea is as follows: a subsidy which reduces the costs of a domestic firm, or a procurement policy or tariff which raises its potential flow of revenue while reducing that of its foreign rival, will in general change the (several) available equilibria. In an extreme case, we might find that a large country, by blocking access to its domestic market, might exclude an otherwise available equilibrium in which a foreign producer entered the market.

The point to be emphasized is this: such policies 'work' only in so far as they change the product-development strategies of *foreign* producers. This is the difference between the present kind of argument and the familiar argument on R&D subsidies discussed earlier, which supposed that such policies would affect *domestic* R&D levels, leaving that of foreign rivals unaffected. It is the fact that domestic policy may affect foreign producers' decisions which is the novel element here; and once this point is appreciated, it will be clear that the range of industries over which such policies might plausibly succeed is extremely restricted. Their role is well illustrated by recent developments in the Airbus project, to which we now turn.

The Airbus project. The new 150-seat European Airbus is the third, and smallest, of the Airbus family.[9] It involves French, West German, Spanish and UK partnership. While commentators differ in the degree of optimism as to likely demand, it is generally felt that this size of plane fills an important market niche: on the (arguably optimistic) forecast of British Aerospace, up to 3,000 aircraft in the 100–175 seat range could be sold by the end of the century. None the less, it seems generally agreed that the market will be dominated by some two or three competitors, at most. As late as October 1983, there were three main contenders. The two rivals to Airbus were the Boeing 737–300, which was already well advanced (the first being scheduled for production early in 1984); and the MD–80 series from McDonnell Douglas. It is estimated, moreover, that Airbus will be 18 per cent more fuel-efficient than the Boeing 737–300 and 20 per cent more efficient than the MD–80.[10] Thus, all things considered, it seems unlikely that the third Airbus is destined to be a 'new Concorde'.

In November 1983, McDonnell Douglas decided to opt out of the market. The precise reasoning involved must be, to some extent, a matter for conjecture – but certain considerations are believed to have played an important part in the decision. These amounted to grounds for believing that, whatever its decision, Airbus would remain in. (Its exit, of course, made the survival of Airbus even more certain.) The first is the heavy degree of subsidy enjoyed by the Airbus project. Boeing claims that subsidies to Airbus to date amount to over $5 billion. The French reply, that launch aid is being repaid with every aircraft sold, is not to the point. Even if all aid were repaid, the government is still underwriting potential losses – thus protecting Airbus, to a degree which makes its withdrawal from the market that much less likely. (Much more to the point is the other strand of the French retort: that Boeing is heavily supported by way of defence contracts.)

The second factor relevant to the McDonnell Douglas withdrawal lies in the record of orders received for Airbus, especially in late 1983. One source of these derives from French procurement policy, the fruits of which brought orders from Air France and Air Inter. (The strategic use of such procurement policies here is evident, each order guaranteed to one supplier reducing the expected profitability of each rival product.) This came as no surprise to commentators; what was much less clear was whether Britain would follow suit. British Aerospace was to have a 20 per cent risk-bearing share in the project, and aimed to employ 8,000 workers in constructing the wings of the plane. The UK government was initially to subsidize BAe, in this respect, to the extent of some £300–£400 million. It seemed likely, under these circumstances, that Airbus might anticipate orders from British Airways.

In the event, however, such plans ran counter to the government's quite separate policy aim, of privatizing British Airways. It was decided to allow BA to lease from Boeing, which the airline regarded as the cheaper option. Fortunately for the future of the project, this loss was offset by the first important 'commercial' order, from British Caledonian, in late 1983. British involvement remained in question until March 1984, when the project was given final approval. The British government agreed to inject £250 million into the project (less than 60 per cent of the amount originally sought by British Aerospace). The UK now holds a 20 per cent stake in the project, and it is estimated that its contribution – the manufacture of the wings – constitutes 27 per cent of the total effort on the venture. The first flight is currently set for March 1987, with certification in February 1988. By April 1984, firm orders for Airbus amounted to somewhat over fifty aircraft, with options on a similar number. Meanwhile, competition between Boeing and Airbus for orders is becoming extremely keen.

Policy procurement practices. From the standpoint of GATT, procurement rules are 'disguised protectionism', pure and simple, and their removal is a matter of concern. The UK has given some signs of late of being strongly inclined to follow the GATT line on this matter. The case of the British Airways initial decision to buy Boeing is not really to the point here: as noted already, that decision was almost certainly a by-product of the quite separate aim of privatizing the airline (and, in fact, industry commentators have suggested that the decision might still be reversed, in the light of Pan-Am's recent decision to buy Airbus). More telling by far is the decision made in 1983, to put out the construction of British Rail's rolling stock for international tender.

Notwithstanding such exceptions, the general tendency in the recent past has been for countries to show great slowness in removing such arrangements. What the French memorandum advocates is the removal of such barriers among *EEC member states*; in other words, a bias by members in favour of Community-based producers. Moreover, the text of the memorandum appears to imply that a narrow definition of a Community producer is desirable.

What are the prospects for such a move? It may be feasible to obtain a formal agreement on this question, but any attempt seriously to tackle the procurement issue must come to grips with the fact that the practice of public procurement is likely to be little affected by the removal of any formal rules, or understandings, which underpin it at present. For one thing, national standards are typically used to favour domestic products – especially as domestic manufacturers will normally be involved in consultations as to the design of those standards. The French memorandum takes note of this and stresses that one road to the establishment of a 'European' market lies in the replacement of such national standards by a common European standard. This, in itself, is not easy of achievement; more to the point, its achievement of itself will not operate specifically to the advantage of European firms but, necessarily, to all foreign suppliers.

The second barrier to the removal of such practices within the Community lies in the fact that, quite apart from any rules or regulations, the purchasing decision typically involves making a choice on the basis of a somewhat arbitrary assessment of the various attributes of rival products. Officials faced with such a choice may well favour the 'safe' alternative of sticking to the domestic supplier – particularly if that supplier is likely to question its loss of a government order, while a foreign supplier is not.

Thus, all in all, a bias towards local suppliers in public purchasing is difficult to remove. This is equally a problem for liberals, who favour general relaxation, and Europrotectionists, who see such practices as a barrier to a unified European market. But the reality of nationally biased public procurement is likely to be with us indefinitely.

A summing-up

The desirability of a common policy

In certain spheres, such as information technology, a plausible case for intervention can be made (though this does not amount to justifying the level of current subsidies, in the UK or elsewhere, which seems to be decided on non-economic grounds). The merit of a European solution in this sphere lies in avoiding duplication of research efforts. Thus there is a prima facie case for a European approach. The French view differs from that of the UK and Germany, for example, in claiming that such efforts should be accompanied by protection. The attempt to justify the latter on infant-industry grounds has little economic merit.

The targeted use of subsidies and public procurement in highly concentrated industries such as aerospace has had a mixed degree of success: the Airbus case is one of the happier examples of such a strategy. While an economic rationale for such efforts can be offered, it offers no general prescription as to how to 'pick winners'.

The feasibility of a common policy

In respect of joint European programmes to subsidize R&D on infant-industry grounds, the main obstacle to a joint approach appears to lie in a lack of confidence among some member countries (including France and the UK) that their domestic firms will reap a fair share of the benefits resulting from commercial exploitation of the body of common knowledge developed. The history of events surrounding the Japanese initiative on fifth-generation computers underlines the reality of such fears.

On the other hand, common efforts on joint projects of the Airbus variety are likely to continue; particularly in the light of the apparent success of the latest member of the Airbus family.

As regards commercial policy, it is unlikely that the French suggestion of combining subsidies with protection will meet with support in the UK, judging by the difference in approach between the French memorandum and the report of the Alvey committee on this issue. It is quite clear that it will not find favour in Germany, where the notion of using commercial policies to foster infant industries is regarded as extremely unwise (see Chapter 5 above, and Chapter 12 below). Since this is seen by the French as a central element in their strategy, it is quite likely that this issue will prove the most serious stumbling-block in framing a joint policy.

12 The Grundig/Thomson-Brandt affair: competition policy and the French memorandum

The second theme explored in the French memorandum on industrial policy stresses the need for cooperative ventures among European firms, if they are to achieve the scale necessary to compete effectively on world markets. This raises two crucial questions, both of which are addressed explicitly in the memorandum.

1. European antitrust

The first question concerns the problem that cooperation may run foul of antitrust legislation in member countries. The memorandum states, in this regard, that: 'The legislation of each Member State should explicitly recognize that the risk of excessive concentration should be assessed in the light of the economic area constituted by the Community and not in the context of each individual state.'

This assertion raised, by innuendo, the controversial issue of whether German antitrust law – the strictest in the Community – is not an unwarranted bar to the formation of effective European conglomerates. This warning is timely, given increasing awareness of this problem in the United States, and the dramatic loosening of stance on antitrust issues (the dropping of the USA v. IBM suit as 'without merit' being the most striking instance of this). Many companies, of their nature, must face a world market – it is the level of concentration in the international market which, under a liberal trading regime, is the relevant parameter to look at in assessing the prospects for effective competition. The point is not a novel one, and the charge of failing to acknowledge this has been brought before. But in the present context, it deserves particular emphasis – for if a case is to be made for an open and liberal trading environment, then a necessary concomitant of this must be a willingness not to bar European firms from effectively competing in world markets on the basis of inappropriate 'domestic' criteria.

2. Cooperation with non-European partners

A second question is raised by this call for cooperation between European firms. Will not cooperative ventures with US or Japanese partners meet, equally well, the aim of achieving a scale sufficient to allow European firms to compete effectively? Here, the memorandum offers a three-pronged argument, as follows:

> It goes without saying that such alliances must be able to continue inside or outside the Community, including the most advanced countries such as the United States or Japan.
>
> It can now be seen, however, that European undertakings favour cooperation with non-European firms, such an approach appearing to them to be more conducive to strengthening their position on the world market than an alliance with another European firm in direct competition with them. . . . The advantages of a well-planned alliance between European firms are, in fact, quite considerable:
> – economies of scale, spread of activities over the territory of the EEC and an increase in the technological and industrial potential of the undertakings concerned;
> – increased capacity for achieving the critical size needed to launch new products on the European market and in the rest of the world;
> – setting up of European groups capable, should the need be felt, of thereafter achieving balanced cooperation with a non-European firm, whereas premature external alliances could lead to European firms sliding into a subcontracting role.

Now the first two arguments do not bear on this issue at all: they are arguments for *some* kind of cooperative venture, internal or external. Their introduction in this context suggests an underlying assumption, that external alliances will be penalized via commercial policy in respect of their access to European markets. The crucial argument here is the last of the three, and this echoes the fear which we noted earlier, that the European partner will gain little out of the external alliance.

The Grundig/Thomson-Brandt affair[1]

Both of the issues we have just raised play a central part in the rather instructive case, which, as *Le Monde* was quick to note, motivates much of this part of the memorandum: the Grundig/Thomson-Brandt affair. The case merits a rather detailed scrutiny.

Continuing Japanese competition in electronics has in recent years led to various attempts at cooperation among European firms. By the late 1970s, a new pattern for the European industry seemed to be emerging. The French group, Thomson-Brandt, took over two German firms, Nordmende and Saba. Philips, the Dutch multinational, took a 24½ per cent share in the German Grundig, and signed agreements on cooperation on TV tubes and videos. But in May 1981, the Japanese Victor Company (JVC), maker of the leading videotape recorder (the VHS) succeeded in reaching an agreement with three European companies: Thomson-Brandt, the British Thorn-EMI, and the German AEG-Telefunken (the so-called J3T arrangement). Under the terms of this plan, the four companies would form an equal partnership group which would manage three factories, each specializing in a single product. Thorn-EMI would make video-disc equipment using JVC technology, AEG-Telefunken would make VHS videos, and Thomson-Brandt would manufacture specialized cameras for these products. Each of the three European firms would then buy the output of the three factories involved, which it would then sell under its own brand name. Of the companies involved here, Thomson-Brandt was the newcomer: Thorn-EMI and Telefunken were already involved in an earlier deal with JVC, under which the three companies jointly operated a video factory in Berlin. (The J2T arrangement; Thomson-Brandt's arrival made it J3T.)

It was the reaction of the Mitterrand government, on receiving this plan for approval, which sparked off the affair. The newly elected socialist government, in line with its views of the desirability of achieving European cooperation in this area, requested Thomson-Brandt not to proceed with the signing of the agreement, but to explore instead the possibility of a European solution. The plans were accordingly shelved until the following spring.

The solution which emerged was that of a link between

Thomson-Brandt and Grundig. On the face of it, it seemed an ideal solution. The resulting group would be of a similar scale to Philips, and the two giants would dominate European consumer electronics. Max Grundig, the firm's founder, retained a 75½ per cent share: he was seventy-four years old, and keen to arrange a succession. He personally favoured the idea of a European group strong enough to compete with Japan. The plan envisaged a purchase by Thomson-Brandt of Max Grundig's shareholding, followed by large-scale technical cooperation, directed in particular towards the next generation of videos. The plan required approval by both the French and the German authorities: as indirect sponsors of the scheme, the former however could confidently be expected to be favourable. Thus the outcome, at least from a legal standpoint, now rested solely on the German response.

Two complications

There were, however, two complications. The first concerned the role of Philips; in so far as they held a 24½ per cent share in Grundig, the two dominant European producers to emerge from the deal would not be independent. This, as we will see below, was of material concern to the German cartel office. However, from the point of view of Philips, it was just this which sweetened the pill of a strengthened European competitor. The key aspect of the deal for Philips concerned the future of their v2000 video.

Thomson-Brandt had already been importing videos from JVC. The competing Philips product was described as 'technically superb but over-engineered and overpriced', though Philips did envisage offering a less expensive variant. As things stood, they had achieved a 20 per cent share in the Dutch and German markets, but had little impact elsewhere. There are three (mutually incompatible) standards for videos; besides Philips, JVC's system (vHS) accounts for 70 per cent of the world market and Sony's Betamax for 20 per cent. The main advantage of the Thomson–Grundig link from the point of view of Philips was that it would strengthen the case for Thomson aligning itself with the Philips/Grundig v2000 standard – a possibility which had already been under discussion for some time.

The second complicating factor in the affair concerned the role of the ailing AEG-Telefunken. It had already been planned that they would be rescued by Grundig, who would acquire 51 per cent of their interests in consumer electronics. It was felt, however, that if such a move preceded the Thomson-Brandt link, then it might constitute the last straw with the German cartel office; and so the move was, for the moment, shelved.

Reactions: the countries

The prime mover now was the German cartel office (the Bundeskartellamt). Composed of lawyers, magistrates and indus-trialists, it acts as a watchdog on merger activity among large firms. It will, as a general rule, make a negative ruling in cases where the planned enterprise would enjoy a market share exceeding 25 per cent, if the three leading firms control more than 50 per cent of the market. The planned Thomson–Grundig link constituted a case in point; the group would have 55 per cent of the German market in consumer electronics. A negative ruling by the cartel office, however, can be overturned by the federal economics minister – this has happened in the case of six of the forty-eight negative rulings made by the cartel office in its twenty-five year history. German antitrust law, then, as it stands, constituted a serious barrier to the merger – but it could still be dealt with as an exceptional case.

There was, however, a second German dimension. Over a period of months, public opinion in Germany moved towards an unfavourable view of the arrangement. It was increasingly noted that this was not so much a matter of Grundig merging with Thomson-Brandt, as of being taken over by the French company. Press comment on the subject drew attention to a recent closure by Thomson of a German factory producing TV tubes (at Ulm). Would future contractions or rationalizations within the Grundig/Thomson-Brandt group occur to a disproportionate extent at its German plants? The fact that Thomson-Brandt was now nationalized was said to heighten such fears. Finally, Grundig workers petitioned Chancellor Kohl not to allow the deal in the absence of guarantees concerning lay-offs.

French reaction to the plan was, predictably, more favourable. Press comment seemed more concerned to assuage German fears;

Le Monde argued that the worries just noted were counterbalanced by the lack of any alternative which Germans would find attractive. The only possible German partner would be Bosch-Blaupunkt and, at least in so far as the cartel office was concerned, this would lead to similar objections. More to the point, however, was the argument that a failure of the deal would inevitably lead Thomson to seek a partner outside the EEC. Indeed, the threat of a Japanese deal was a card repeatedly waved by Thomson-Brandt. French rhetoric waxed strong on the issue; if it failed, remarked *Le Monde,* the very idea of Europe would risk a loss of credibility.

Two final issues further separated the French and German positions. The first concerned their differing attitudes to commercial and industrial policies. The French, as we have seen, view a protectionist stance as the natural concomitant of industrial policy. Germany, as the leading liberal in the EEC on trade in manufactures, views things quite differently. The view of those in Germany who were more favourably disposed towards the merger might be summarized as follows: increasing concentration in Europe might indeed be tolerated if the European market were completely open to overseas producers. The judgment of the cartel office would depend on the weight given to the following familiar argument: that the force of international competition on firms in this industry was sufficiently strong to eliminate any monopoly power which they might otherwise enjoy, so that, despite there being so few European producers, there was no need for any antitrust action. Thus the very logic of the pro-merger position in Germany led to genuine fears that the industry might subsequently fall victim to French-inspired protectionist policies.

The two parties were also separated by a general lack of confidence among Germans as to the good faith of their French partners. Repeated references were made in the press to the ill-starred precedent of the Unidata case: in the early 1970s, Philips, Siemens and CII of France pooled their computer interests in Unidata – but the partnership was broken up by the French, who turned instead to the US company, Honeywell. German antitrust law, then, was the primary barrier, but it could be circumvented. Beyond it, however, lay a further, political obstacle.

Reactions: the companies

The views of two of the companies involved played a possibly crucial, though necessarily somewhat obscure, role in subsequent events. First, some commentators argued that the proposed Grundig deal was a second best for Thomson-Brandt, whose initial intention was to seek a Japanese partner. It was asserted in the press that senior executives within the company were divided as to the relative merits of a Grundig link.

Second, Philips were initially reported as being, on balance, unfavourable to the deal. The balance of advantage, given their position as outlined above, was not obvious. However, it was reported in January 1983 that Philips had won guarantees that the arrangements whereby they supplied 1 million TV tubes per annum to Grundig would be continued under the new regime. It was also noted in the press that Philips' mistrust of French collaboration, based on the Unidata episode, seemed to be weakening: they had just signed an agreement with the French state telecommunications group CIT-Alcatel, to jointly produce mobile telephones. Finally, on 30 January, Dr Wisse Dekker, president of Philips, came out publicly in support of the proposed arrangement – though in so doing he re-expressed the hope that Thomson would indeed proceed to produce the Philips-Grundig V2000. In spite of the frequently expressed doubts as to the role of Philips in the affair, their public statements indicated a favourable stance.

The outcome

During the first few weeks of 1983 the press was reporting the development of thinking in the cartel office – and the consensus was that a favourable decision was unlikely. On 7 February, *Le Monde* reported, however, that a favourable judgment was still possible *if Philips gave up its holding in Grundig*. This idea now played a crucial role; clearly, such a move would make quite clear the strength of the case, for the German cartel office could now retain unblemished its goal of two quite independent 'poles' in the European market. But from the Philips point of view – and as part-owners of Grundig their view remained a critical, if not always visible, factor – this switched the balance of advantage very heavily against the deal.

By 5 March, the president of the cartel office, Dr Wolfgang Kartten, was telling a meeting in Munich that his office were looking at the deal 'very questioningly'. 'Authoritative German sources' were reported in the *International Herald Tribune,* on 6 March, as stating that the cartel office planned to notify Thomson early the following week that its bid had been rejected. From that point forward, events moved with surprising speed. On 9 March the cartel office let Thomson-Brandt know that they would veto the plan.[2] Thomson-Brandt immediately dropped their bid for Grundig,[3] and consequently no formal decision was issued by the cartel office. On 10 March, the French group announced the signing of an agreement with Telefunken to buy a 75 per cent interest in its consumer electronics business (an arrangement later agreed by the cartel office).

Thus, Thomson-Brandt's immediate response to the failure of the Grundig proposal was to pre-empt Grundig's 'frozen' plan to take over Telefunken – and thereby gain a one-third share in the 'J2T' factory in Berlin, producing Japanese videos. Later in March, Thomson-Brandt announced plans to begin the manufacture of videos early in 1984, using the Japanese JVC standard; on 26 April the company announced a 'landmark' agreement whereby JVC had granted it a licence to manufacture its VCR products for all markets except Japan. The speed, as well as the direction, of these final developments led to considerable soul-searching among some of the parties involved.

Post-mortem

Views differed, inevitably, on the apportioning of blame. For some (including the *Financial Times*), it was the determination of Philips to maintain its control of Grundig which was the root of the problem. An alternative line of argument exists, however, which is particularly pertinent to our present concerns: this alleges that the blame for the failure lies squarely on the part played by internal pressures within Thomson-Brandt, by those who favoured a Japanese solution. This argument rests on circumstantial evidence: its proponents pointed to the speed with which, once the Grundig merger had collapsed, Thomson switched to a deal with JVC. It must be said, however, that the force of this argument is somewhat weakened by the fact that the cartel office's decision was long anticipated and came as no surprise. Commitment to the Grundig deal was not inconsistent with the elaboration of contingency plans against its failure.

Perhaps the simplest explanation rests on the proximate cause of the problem: the cartel office decision. That the rigour of German antitrust rulings should be seen as a substantial barrier to desirable mergers was a theme which did not lack advocates within Germany: as *Le Monde* reminded its readers, it is the Japanese who win in these affairs. Those seeking a deeper explanation, however, asked why Thomson could not have awaited a formal decision, and then queried it, as they were entitled to do, thus passing the decision on to the economics ministry. This might suggest, once again, a lack of will within Thomson-Brandt; it might also reflect a belief on the French side that the cartel office decision was only a veil behind which German political pressures were operating to block the deal. On this reading, an appeal would be futile.

This was not the opinion of the European Commission, however. In Brussels, the reaction to the collapse of the Grundig plan was one of dismay. Viscount Etienne Davignon, the commissioner responsible for industrial policy, had followed, and encouraged, the plan from the outset. He now came in for some French criticism: it was charged that, had he taken a more active part, the affair might have succeeded. The idea that German public opinion was the real culprit was dismissed by Grundig, now the clear losers in the fight – they believed they could have obtained a go-ahead from the authorities. This would leave Thomson-Brandt's unseemly haste as the final culprit. *Le Monde* offered some support to the thesis that a lack of will within the French concern was an important factor; the French tendency to place all the blame on the Germans, now the clear losers, was simply 'audacious'.

The aftermath

Early in 1984, Philips increased its 24½ per cent stake in Grundig to a controlling interest. In June 1984, Philips announced its intention of selling VHS-format videos in Europe – while protesting strongly its commitment to continue producing and marketing its own V2000 format. While these will be made under licence from Matsushita (which owns a 51 per cent stake in JVC), a vice-president of Philips was quoted as saying: 'We will introduce our own technological standards and they (the VCRs) will always be recognizable as Philips' sets – totally and completely made by Philips in Europe.'

Meanwhile, Thomson is currently assembling VCR mechanisms in France from parts supplied by JVC in France. Thomson is working on its own designs for VCRs, however, and is determined to develop an R&D capability which will give it total independence from the Japanese. This seems likely to be a growing source of tension in J2T, which has so far been a remarkably successful European–Japanese collaboration.

A summing-up

We have seen that Thomson-Brandt executives apparently favoured a Japanese solution from the outset, in contrast to the European solution favoured by the French government. Now it is a basic theme of the French memorandum that decision-making must remain in the hands of the enterprises themselves. The memorandum also notes, indeed, that European firms have in practice tended to favour external alliances. Now this leads to a worrying inconsistency: for the key argument offered by the memorandum here is that the European partner would tend to be in a relatively disadvantaged position in an external alliance; this does not square with the view of the firms themselves. The only way in which one can rationalize the choices made by European enterprises, then, is by positing some kind of dynamic effect whereby a large European unit will catch up on its international rivals, in spite of the fact that the short-run pay-offs favour an external alliance. Even then, one must either posit the existence of benefits to the economy as a whole, in addition to those gains accruing to the firms concerned (it is quite unclear how), or else claim that firms are more short-sighted than governments. On any view, this line of argument remains unconvincing.

None the less, the German position is also open to serious criticism. A key factor in the Grundig/Thomson-Brandt affair was played by the insistence of the German cartel office that the two major European groups (Philips and Thomson-Brandt) must remain completely independent. Such an aim would be quite reasonable within an isolated European economy; moreover, if the European industry were to be heavily protected, such considerations would again be appropriate. But the main thrust of the German position in this sphere is towards a quite open trading environment, in which case competition must be seen in the setting of the world market, and any such constraints on European firms must be imposed with great caution.

The position of the French memorandum precisely reverses the emphasis of the German stance, calling for a more relaxed approach to antitrust law – but coupling this with an increased reliance on protection.

Both these approaches seem to fall between two stools. If a tougher commercial policy is to be followed, then a serious danger exists regarding the relaxation of competitive pressures between European firms. But if we are to operate in a more open trading environment, then a more relaxed approach to competition law is essential. Our present state represents, in this respect, the worst of both worlds. Neither the French stance, nor the German, come to grips with the dilemma. This is an area in which a clear policy lead is wanting within the Community. It is also one in which Britain, with its traditionally pragmatic approach to antitrust issues, may be unusually well qualified to provide such a lead.

13   Protection and exchange-rate policy in Europe

Introduction

Economists find it convenient to pigeonhole economic problems as either 'microeconomic' or 'macroeconomic' in nature. Traditionally, economists have analysed protection as a microeconomic problem, emphasizing its effects on consumers and producers in the protected market and in related sectors of the economy. The strength of this approach is that it is technically non-controversial. Most economists share a common view of how individual markets function. Most agree with the classical analysis of protection presented in Chapter 7. Protection is costly in economic terms relative to free trade, and some types of protection, such as quotas, are more costly than others, such as tariffs. The case for protection can then be rationally argued by setting these economic costs against possible social benefits from protection – the conservation of declining industries or regions, say – and possible political benefits (such as the avoidance of retaliation) from second-best forms of protection.

Historically, however, practical people and their political representatives have not regarded protection only in this way. Tariffs and import restrictions have often instead been treated as instruments of macroeconomic policy. Calls for protection have certainly been heard as particular individual industries in the European economy have been overtaken by foreign competition or by a contraction of demand caused by rising living standards. But the calls have been loudest when the economy as a whole has been in decline – when aggregate unemployment is high, the general rate of economic growth low, or the balance of trade persistently in deficit. Much of this volume is concerned with identifying sectors where protection would be politically feasible and provide net economic benefits, using standard microeconomic arguments. The ground for debate over the macroeconomic effects of protection is, however, rather different. It is that protection, though costly in microeconomic terms, can circumvent rigidities in the economic system (in practice, wage rigidities of some kind) which prevent a country achieving its full potential with respect to output and job creation. In this chapter, we look at policies of protection from this macroeconomic standpoint, with the aim of establishing whether or not the above argument – that protection in itself causes, or at least can contribute to, a permanent and significant expansion in economic activity – is correct.

Taking this macroeconomic perspective complicates the analysis of protection in two ways. First, just as conventional protectionist policies have macroeconomic consequences, so also do conventional macroeconomic policies have protectionist effects. Even if we have the limited objective of preserving employment in a declining sector, it is necessary to consider how far this could be met by general policy actions rather than by specific tariffs or quotas. Most types of macroeconomic policy result in some groups benefiting relative to others. A monetary expansion will, for example, benefit the first holders of the new money. However, the closest parallel arises between tariff and quota protection, and policies aimed at exchange-rate devaluation. In both cases the primary beneficiaries are producers of tradable goods, and the primary impact of policy is on the trade balance. The first part of this chapter looks at this use of macroeconomic policy for protectionist purposes – 'exchange-rate protection' – in more detail.

The second set of issues concerns precisely how we should analyse the macroeconomic consequences of protection, and how we should then rank protection against alternative policies for economic expansion. The macroeconomic consequences of protection in one industry can be explored only if we set the protected sector in a framework which allows us to analyse repercussions in other related but unprotected sectors, and in money and foreign-exchange markets as well as the 'real' side of the economy. In short, we need a macroeconomic model. Unfortunately, whereas economists are in broad agreement over how the market mechanism works in a single industry, they are notoriously divided over how to model the functioning of the economy as a whole. For the best part of two centuries economists thought that the aggregate effects of protection arose mainly through its effects on the allocation of resources within a fully employed economy. This was essentially because the whole economy was regarded as a collection of efficiently functioning markets; the expansion of activity in the protected sector simply bid resources away from others, a process which might or might not lead to a higher level of national income or employment, but which would certainly involve a reduction in economic welfare. Recent debate has centred on the rather different analysis of the macroeconomics of protection set out by the Cambridge Economic Policy Group (CEPG) (see, for example, Godley and May, 1977, and the critical articles surveyed in Godley, 1980). These arguments rely on a very different, non-classical view of the macroeconomy, in which markets do not function well, and protection creates employment and growth by drawing on a pool of otherwise idle resources and unexploited economies of scale. The logic of both these arguments over the macroeconomic effects of protection is explained in the second part of this chapter, the final section of which draws together our conclusions on the macroeconomics of a Europe-wide protectionist regime.

On the possibility of conducting protection through a concerted depreciation of European currencies, our conclusions are that such a policy of exchange-rate protection would be hard to coordinate, inequitable in its impact on individual countries within the EEC, and hard to sustain for more than two or three years. While it may be feasible and desirable to stabilize exchange rates vis-à-vis the US dollar around their long-term trend, there is no reason to suppose competitiveness could in fact be permanently improved by trying to drive rates below this trend.

As for the possibility of expanding aggregate output and employment by means of more conventional protectionist measures, our conclusions must be a little more equivocal. In the right circumstances – with wages and prices in protected industries being set without regard to the opportunities for profit offered by protection, protected industries benefiting from economies of scale and the tariff revenues ploughed back as a production subsidy – tariff protection can raise aggregate activity permanently, in spite of the fact that the exchange rate will tend to rise to restore external balance. The fact that protection can create employment when market forces are suspended should not come as a surprise;

after all, we have before us the example of the highly protected, centrally planned, but fully employed economies of Eastern Europe. The issue is not, then, whether protection could possibly be made to work for full employment in Western Europe, but rather whether it can fulfil this role within a mixed economic structure and a fundamentally liberal ideology. It is hard to believe that in a free society protected groups would not attempt to raise their own wages and prices, and hard, therefore, also to believe that the policy could work without the introduction of state control over wages and prices.

Our calculations suggest that a tariff sufficient to make a significant impact on employment at the European level would have to be very high indeed. This, of course, makes it even more unlikely that workers and producers in protected sectors will fail to exploit their privileged position. It may also be impractical, inviting either retaliation by trading partners, or the negotiated substitution of more politically acceptable quota or voluntary export restriction schemes. In both cases, any employment-creating potential from the scheme would be lost.

Even if the tariff were feasible, however, a fundamental doubt must arise over whether it is anything but a second-best way of tackling Europe's adjustment problems. The tariff is acknowledged by its proponents to be effective at the macroeconomic level only because certain market imperfections, notably the effective indexation of wages – 'real-wage rigidity' – in (now) declining industries, have become institutionalized. The case for the tariff takes as given the subsidies to certain labour and producer interests implicit in these arrangements. But these arrangements are not immutable. They are economically inefficient, and by the protectionists' own argument they constitute a major cause of unnecessarily high unemployment in the European economy. The removal of barriers to relative wage movements, and not increased protection, represents the first-best solution to the unemployment problem.

The protectionist consequences of macroeconomic policy

Before looking at the possibilities of achieving protection by means of macroeconomic policy actions, it may be useful to summarize what is entailed in conventional, microeconomic, protection.

Protection is generally associated with the use of selective devices such as tariffs, quotas or subsidies applied to trade in, or production of, specific goods. The effect of such policies is to increase activity in the protected industry (and closely related industries) by allowing profits and wages in that sector to be higher – relative to those in the rest of the economy – than they otherwise would have been.

A case can be made for protection in two very different circumstances. One arises when the industry concerned faces a sudden loss of competitive advantage. To adjust immediately by contracting output and employment in the industry would be costly in three respects. There might be substantial social costs to contraction (or the industry might be a 'strategic' one); there might be undesirably high short-run unemployment during the time it takes for real wages in the contracting industry to find their new, lower, equilibrium level; and, finally, there is always a risk that the loss of competitive advantage is temporary, rather than permanent, the result perhaps of 'dumping' by foreign competitors, so that irrevocable adjustments, such as the run-down of capital in the affected industries, would be inappropriate.

The second case for protection arises when the industry concerned has the capacity to generate rapid productivity growth, given the right circumstances. One condition might be market size. Protection of an industry from foreign competition could let it reach the critical minimum size necessary for the achievement of scale economies. A second condition for productivity growth might be the reduction of risk. Insulation of a domestic industry from the vicissitudes of competition and fluctuations in market size could lead to a higher rate of investment and greater productivity. However, as we have seen in Chapter 9, economies of scale alone are by no means sufficient justification for protecting an industry; at the macroeconomic level, a great deal depends on whether the gains from scale economies are passed on to consumers in the form of lower prices.

Concern with the rate of deindustrialization in Europe, and calls for a protectionist response, reflect a mixture of all the above arguments. It is undoubtedly felt that on strategic grounds Western Europe should preserve capacity in food production, transport, communication and armaments. It is also felt that, while contraction in many traditional industries is necessary in the face of competition, particularly from newly industrializing countries and from Eastern Europe, this process should occur at a pace which minimizes the transitional unemployment costs; and that in some cases, the process should not be encouraged at all since the competition is 'unfair'. In addition, the notion that manufacturing industry is peculiarly liable to growth-creating 'dynamic economies of scale' has been a theme of economists in the UK from the ideas of Kaldor (1966) down to those more recently expressed by the new Cambridge school (Godley and May, 1977); and the notion that protection, or at least export promotion, has beneficial effects in reducing risk is a recurrent theme in the older European tradition of 'export-led growth' (Lamfalussy, 1963).

It is important to note that all of these arguments, except that based on the idea of strategically or socially essential industries, view protectionist policies as temporary and self-liquidating. Industries facing a permanent loss of competitive advantage must eventually contract; industries facing temporary problems will in time see their competitive position restored. The tariff or subsidy scheme simply plays a buffering role. Similarly, industries subject to scale economies, or to productivity gains from investment, will find their costs falling to the point where the tariff is no longer necessary. The fact that in practice tariffs on many industries tend to persist must reflect either the incorrectness of these arguments applied to those particular industries, or the unwillingness of those engaged in the industry to surrender the excessively high returns with which the tariff endows them.

Such arguments over the merits of protectionism generally envisage the policy being effected by means of either import restraint, through a tariff or quota scheme, or export expansion, resulting from an export subsidy. However, precisely the same arguments underlie most discussions of exchange-rate policy, and the effects of such a policy are in many respects analogous to those of more conventional protectionist measures. We look below at three aspects of exchange-rate policy: first, at what protectionist effects arise from such policies; second, at an important distinction between exchange-rate stabilization policies and policies aimed at achieving a permanent competitive advantage; and finally at the costs and benefits from protection by means of exchange-rate management as against tariff and quota protection, in terms of the distribution of rents, the probability of retaliation and the efficiency and equity of the two programmes.

To keep the argument simple, let us assume that we can talk about the exchange rate of the whole EEC bloc vis-à-vis the outside world. That is, we will focus on the effective rate of some common currency unit such as the ECU, a rate formed by weighting together its bilateral rates of exchange against the dollar, the yen and the currencies of Europe's other major trading partners, in a way which reflects their importance in trade, and the responsiveness of trade flows to changes in these bilateral rates. And we will assume for the moment that problems of policy coordination within the Community have been resolved, so that the network of bilateral rates inside the EMS is always optimal, the burden of intervention necessary to achieve a given target for the effective ECU rate is equitably shared, and the whole bloc can be treated as if it were a single economy. This set of assumptions does, of course, beg a number of questions over the technical feasibility of a Europe-wide exchange-rate policy, to which we return later.

On the above assumptions, there will be some effective ECU rate of exchange which, given the level of goods prices in Europe and the rest of the world, will in the long run result in current-account balance. So long as the nominal effective ECU rate continuously moves so as to offset changes in price competitiveness, appreciating when European inflation is below the rate in the rest of the world, and depreciating when European inflation rates are relatively high, the real (i.e. inflation-adjusted) effective ECU rate will remain fixed at this level. We might characterize this as the 'fundamental equilibrium' rate of exchange, or as the rate which preserves 'purchasing-power parity' between European and non-European currencies.

The experience of over a decade of floating rates shows, first, that *on average* over a long period rates do gravitate to this equilibrium, but, second, that fundamental equilibrium is in no sense the *typical* or normal state of the international monetary system. Individual countries, and indeed the European economy as a whole, typically experience runs of persistent current-account deficits or surpluses, and runs of exchange rates above or below trend. The cyclical behaviour of the EEC current account is

Table 1   *The ECU effective exchange rate and the European Community current-account balance*

Year	Real ECU exchange rate* (index, 1971–83 = 100)	Current-account balance (percentage of GDP)
1971	94.4	0.8
1972	90.7	0.8
1973	101.0	0.0
1974	114.0	−1.0
1975	104.7	0.0
1976	105.6	−0.5
1977	99.6	0.1
1978	92.5	0.8
1979	91.1	−0.4
1980	92.8	−1.3
1981	107.2	−0.6
1982	106.5	−0.5
1983	107.8	0.1
1984†	113.5	0.0

* ECU price of trade-weighted foreign currencies, deflated by ratio of 'world' price index to EEC price index. *Sources*: Commission of the European Communities, *European Economy*, November 1984; IMF, *International Financial Statistics*, various issues. A rise in the index indicates a real depreciation of the ECU.
† Estimated.

illustrated in Figure 1, alongside the cycle in the real effective exchange rate. The two series are, of course, intimately connected. A depreciation of the real effective exchange rate, for example, has an effect similar to that of a policy of generalized protection. By increasing the domestic currency equivalent of exporters' foreign-currency selling prices, it amounts to a subsidy to all exports; by increasing the domestic-currency equivalent of importers' foreign-currency selling prices, it also involves an implicit tariff on all imports. The whole of the tradable-goods sector – export industries and producers of import substitutes – is thereby protected by a real devaluation. Conversely the whole tradable-goods sector is penalized by real-exchange-rate appreciation. The immediate effect of a real-exchange-rate depreciation is to increase activity in the tradable-goods sector of the economy, as wages, prices and profits in protected industries rise relative to those in non-protected, non-tradable industries. Conversely, a

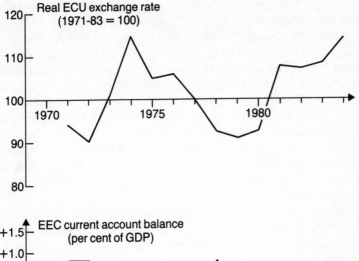

Figure 1 *The real effective EEC exchange rate and the EEC current-account balance*

real-exchange-rate appreciation tends to cause the tradable-goods sector to contract, and the non-tradables sector to expand.

The impact of real-exchange-rate changes on individual economies will therefore depend on the size of the tradable-goods sector, and the demand and supply conditions facing producers in that sector. A uniform depreciation of all European currencies would probably tend to benefit output and trade in economies relatively open to extra-European trade (Belgium, Denmark, United Kingdom), but have a smaller impact on low-extra-trade economies (France, Ireland, Italy). On average over the Community, the patterns of Figure 1 suggest that a 5 per cent general depreciation/appreciation – roughly what occurred in 1974–6 and

1978–80 – is followed, over two to three years, by a turn-around in the current account of around ¾ per cent of Community national output, or around 15 billion ECUs at 1980 prices. For most individual economies within the EEC, real-exchange-rate changes over the last decade have been even larger, and the fluctuations in trade and tradable-goods production greater, than this average suggests. Following the exploitation of natural-gas resources in the mid-1970s, the Netherlands experienced a real-exchange-rate appreciation of around 20 per cent; the exchange rate of sterling reacted similarly to the development of North Sea oil resources in 1979–81. In both cases, the outcome was a turn-around in the current account of the balance of payments amounting to roughly 3 per cent of GDP.

Departures of real exchange rates from their fundamental equilibrium values have, then, been important factors causing real changes in the European economy. Such exchange-rate movements need not, and typically do not, reflect irrationality or disequilibrium in the foreign-exchange market. They simply reflect the fact that in the short term real exchange rates are dominated by the demand for and supply of internationally mobile capital and money, rather than the behaviour of trade in goods. There is, in a terminology suggested by Bergsten and Williamson (1983), in general liable to be a difference between this 'market equilibrium' and the 'fundamental equilibrium' indicated by purchasing-power-parity considerations. The protectionist consequences of depreciation of real exchange rates, and the sensitivity of exchange rates to money and capital flows, open the possibility that the exchange rate can be *managed* as an instrument of protection. To understand how this can occur, it is helpful further to distinguish what we might call the 'private-market equilibrium' exchange rate from the realized 'market equilibrium' exchange rate. The private-market-equilibrium rate is that achieved in the absence of any public-policy action to encourage (or discourage) net inflows of foreign capital. The actual market equilibrium deviates from the private-market equilibrium as a result of official exchange-market intervention or capital controls. 'Exchange-rate protection' – a term coined by Max Corden (1982) – can then be defined as any attempt to reduce the market equilibrium rate below the private-market equilibrium rate.

All talk of an exchange rate being 'too high' is implicitly a call for exchange-rate protection. However, as with more conventional forms of protectionist argument, it is useful to distinguish policies designed to offset temporary losses of competitive advantage, and hence stabilizing the size of the tradable-goods sector, from policies aimed at permanently expanding the tradables sector. In the first case, policy action is envisaged whenever the private-market-equilibrium exchange rate exceeds purchasing-power parity. It takes the form of intervention to reduce the market equilibrium rate towards its fundamental equilibrium. This we might term 'temporary exchange-rate protection', or better, simply 'exchange-rate stabilization' policy. In the second case, action is envisaged even when the private market is pricing the currency at its purchasing-power-parity level. It involves an attempt to reduce the exchange rate below its fundamental equilibrium. This constitutes genuine 'permanent exchange-rate protection' in that it is clearly aimed at subsidizing the tradables sector to a degree which would not occur in a situation of long-term equilibrium.

In a flexible exchange-rate system the market rate of exchange will almost always differ from its fundamental value, as shocks hit international money and capital markets. The competitive position of exporters and producers of import substitutes is changing continuously, and is only rarely at the 'right' level for balanced trade. This does impose costs on such firms, since they must live with uncertainties concerning the real value of future selling prices, or pay a premium to hedge such risks in the forward exchange market. But these costs of random exchange-rate fluctuation are really an argument for preferring permanently fixed to flexible exchange rates, and do not constitute an argument for exchange-rate protection. Under fixed exchange rates, shocks tend to be transmitted to domestic money growth and prices rather than to exchange rates, and so the burden of risk is transferred from the tradable-goods sector towards all groups in the economy with incomes which are not tied to the price level by means of indexation agreements. Whether the government ought to inter-vene to reduce the risks for the tradable-goods sector (by pegging the exchange rate) or to reduce the risks facing individuals with relatively fixed nominal incomes (by letting the exchange rate float) depends on the relative efficiency of forward exchange markets and indexation arrangements.

The case for temporary exchange-rate protection is based not on the fact that floating exchange rates tend to depart temporarily from their fundamental equilibria, but rather on the fact that they seem to depart *persistently* from their fundamental equilibria. We have already seen in Figure 1 that whenever the real effective ECU rate rose above trend, it tended to stay there for a number of years (say, 1970–3, and 1978–80); similarly whenever the rate fell below trend, as in the mid-1970s, and in the early 1980s, the undervaluation was not simply temporary. There are theoretical reasons for thinking that such persistent 'overshooting' and 'undershooting' of equilibrium is an inevitable feature of any floating-rate regime (see, for example, Dornbusch, 1976). Suppose some shock occurs which raises money demand in Europe above money supply. The shock might take the form of a monetary event, say a tightening of European monetary policies, or a relaxation in monetary policy in the United States; or it might be in the nature of a 'real' event – an acceleration of productivity growth in Europe, a slow-down in growth abroad. In either case, the market will expect an eventual (relative) fall in the European price level and an appreciation in the nominal effective European exchange rate. These expectations will be reflected in an immediate appreciation of the forward exchange rates. However, the prices of goods typically do not react quickly to such shocks. In order to match higher money demand with a fixed real supply of money, interest rates in Europe must rise, to induce investors to hold bills and bonds rather than money. However, the higher European interest rates will induce an inflow of foreign capital which will only be arrested if the appreciation of the spot exchange rate exceeds the appreciation of the forward rate by the amount of the interest-rate rise. US investors buying European assets on a covered basis will then gain from the higher European interest rates but lose an equal amount from the forward discount on the ECU. In time, European prices will fall, interest rates rise and the spot rate of the ECU will fall towards the forward rate. However, throughout the transitional period, the nominal rate of exchange has been above its long-run equilibrium value, and the real rate of exchange has been even further above purchasing-power parity. The two-to-three-year duration of deviations of the real European exchange rate from its equilibrium value is obviously consistent with the lag commonly observed between monetary change and its effect on the price level.

The effects of real-exchange-rate 'overshooting', and the relative sluggishness of price changes in response to monetary and real shocks, are analogous to those of a programme of 'dumping' by a foreign competitor. Firms may be forced to write off capital or leave the industry even though their long-term competitive position is sound. In such circumstances there may be a case for public action to limit the extent of the exchange-rate fluctuation, to help give private markets a better idea of the long-term competitive position of domestic industry, just as there is a case for public action to signal the presence of 'dumping'. This sort of temporary, countercyclical, action against persistent deviations from purchasing-power parity is very different in nature from action aimed at a permanent reduction of the exchange rate below its current purchasing-power-parity level. So long as it is recognized as a temporary measure, countercyclical exchange-rate protection has no implications for trend income growth or trend inflation. By contrast, permanent exchange-rate protection has important macro-economic consequences. These will, except in certain special circumstances, tend to offset any beneficial effects of devaluation.

To see what limits exist on the operation of exchange-rate protection, it is necessary to be a little more precise about how the exchange rate is managed. The target of policy is the current account of the balance of payments. This must at all times be equal in size, but opposite in sign, to the sum of the capital account (measuring net inflows of foreign investment) and the change in foreign-exchange reserves (measuring net domestic purchases of foreign money). Disturbances to the current account can be dealt with either by inducing changes in the capital account, by means of capital controls or taxes, or they can be dealt with by official intervention in the foreign-exchange market, designed to increase or decrease the level of foreign-currency reserves. In the scenario justifying temporary exchange-rate protection, a rise in European interest rates causes the capital account to move into surplus. In order to offset this, the current account must be pushed into deficit. The rise in the exchange rate is simply the means by which the market mechanism seeks to bring this about. The authorities may prefer one of two alternative non-market solutions. The first is to remove the incentive for capital inflows, by limiting or taxing capital inflows. Ideally, a tax should be levied to equalize *ex ante* real expected returns from investing in Europe with those from investing in the rest of the world. However, this sort of real-interest-rate equalization tax seems an impractical device – it would, for example, involve discriminating between, say, Japanese-based and US-based investors whenever US and Japanese interest rates differed; and it would involve a difficult judgment over which relative interest-rate changes were permanent, requiring a relocation of international capital, and which were transitory, and should be taxed away.

The second option for the authorities is to intervene directly in the foreign-exchange market, buying dollars, say, as fast as foreign investors buy European currencies. The capital-account surplus would then be offset by an official-settlements deficit, rather than a current-account deficit. There would be no pressure for an exchange-rate appreciation. However, this sort of action seems helpful only if the 'overshooting' has a real origin. If the overshooting is due to monetary contraction, then the effect of intervention will be simply to reverse this monetary stance, since the reserve inflow will add to the monetary base and, in time, to the money stock. If the authorities attempt to sterilize the monetary effects of the reserve inflow, by selling domestic bonds, then European interest rates are liable to be driven up further, creating a yet greater incentive for capital inflows. The policy is really only sustainable if the authorities create room for the absorption of new debt by redeeming old debt, by running a budgetary surplus. This may seem a paradoxical course of action; but the sense of it is that more resources can be devoted to exports only if fewer are devoted to meeting domestic demand.

The limits to exchange-rate protection are even more evident in a scenario in which permanent protection is sought. In this case, current and capital accounts are initially in balance. Action is taken to move the current account into permanent surplus. Again, there are two options. Either the capital account may be forced into permanent deficit, or the authorities may continuously intervene to buy foreign currency. The first type of policy requires controls or taxes on capital inflows, or subsidies to outflows. West Germany and Switzerland consistently operated such policies in the 1960s and early 1970s. They impose a welfare cost on the country concerned which is in many respects similar to that which would be incurred if one type of industry were taxed in order to permit others to expand. There will be an unjustified shift of resources away from the disadvantaged sector – in this case, sectors which are relatively (foreign-)capital-intensive – and towards relatively labour-intensive, tradable-goods industries. Continuous foreign-exchange intervention may appear to avoid the losses associated with capital restrictions. However, the policy is by no means costless. Suppose first that no attempt is made to sterilize the effects on the European monetary base of the buildup of dollar reserves. In this case, the money supply in Europe will rise, the price level will rise and purchasing-power parity will be re-established. The nominal ECU exchange rate will have been lowered; but the real exchange rate will be unchanged, since inflation in Europe has run ahead of that in the rest of the world. The policy, then, will only work if the European monetary base is instead stabilized through sales of public debt inside Europe. This increased debt, however, can again be absorbed only if either European interest rates rise or the public sector simultaneously runs a fiscal surplus in order to reduce the stock of outstanding debt held by the private sector. The first situation does not represent a position of equilibrium. If interest rates rise capital will migrate to Europe, and a further tranche of dollar purchases will be necessary to prevent the exchange rate returning to its original level. The running of permanent fiscal surpluses in tandem with the exchange intervention does represent a feasible policy package, but this implies a permanent contraction in aggregate demand in the European economy. In effect, a redistribution of income towards the tradables sector is being paid for by running the economy permanently below its potential income level. Whereas a temporary fall in absorption might be a reasonable price to pay to offset the effects of a temporary overshoot in the real exchange rate, the benefits from subsidizing the tradables sector must be large indeed to justify a permanent income loss. In fact, if there were no implications for future income growth from an expanded tradable-goods sector, then continuous sterilized intervention would be neither a desirable nor a tenable long-run policy. Any justification for attempts to reduce the nominal exchange rate below its fundamental equilibrium must therefore rest on the notion that the larger tradables sector offers a prospect of productivity growth, in the future, sufficient to offset the current fall in domestic aggregate demand. If such dynamic increasing returns are associated with the tradables sector, then current account balance will be restored at the lower real rate of exchange, as a result of income growth in the European economy.

In view of these limitations on the efficacy of exchange-rate management as a protectionist device, how does it rank against more conventional tariff and quota programmes? At first blush, it might seem that there is a simple difference between the two types of policy. Devaluation is, except under certain special circumstances – dynamic increasing returns in the protected sector – at best only temporarily effective. Market forces operate which tend to offset the impact of intervention on the exchange rate. In contrast, tariffs and quotas can be imposed and maintained at the government's discretion. However, this distinction is rather illusory. Tariff and quota protection also have, as we shall see in the next part of this chapter, macroeconomic consequences which tend to offset their impact, and tariff protection proves efficacious in much the same circumstances as exchange-rate protection. Any case for preferring one form of protection over the other must be made on microeconomic rather than macroeconomic grounds, on considerations of efficiency, equity and practicality.

As we have seen, devaluation works by subsidizing exports and taxing import substitutes. In order to achieve the desired contraction in non-tradables, however, devaluation also reduces domestic demand for domestic output. The same effect could be achieved simply by subsidizing exports and import-substitute industries directly, and financing the subsidy by means of taxes on non-tradable goods (the old United Kingdom Selective Employment Tax, which hit labour-intensive service industries preferentially, provides a model for such a tax). This subsidy/tax scheme would induce a switch of resources from the non-tradable sector without the necessity of a reduction in domestic demand. Devaluation is in this sense a technically inefficient way of achieving protection of tradable-goods industries.

Differing protectionist devices also give rise to different distributions of 'rents'. A depreciation in European rates of exchange will confer a windfall gain on European holders of non-European assets. Quantitative restrictions on imports, unless they are regulated by an auction of import licences, will actually confer benefits to *non*-European exporters, since they can raise selling prices in the rationed European market. Which of these arrangements is most favourable to activity in Europe depends on the spending habits of the *rentiers*. Clearly, it is least likely that quota schemes will raise income and employment, most likely that tariffs will. Precisely because of these properties, quota restrictions are the easiest to implement without fear of retaliation, and tariffs the most likely to invite retaliation. In terms of its international acceptability, exchange-rate policy probably lies somewhere between these extremes. However, retaliation against exchange-rate policy does raise a particular problem of asymmetry not encountered in a trade war fought with more conventional weapons. It is that the depreciation of the European currencies might be met not by a competitive devaluation by the United States or Japan, but by the imposition of tariffs or quota restrictions. Whereas devaluation is, as we have seen, typically self-destructive, and almost inevitably temporary, such tariff and quota hikes can easily become permanent. This asymmetry in policy actions does seem to be a feature of recent history, with governments most willing to consider trade liberalization when the real exchange rate is, for whatever reason, low, but ready to initiate new trade restrictions, when the real exchange rate is high.

Even assuming that we do want to protect tradable-goods industries, devaluation appears a technically inefficient and politically rather sensitive route to follow. But do we, in the context of the current situation in Europe, really want to protect the entire tradable-goods sectors of all EEC countries to the same extent and at the same time? This is what would be entailed in a coordinated programme of exchange-rate management. As a vehicle for protection it would be a blunt instrument indeed. The message of the earlier chapters of this report has been that all countries in Europe face challenges in broadly the same industries, from broadly the same group of competitors. However, these industries are by no means coextensive with the tradable-goods sector. Indeed, in many countries, part of the tradables sector is very successful indeed, and its success – as much as the severity of foreign competition – has been responsible for squeezing the relatively unsuccessful sectors. Devaluation in such circumstances would certainly alleviate the squeeze on the lagging sectors, but would also unnecessarily promote already successful sectors. Given that our objective is to solve the problems of a small range of industries, faced with competition from a small number of (important) overseas producers, it is also clear that a uniform devaluation in all EEC currencies would have very non-uniform effects. Countries which have tradables sectors that are dominated by problem industries, or which trade intensively with aggressive foreign exporters, would benefit most. Countries which deal in less sensitive commodities, and which are committed most to intra-European trade, would gain least.

Finally, there is no guarantee that a concerted depreciation would leave all national currencies inside Europe at the same level relative to their initial purchasing-power parity. In spite of the operation of the EMS, and attempts at policy coordination, fluctuations in real exchange rates *within* Europe have been scarcely less than fluctuations in the ECU vis-à-vis the dollar and the yen. To illustrate the problems that might arise, imagine that in 1978 an attempt had been made to engineer a 10 per cent devaluation across the board in Europe. This would have roughly re-established the average effective rate of exchange observed in the years 1971–83. However, within Europe, in 1978, two countries – Ireland and Italy – were already about 10 per cent below purchasing-power parity, and France was perhaps 5 per cent below; and Belgium, Denmark, Germany and the Netherlands were already relatively overvalued by 5–10 per cent. The United Kingdom, of course, was on the point of a 20 per cent swing from under- to over-valuation. The effect of the European policy would be to make the already undervalued countries super-competitive, by driving the real effective rate well below its fundamental equilibrium. The already overvalued countries would find that the policy simply stabilized the rate at its purchasing-power-parity level. The differential effects solely relate to the initial conditions under which the policy was implemented, and bear no relation to the industrial adjustment problems, and hence the protectionist 'needs' of the economies concerned. Moreover, the appropriate supportive macroeconomic policies in individual countries of the Community would be different, with deflation required in countries with initially undervalued currencies, but not in the others. A common exchange-rate policy cannot in general be linked to common internal policies unless the initial EMS parities happen to be close to their equilibrium values.

Our verdict on exchange-rate protection must be that protection of economies, rather than protection of industries, is liable to lead to difficult and unnecessary problems of policy coordination, and dissension inside the Community over the distribution of the costs and benefits of the policy. Unless there is a strong feeling that the tradables sector in all countries possesses a magic ingredient for growth, simultaneous depreciation of European currencies seems in any case a short-sighted and haphazard means of improving industrial performance.

The macroeconomic consequences of protectionist policies

A tariff has clear advantages over devaluation as an instrument of protection. The final question is: what are its merits as an instrument of macroeconomic policy?

To answer this, it is helpful to start by tracing through the effects of a tariff on the assumption that all the markets which make up the European economy – markets for money, goods and labour – function efficiently, the prices in each rising when demand is increased, falling when excess supply emerges. Of course, in such a Europe, there would be no macroeconomic problem to solve. Aggregate demand could not fall persistently below supply; interest rates and prices would fall to provide the necessary stimulus. Equally, there would be no involuntary unemployment; wages would fall relative to producers' output prices, so as to make it more attractive to hire labour. The fact that output and employment in Europe fluctuate considerably, and, some would argue, have persistently fallen below their potential equilibrium levels, shows that the market mechanism does not function perfectly. We start, then, with this assumption of efficient markets not because we believe it to be true, but simply to provide a background to subsequent discussion of how the tariff might operate under different kinds of market imperfection. We then look at two particular sets of causes of involuntary unemployment: a poorly functioning foreign-exchange market, and a poorly functioning labour market. Problems arise in the foreign-exchange market mainly if the authorities attempt to peg the exchange rate at an unrealistically high level. In contrast there are several ways in which institutional arrangements can render the labour market inefficient. As a result of long-lived contracts or 'money illusion', for example, money wages may be relatively insensitive to demand and supply conditions. Alternatively, as a result of indexation arrangements, wages in individual industries may respond only to general price-level changes, and not to conditions in the industry. We look below at the effects of a tariff under these cases of, respectively, nominal and real wage rigidity.

First, however, consider the effects of a tariff under ideal market conditions. Suppose the tariff is imposed on a small range of imported goods, for which domestically produced substitutes exist. An immediate effect of the tariff is to create a balance-of-trade surplus, which is reflected in a net demand by non-EEC countries for EEC currency. The exchange rate of the ECU will appreciate. This exchange-rate appreciation will tend to make EEC exports uncompetitive, and it will also put at a disadvantage those EEC producers of import substitutes who have not benefited from the tariff. In short, there will be a reduced demand for non-protected tradable goods. Conversely, demand for the relatively cheaper non-tradable goods will rise. These market pressures will cause prices (in ECU terms) to fall in the non-protected-tradables sector, and output to contract, while in the non-tradables sector prices will rise and activity will expand. As far as the protected industries are concerned, the exchange-rate appreciation will reduce, but not offset, the demand expansion caused by the tariff, so prices will rise and output increase.

These changes in the output plans of producers cause increases in the demand for labour in the expanding sectors – in the non-tradables sector and the protected sector – and a fall in the demand for labour in the unprotected-tradables sector. Real wages and employment will rise in the expanding sectors, contract in the declining sectors.

Whether or not the tariff results in increased employment, then, depends on the relative size of the expanding sectors and on whether they use labour more intensively than do the contracting sectors. In most European economies, and certainly in the United Kingdom, the non-tradables (service) sector is indeed relatively labour-intensive, so that employment in aggregate might benefit from a tariff. However, it is somewhat ironical to be looking for the employment-creating effects of a tariff on, say, automobile imports in the jobs it decants from more successful but unprotected sectors, say computers, into the fast-food business.

A number of more convincing arguments for the tariff can be made. All of them, however, rely on the presence of rigidities or imperfections which in some way break the chain of adjustments outlined above. A tariff can, for example, be helpful if the exchange rate is pegged. In the 1960s, it was (correctly) argued that tariffs could help relax the 'external constraint' on the growth of the United Kingdom and other European economies. The constraint consisted of the fact that any country engaging in domestic demand reflation under the Bretton Woods system quickly found its imports increasing. This meant, first, that the impact of the demand expansion on domestic output and employment was diluted; and, second, that the demand expansion itself was choked off by the monetary contraction which ensued as foreign-currency reserves fell in the face of the current-account deficit. A domestic reflation coupled with a tariff, however, was a viable package, since the tariff could, if it was sufficiently high, prevent the damaging deterioration in the trade balance.

In practice, countries in which this policy mix was advocated tended also to be countries which had already overvalued exchange rates. In the UK and France, relatively high inflation rates in the 1960s led to deteriorating trade balances, and an automatic tendency towards monetary deflation. Fiscal reflation was advocated as a means to cushion the effects of this on output and employment. Out of this experience came a view that certain countries in the world economy were chronically in deficit, while others were chronically in surplus; and that the only escape route for the first group was to institute a policy of reflation combined with tariff protection.

While this view is clearly relevant in an era of fixed exchange rates, it is less obviously relevant when exchange rates are floating. The only circumstances under which it would have force occur if either exchange rates did not move in an appropriate direction or, if appropriate, exchange-rate variations had no net effect on the current account of the balance of payments. On the first point, we have seen earlier, in our discussion of exchange-rate protection, that the main problem with exchange-rate fluctuations in the 1970s has been not that they have been inappropriate, but rather that they have been too appropriate, frequently overshooting their eventual equilibrium level. Overshooting does, of course, represent an inefficiency of a sort, and with overshooting exchange rates tariffs would have a role. It would, however, be temporary, and it would be extremely perverse. As reflation occurred, the exchange rate would depreciate by too much, and tariffs would have to be reduced to compensate; conversely, tariffs might be raised during a deflation in order to compensate for the excessive appreciation in the exchange rate. This is decidedly not what advocates of tariffs have in mind; but it is the logical use for such devices in a regime of chronically overshooting exchange rates. On the second point, the conditions which have to be satisfied for exchange rates to 'work' (the so-called Marshall-Lerner conditions) are well known: namely, the 'real' effects of a devaluation, in increasing export volume and decreasing import volume, must exceed the nominal effects of the devaluation, which are to make existing imports instantly more expensive in terms of domestic currency. Experience with floating exchange rates shows that, although the initial effects of devaluation are adverse, in the long run, after about three years, the trade balance will turn around – the J-curve phenomenon. Indeed, the chronic imbalances in the external trade of the United Kingdom and France of the 1960s were, eventually, permanently eliminated by step devaluations and a downward-trend float in the currencies of both countries through the 1970s. As Figure 1 shows, Europe as a whole has also remained on average in balance throughout the 1970s.

Since floating exchange rates do fulfil this stabilizing function, the case for using tariffs to relax external constraints on growth seems doubtful, as does the very concept of an 'external constraint'. Domestic reflation in a floating-exchange-rate regime will simply cause exchange-rate depreciation. This will, in time, eliminate the trade deficit. The best that can be said for using the tariff is that it will operate *faster* than the devaluation; the worst is that the efficiency costs it imposes are permanent. Calculations by Batchelor and Minford (1977) indicate that, unless governments are very short-sighted indeed, and give an overwhelming weight to the early benefits of the tariff, the floating-exchange-rate option is to be preferred.

A tariff can, then, be helpful if there is an imperfection in the external sector – if the exchange rate is pegged. However, if the exchange rate is freely floating this case has less force. The 'external constraint' argument in this form appears nowadays to be rather old-fashioned. Current arguments for protection rest not so much on exchange-rate fixity as the source of imperfection in market adjustments to shocks, but rather on the existence of some inflexibilities in prices in domestic goods and labour markets. A number of these arguments are usefully reviewed in Krugman (1982).

Much early analysis of the macroeconomic effects of tariffs assumed that prices and wages were rigid in money terms, and did not react to changes in demand. These assumptions led to the quite startling conclusion that although a tariff might seem to increase output and employment by expanding production of import substitutes, its aggregate effect is actually deflationary.

There are two lines of reasoning which lead to this conclusion. One, due to Laursen and Metzler (1950), focuses only on the real sector of the economy. Suppose trade is initially balanced, and a general tariff is imposed on imports. The trade balance will improve and domestic demand for domestic output will increase. These two imbalances can be corrected by movements in two variables – an exchange-rate appreciation and a fall in domestic real income. In general, both effects will occur. Although the import-substitute sector will expand, there will be contraction elsewhere in the economy which will result in a net contractionary effect from the tariff. The second line of reasoning over the effects of tariffs with rigid money wages looks not only at adjustments in the real sector, but also at monetary repercussions. If the revenues from the tariff are redistributed, aggregate money income will be raised and the general price level will be raised. In both cases, the demand for money will rise. How can money-market equilibrium be restored? Again, the imbalance can be corrected by movements in two variables: by a rise in interest rates and by a fall in real income (since we are assuming prices and wages to be rigid). In general, both effects will occur, so that the tariff is again deflationary, the interest rate rising in the short term, income falling in the long term. The rising interest rate will cause the exchange rate to overshoot – to appreciate further than is necessary to restore equilibrium in the external balance. The falling income means that, for a time, the tariff may also be unnecessarily deflationary, reducing income by more than is necessary to restore real internal balance. These adverse dynamic effects of the tariff add up to a decisive argument against using tariffs as a macroeconomic policy when nominal wages and prices are fixed – the traditional Keynesian view of the economy.

Complete rigidity in money wages and prices is, however, a

rather extreme form of economic imperfection. The main academic proponents of protectionism – the Cambridge Economic Policy Group – do not adhere to these assumptions, but to an alternative, so-called 'new Keynesian', view of goods and labour markets. The two crucial premises of the CEPG analysis are: (1) that goods prices are flexible but do not respond to excess demands for or supplies of goods, being simply calculated as a (roughly) fixed mark-up over costs; and (2) that money wages similarly are flexible but do not respond to excess demands for or supplies of labour, being simply tied to the general price level. These assumptions, of mark-up pricing and real wage rigidity, are felt to reflect the facts of life in the modern corporation and in the employer–union wage-bargaining process. They are supported by a number of studies of profit margins (Godley and Nordhaus, 1972; Coutts, Godley and Nordhaus, 1978), and by studies of wage–price relationships (Godley *et al.*, 1980; Lawson, 1981).

These assumptions on their own leave no room for tariffs to improve employment. A tariff should lead to an appreciation in the exchange rate, and a matched rise in prices and wages, leaving the real economy undisturbed. Since the CEPG proposal is to protect almost all manufactured goods for which domestic substitutes exist, there will not even be a distributional effect resulting from switches of resources from unprotected to protected tradable-goods sectors. However, the tariff can under CEPG assumptions raise activity if two circumstances both occur. First, the tariff revenues must be returned to the economy in a way which leaves the aggregate price level – an average of the prices of goods in the protected and unprotected sectors – unchanged. The significance of this is that if the aggregate price level is unchanged, there will be no upward pressure on money wages. Since the tendency of protection will be to raise import prices, the tariff revenues must be used either to subsidize domestic producers of import substitutes (hence lowering their costs and prices) or to reduce indirect taxation across the board.

Second, economies of scale must exist in the protected sector. The significance of this is that, if economies of scale exist, the natural tendency of costs to rise as domestic production of import substitutes is stepped up will be offset by increased productivity at the new higher level of output. This can in fact obviate the need for any subsidy to the expanding import-substitutes sector, since scale economies in effect mean that producers are being subsidized not by the government but by an accident of technology. Under these conditions it is indeed true that a tariff will increase aggregate activity and employment. The question to be answered is: do these conditions characterize the present state of the European economy?

A major difficulty is that the behaviour of firms and workers (and their unions) in the CEPG argument does not seem to correspond to the profit-maximizing self-interested stereotype which Western economists have found useful in analysing many other economic problems. The tariff, together with the production subsidy and the economies of scale, puts firms and workers in protected industries into a situation which they could exploit to their own benefit. Producers could, for example, raise prices by the amount of the tariff, thus increasing profits. Equally, they could hold on to the subsidy, or gains from scale economies. Equally, workers might seek to negotiate higher wages. The exact mechanism by which wages are fixed at their 'rigid' real level is not spelled out in the CEPG argument, but any sensible theory of bargaining would predict upward pressure on this level as profits in the protected sector rose. But neither price nor wage reactions are assumed to occur. This behaviour might be plausible as a description of reactions to a small or temporary change in the competitive position of the protected industry. It might be costly to make frequent small price and wage adjustments. However, if the tariff is large, visible and expected to be fairly long-lived, then it seems scarcely conceivable that prices and wages would not react to raise the standard of living of producers and workers in the sheltered sector.

In the end, of course, the plausibility of the CEPG case is an empirical issue, not a matter for conjecture. The CEPG evidence is largely based on a demonstration of the (in)dependence of price–cost margins in various United Kingdom manufacturing industries from the prices of competing imports, and the independence of average wage settlements from labour market conditions. These do not seem satisfactory tests of the assumptions of the analysis, for two reasons. First, price–cost margins might be stable in the protected sector, but both prices and costs might be heavily influenced by the prices of competing imports. This would happen if wages in that sector rapidly rose to absorb any profits resulting from exchange-rate or tariff changes. Indeed, since there is considerable evidence that exporters raise domestic-currency prices rapidly in response to exchange-rate changes, and that the price of domestic output rises by more than the impact of such exchange-rate changes on costs, it does seem as though the stable mark-up is really a reflection of the reaction of wages to market forces. The CEPG evidence on aggregate wage movements does not constitute a refutation of this idea, since the average wage movement may conceal a great variety of market-related wage movements. The second problem with the CEPG analysis is that it relates to a period when no policy change of the type they propose was actually implemented. No large and permanent tariff barrier was raised. Changes in competitive position arose from real-exchange-rate fluctuations of a temporary nature, and from a series of tariff reductions which were permanent, but very small relative to the exchange-rate changes. Reactions of firms to transitory fluctuations are likely to be minor compared with reactions to a permanent change in their status. It is not clear, then, how far an analysis of the past few decades of industrial pricing and wage behaviour helps build a picture of what might happen if a large (say 30 per cent) general tariff were permanently imposed. The force of the CEPG evidence must be even less if we try to extend their argument to the European economy. In some economies – Belgium, Italy – where there is widespread institutionalized indexation of wages, the CEPG case might hold; in others where relative wage flexibility is greater, the case clearly will not apply.

Moreover, where institutionalized wage rigidities currently exist, it is not clear that they would continue to do so in the face of a tariff hike. Institutions can change. The indexation of wages was the reaction of powerful unions in declining industries to the falling relative standard of living of their members. Evidence of wage rigidity in Europe is largely evidence of *downward* real-wage rigidity. The tariff, on the other hand, opens the prospect of a rising relative wage. The observations that real wages in many countries are downwardly rigid does not mean that real wages can then be guaranteed also to be upwardly rigid, after the tariff is imposed.

An alternative to examining the assumptions of any theory is of course to examine the validity of its predictions – in this case, that protection causes high employment and growth. As Hindley (1983b) has pointed out, the historical record is, to say the least, mixed. Many highly protected developing countries have signally failed to perform well; the fastest growing developing economies – such as Hong Kong – do not rely on protection at all. Most developed economies – including the United Kingdom and, in spite of popular mythology, Japan and Germany – also grew rapidly in the early stages of industrialization within a regime of free trade. So protection has not, historically, proved a necessary condition for growth. Indeed, the world market has proved a better vehicle than the home market on which to exploit economies of scale in expanding industries.

Protectionism in Europe

Our aim in this chapter has been to review macroeconomic aspects of a policy of protection applied to the European economy. This has involved looking beyond the impact of protection on the protected industry, at its repercussions in unprotected sectors of the real economy, and in money and foreign-exchange markets. These secondary effects are complex. To understand them we have been obliged to analyse the protectionist policy in the context of a series of simplified, abstract, models of the economy. The advantage of this approach is that it does let us identify conditions under which protectionist policies have favourable and unfavourable aggregate effects. Its drawback is that such abstract reasoning may seem rather remote from the realities of the current debate over protection and employment in Europe. In this tailpiece, it might be helpful to summarize the practical conclusions of the analysis.

We have addressed two questions. First, if a policy of protection is felt necessary, is it better carried out through conventional tariff and quota devices or through some macroeconomic measure, such as devaluation? Second, if conventional tariff protection is undertaken, is it guaranteed to raise aggregate output and employment?

On the first issue our conclusions are clear-cut. Exchange-rate policy will shelter exporting industries and industries competing with foreign imports. However, the protection afforded is likely to be temporary. Furthermore, such a policy would be difficult to organize at the European level; and it is not in any case desirable that all tradable-goods sectors in all European economies receive an equal degree of protection. On the second issue, our conclusions are that protection can raise employment temporarily if prices and wages eventually respond to market forces, permanently if firms and workers in protected industries do not attempt to exploit their privileged position. Such altruistic behaviour is at odds with the self-interested actions we observe when firms and individuals are confronted with permanent changes in other types of subsidy and tax.

Even if the wage and price rigidities necessary to make tariffs work do exist, a more fundamental question arises. These rigidities in effect prevent labour from being attracted into growing industries and trap workers into sectors which in the long run will prove unviable. In such circumstances, microeconomic policies aimed at increasing competition, encouraging relative wage movements and removing automatic indexation would have a much greater macroeconomic impact than a policy of protection. Calls for protection rely on the continuation of precisely those distortions which have led to adjustment problems in Europe. Removing these distortions would seem preferable to adding to them the classic inefficiencies associated with protection, particularly since the pay-off to employment is so uncertain.

14 A summing-up

Most of this book has been concerned with the idea that for specific industries the European Community as a whole should adopt more protectionist measures, often directed against imports from specific countries. In this chapter we summarize what is being proposed and why, the case that can be made for greater protection, and the outlook for trade and industrial policy in Europe.

In broad terms increased protection is advocated for two categories of industry whose competitiveness is seen to be in doubt. These are either old, established industries which are declining because of competition from new producers (e.g. textiles, cars), or new industries offering good prospects for expansion which have been launched more successfully elsewhere than they have in Europe (e.g. micro-electronics).

It is often suggested that greater protection is needed for declining industries from NICs, and for high-technology industries from Japan, although in some products the United States is at least as competitive as the NICs and Japan. Perhaps for political reasons it is thought advisable to avoid problems in relations with the United States; or the United States is believed to be more likely than Japan or the NICs to retaliate because of its large trade deficits.

The proposals envisage strengthening protection at the European level partly for the obvious reasons that Europe is supposed to have a common commercial policy, that such measures will have more impact if they are adopted by all member states than by only one or two, and that member governments should not pursue national policies which may have adverse effects on other member states. More radically, increased protection is linked to proposals for lowering internal barriers to create a unified internal market from which European firms could reap economies of scale.

The case for protection

In Chapter 7 we set out the analysis of commercial policy within the classical model of international trade. This model depicts trade flows as being generated by differences in comparative advantage across countries. Each country gains by specializing in the production of those goods which, given its endowment of resources (labour, capital and raw materials), it can produce most efficiently relative to its trading partners.

If free trade has unacceptable social repercussions, a case can be made for intervening, but this should be done in a way that interferes as little as possible with free trade. If distortions are impeding the efficient allocation of resources, intervention to remove the impediments may be justified. Protection is to be avoided because it imposes an efficiency loss on the economy as a whole. One situation in which protection may be justified is in association with an employment subsidy to ease adjustment problems in a contracting industry. For an industry where import penetration fluctuates unpredictably it is hard to calculate the optimal subsidy, so some form of quantitative restriction may be desirable which takes effect when imports surge above the anticipated level.

The classical model implicitly admits that, when rapid shifts in comparative advantage entail heavy adjustment costs, these can be offset by suitable compensatory schemes, but it is unaffected by the reasons for shifts in comparative advantage. Hence no special case can be made for protection on the grounds that competitors operate under different socio-economic arrangements, or that new producers have entered the market.

The discussion indicates that there was a case for intervening in the European textiles industry to help it adjust more easily to changes in comparative advantage, and that an adjustment package could justifiably include quantitative restrictions to cope with surges in imports. It does not, however, justify either member states continuing to channel industrial aids into the textiles sector, or the semi-permanent character which the MFA has acquired.

Several features of international trade in recent years cannot be analysed within the classical model. Detailed investigation, however, shows that even outside the classical model protection is unambiguously advantageous in only a few closely circumscribed situations.

Economies of scale introduce the possibility of beneficial intra-industry trade, where a country both imports and exports rival brands of the same product. Scale economies imply imperfect competition and so complicate the welfare analysis of protection. Imperfect competition comes in various forms. In Chapter 9 we showed that there may be a case for subsidizing a domestic producer faced with increasing returns to scale if this would enable him to capture enough of the domestic market to bring his costs down to, or below, the world price. Protection, however, would be detrimental. In oligopolistic markets protection may make things better or worse relative to *laissez-faire*; even if it makes them better, there may be a superior alternative. In Chapter 10 we examined the argument for protecting an increasing-returns sector, such as the car industy, and showed that it is very restricted. Protection might at best bring about a migration of foreign firms to Europe, which could benefit the economy as a whole. Even then, in so far as European producers would be likely to respond to the relaxation of competition from overseas producers by raising their price–cost margins, the overall effect would probably be adverse.

Another area sometimes beyond the scope of the classical model is industrial policy, particularly R&D activity. In R&D-intensive sectors, a firm which invests in developing a product often does not fully capture the the the benefits. This means that the market economy may generate 'too little' R&D, and this creates a rationale for subsidizing R&D activity. Protection is an inferior instrument, however, and 'infant industry' arguments for protection have little validity.

A convincing economic argument exists for subsidizing R&D activity in a programme such as Esprit, on the grounds that individual firms do not wholly capture the benefits of their own R&D efforts, and that a European approach avoids duplication among national efforts. Protection is unlikely to be helpful. The role of public procurement as an indirect subsidy to R&D is uncertain. In industries which are natural oligopolies, however, public procurement can help secure a place in the market for one (domestic) firm rather than a (foreign) competitor. An economic rationale can be provided for using public procurement in this way in highly concentrated industries. In Chapter 11 its role was illustrated by the case of Airbus, but it should be emphasized that this analysis offers no prescription for 'picking winners'.

In Chapter 13 we explored a situation in which wage rigidities of some kind have led to the appearance of aggregate unemployment. This, at first glance, seems to pose the most serious challenge to the classical defence of free trade. For, if in such a situation protection could raise *aggregate* employment, the efficiency gain thereby achieved might greatly exceed any losses of the kind emphasized in the classical model (i.e. distortions in relative prices which lead to a misallocation of resources between one industry and another). An important point is that protection of any one industry will of course tend to raise employment in that industry; but, in a world of floating exchange rates, it will also tend to generate, by way of exchange-rate adjustments, a loss in employment elsewhere. The issue is whether, on balance, aggregate employment can be increased. Our conclusion was that this is likely to happen only under extremely 'optimistic' assumptions regarding the likely response of domestic prices, and wages, to an increase in the level of protection.

Outlook

Although there may be a piecemeal increase in protectionism, the European Community as a whole is unlikely to shift to a systematically more protectionist stance. Such a shift would require a greater similarity among member states' levels of competitiveness and attitudes towards trade and industrial policy. Nor are present circumstances in the Community conducive to unified initiatives. On the contrary, the trend is towards seeking ways to manage heterogeneity. Furthermore, the Mediterranean enlargement of the Community is seen by some member states as tilting the balance in the Council of Ministers and in the Commission towards *dirigisme*. As a result, some member states, such as the Netherlands, which in the past have whole-heartedly endorsed a supranational approach, are beginning to express reservations about arrangements that might commit them to a more interventionist policy than they would choose.

In textiles the divisions are particularly acute since France and Italy, which in any case incline towards protectionism, would be the gainers, while Germany and the Netherlands, whose approach is more liberal, would lose because their industries have been run down relatively rapidly. In view of these divisions and pressures for eventually dismantling the MFA, the Community's position will probably be geared to minimizing the degree of liberalization in MFA 4. There is a comparable situation in cars, where Germany is most in favour of free trade and also has the most competitive industry. If the Community moved to the level of protection at present imposed by France and Italy, they would be the main gainers, while Germany and the non-producing countries would lose most. Consequently, Germany, supported by other member states, would oppose an increase in protection on principle and also because of the practical implications for its domestic economy.

The Community is most likely to adopt a more protectionist position with regard to new products, such as electronics. A recent case was the doubling of the tariff on compact disc-players. This was prompted by Philips, a company with a wide enough base within the Community to be considered 'European' and to make the imbalance between winners and losers less pronounced. Furthermore, the fact that the tariff increase was presented in terms of infant-industry protection lent it a modicum of respectability in the context of GATT. If European products of this sort continue to have difficulty in competing with those from Japan and elsewhere, then a protectionist response from the Community can be expected.

There is little prospect of the Community developing a coordinated industrial policy. Again this reflects a divergence between the interventionist approach of some member states and the more liberal approach of others. In addition there are reservations about the costs of such a policy and fears that the benefits might be distributed very unevenly. Esprit is unlikely to be followed by many similar initiatives since there are few areas in which all member states have an active interest. An alternative to collaboration among all member states is a variable-geometry format, bringing in only those which are interested. This raises other problems if Community funding or protection is involved. Non-participants would be expected in the short run to make sacrifices to the advantage of participants, with no guarantee of themselves benefiting in the long run.

Conclusion

Our conclusion is that a systematic move by the European Community to a more strongly protectionist external trade policy is for the most part neither desirable nor feasible. What, then, would be a desirable and feasible course for the Community's trade and industrial policy? To try to answer that question is beyond the terms of reference of this study, and to do so thoroughly would require much more space. We shall simply review a few policy measures which the study indicates are desirable.

First, some obvious points which bear repeating: if the Community is to become a proper customs union, the member states will need to remove barriers to internal trade and to adopt uniform external barriers. Economic analysis points to the desirability of convergence on a lower rather than a higher level of protection. This amounts to advocating that some member states which are feeling international competition most keenly should reduce their protection. Policy-makers say that this is a counsel of perfection. They are perhaps influenced more by immediate political imperatives than by economic costs which emerge only over some time, may not be attributable to any specific measure, and are borne by the population at large rather than by one section of it. That they should yield to political imperatives is understandable, but they ought not to ignore the economic costs, a proper assessment of which might lead them to reduce the relative weight of political considerations.

Unless all European governments become actively interventionist, which is unlikely for the foreseeable future, the development of a European industrial base will be a matter for firms rather than for governments. If policy-makers wish this development to occur there is much they can do to facilitate it. Financial support for collaborative activities – for example, through programmes like Esprit – can encourage firms to pursue cooperation which they might not otherwise consider. Firms themselves, however, maintain that far more important is the removal of internal barriers and the revision of Community and national laws and regulations so as to make it easier to establish and operate European companies.

Finally, we would draw attention to two specific areas of trade and industrial policy. The policies of member states towards inward investment have recently become more convergent, with the French government's shift towards a more accommodating attitude. This intensifies the danger that member states will compete among themselves to attract foreign investment, to their mutual disadvantage and to the benefit of the foreign investor. In the case of Nissan, Britain was ahead of the field but still paid dearly for the privilege of securing the Japanese company's investment; had other European countries been equally eager the price would have been higher still. To avoid situations in which a foreign firm plays off one Community partner against another, member governments should agree on a common approach to investment incentives.

Also urgently needed is a common view of competition policy. Germany takes a liberal stand on trade issues but insists on applying stringent antitrust laws. France presses for increased external protection but more relaxed implementation of antitrust laws. Neither position is consistent, for a more liberal stance on trade should be accompanied by a more flexible stance on competition policy. Britain, with its relatively pragmatic concept of antitrust and its less extreme position on protection, may be uniquely well placed to take a lead on this issue within the Community.

Notes

Chapter 1

1 The NIESR's contribution was published as Morgan (1984).
2 If an expansionary policy leads to a fall in the exchange rate, then, under 'real-wage rigidity', it will induce an increase in domestic inflation as wages rise to recapture the fall in purchasing power associated with the depreciation of the currency. It is this mechanism which is suggestive of recent French experience.

Chapter 3

1 A succinct description of the GATT is in GATT (1982).
2 The codes are discussed in Baldwin (1979). See also Bergsten and Cline (1982) and Ginman, Pugel and Walter (1980).
3 These issues are discussed in Bergsten and Cline (1982).
4 The future of the GATT is analysed in Balassa *et al.* (1979), Camps and Diebold (1983), Corden (1984) and Díaz-Alejandro and Helleiner (1982).

Chapter 4

1 Commission of the European Communities (1983b).
2 Holmes and Shepherd (1983), p. 18.
3 'Import safeguard problem for GATT', *Financial Times,* 29 September 1982, p. 7.
4 European Communities (1982).
5 The Community's role in the MFA is described in more detail in Chapter 8.
6 MFA is a formal derogation from GATT. In that it involves quantitative restrictions and selective treatment of exporters it is contrary to GATT rules.
7 The average annual increase for sensitive products is 0.9 per cent; for less vulnerable products, 3 per cent; and for non-sensitive products, 4.5 per cent. *Europe,* 15 December 1982, p. 7.

8 A detailed account of the problems between the United States and Europe in steel trade policy is in Jones (1983).

9 The compact-disc case is discussed further in Chapters 5, 6 and 11.

10 Interestingly, senior officials of the Commission cited the sale of wheat flour by the USA to Egypt in January 1983 as an instance of the kind of situation in which the new instrument could be used to retaliate. *Financial Times*, 18 February 1983, p. 1.

11 Commission of the European Communities (1983a). The list summarized here is also reproduced in European Communities (1983).

12 France originally prepared a highly tendentious list. This was redrafted and toned down after other member governments agreed that the Commission should compile an inventory. 'Paris catalogues the EEC tariff trip wires', *Financial Times*, 1 March 1983.

13 'EEC blocks £5m UK aid for new Japanese plant', *Financial Times*, 1 March 1984, p. 9.

14 These are discussed in Hodges (1983) and Jacquemin (1979).

15 An English translation of the French memorandum was published in *Europe Documents*, No. 1274, 16 September 1983. The British memorandum is summarized in HM Treasury, 'Future financing and development of the European Community: British Government ideas', *Economic Progress Report Supplement*, October 1983. The Gyllenhammar group is discussed in: 'The self-help seventeen', *Financial Times*, 15 November 1983; 'Gyllenhammar's vigilantes', *The Economist*, 28 January 1984, p. 69; 'Bosses want the common market Brussels never built', *The Economist*, 26 May 1984, pp. 75–6; 'European venture-capital initiative', *Financial Times*, 26 June 1984, p. 40.

Chapter 5

1 HM Treasury, 'Future financing and development of the European Community: British Government ideas', *Economic Progress Report Supplement*, October 1983, p. 4.

2 See Anthony Moreton, 'Exports lead growth in W. German textiles', *Financial Times*, 7 December 1984, p. 2; letter from Dr Konrad Neundorfer to the *Financial Times*, 22 October 1984, p. 17; and Anthony Moreton, 'Textiles: the struggle at Lake Geneva', *Financial Times*, 29 October 1984, p. 15.

3 The textiles sector is discussed further in Chapter 8.

4 Even without a stipulation on minimum prices, exporters tend to raise their prices in a situation of this kind.

5 The details of the agreement were settled outside of the GATT in negotiations between the USA and the Commission. See *Financial Times*, 1 March 1984.

6 The French explanation is that they were intended to prompt the Community into taking joint action. In this case they mark the

beginning of the new phase in policy rather than the end of the old one.

7   This is discussed in Commission of the European Communities (1983a), pp. 20–1.

8   They are reinforced by the German technical institutes. Students, from Germany and abroad, are made familiar with the norms during their training and when they become purchasers opt for German goods.

9   Paul Cheeseright, 'Britain launches new drive to break down EEC trade barriers', *Financial Times*, 24 July 1984.

10 Institute of Directors (1985) reported in John Wyles, 'UK institute calls for "genuine" common market', *Financial Times*, 4 January 1985.

Chapter 6

1   Much of the analysis underlying the French memorandum is elaborated in Richonnier (1983). A presentation in English of the main arguments is in Richonnier (1984).

2   This argument has been developed in Jeanneney (1978).

3   This view is not held universally. Some officials made a point of saying that the memorandum was not directed against the USA and Japan.

4   This was an important issue in the attempt by Thomson-Brandt to take over Grundig. See Chapter 12.

5   See Rupert Cornwell, 'Hi-tech fears cloud West German optimism on recovery', *Financial Times*, 3 February 1984; 'Bonn to spend DM 3bn on high technology boost', *Financial Times*, 9 March 1984, p. 1; Guy de Jonquières, 'Bonn chips away at an old industrial block', *Financial Times*, 14 March 1984, p. 3; Jonathan Carr, 'West Germany falls back in high tech race', *Financial Times*, 19 April 1984, p. 2; and 'R and D spending set to rise 6%', *Financial Times*, 13 June 1984, p. 3.

6   It is recognized that there have been some examples of a French nationalised company taking over a weak German company and putting it on a more stable basis, for example, Nordmende, Saba and Dual.

7   See 'German equity in the kindergarten', *Financial Times*, 24 April 1984, p. 36.

8   Competition policy and the Grundig/Thomson-Brandt case are examined in detail in Chapter 12.

9   This case is discussed in Steinberger (1984).

10 In Germany too the government is privatizing some nationalized companies.

11 *The Times*, 29 April 1983, p. 26.

12 Ibid.

13 HM Treasury, 'Future financing and development of the European

Community: British Government ideas', *Economic Progress Report Supplement,* October 1983, p. 3.
14   There are powers under the 1975 Industry Act to prevent a foreign company taking over a UK business if it is against the national interest but they have never been used. See Brech and Sharp (1984, p. 9).
15   *Hansard,* 6 June 1984, col. 302.
16   *Le Monde,* 23 November 1982.

Chapter 7

1   It is important to distinguish comparative from absolute advantage. Even if one country is more productive than another in *all* industries (in terms of its ability to transform factors into products), there is still scope for mutually advantageous trade, so long as it is relatively more productive in some industries than in others.
2   The purchases and sales of the 'small' country can be assumed to have a negligible effect on world prices. Thus we are assuming here that it faces an infinitely elastic supply schedule for its imports, and an infinitely elastic demand schedule for its exports. The scope for tilting world relative prices, and so changing the terms of trade in its favour, is greater according as the supply of its imports, and the demand for its exports, are less elastic. (Note that the *elasticity* of the schedule is defined as the ratio of the fractional change in quantity supplied, or demanded, to the associated fractional change in the price.)
3   Or, within the classical model, at least, any scheme of quotas.
4   For a full discussion of such arguments, in a more general context, the reader is referred to Dixit and Norman (1980).
5   Thus, for example, the European Commission has attacked the schemes of several member countries (including those of Belgium, Italy and the UK), using its powers to act in cases in which intra-EEC trade is affected (Woolcock, 1982a, p. 45). Such fears are difficult to rationalize within the classical model, in which the policy-maker's objective was confined to maximizing general welfare, and in which we assumed the availability of an ideal system of compensatory payments to remedy any adverse distributional consequences. But once we admit the case for intervention aimed at slowing down the rate of job loss in certain industries, then it follows that such employment subsidies have a 'beggar my neighbour' aspect, in that they shift some of this sectoral unemployment to the foreign economy.
6   For an industry to be perfectly competitive we require that it consists of a large number of firms, each offering an identical product. It will follow from this that, at equilibrium, the firm chooses a level of output at which its marginal cost (the incremental cost incurred in producing one further unit) coincides with market price. To see this, note that a firm can sell all it wishes at the prevailing price (a tiny

price cut suffices to draw all customers away from its rivals, as they offer an identical product – and its actions can be supposed to have a negligible influence on any other particular firm, so that we can ignore the possibility of any rival responding to its cut). Hence it will maximize its profit if it produces up to the point where marginal cost equals price. (All this presupposes that marginal cost does *rise* as output increases – otherwise we have increasing returns, and the argument fails; see Chapter 9 below.)

7   It is worth noting that the observation that price–cost margins are stable over time, in response to fluctuations in aggregate demand, is not relevant here; the question relates purely to their stability in response to a change in the level of protection.

8   In fact, it is possible that a quantitative restriction might benefit the trading partner, while reducing domestic welfare (Hindley, 1978).

9   We are here going beyond the 'perfect competition' framework. VERs are imposed on specific producers, on the assumption that other foreign producers will not then supply perfect substitute goods at the old price, thus fully offsetting the VER.

10 As a consequence of this, it turns out that the optimum quota will be at a level which restricts trade by less than does the optimum tariff. The optimum level of VER is less restrictive again – in fact it will normally be optimal to have no restriction of this kind. I am grateful to Alasdair Smith for clarifying this point.

Chapter 8

1   The developments prior to the negotiation of MFA3 in 1982 are very well documented in Woolcock (1982a). For the tensions surrounding the Community's stand in regard to the renewal of the MFA in 1982, see: *Financial Times*, 22 December 1982; *Europe*, 20–21 October and 7 November 1980, 25 and 26 February, 5 August, 20 and 28 October, 15 December 1982; S. Islam, *International Economics*, 27 and 28 October 1982; *Guardian*, 8 May 1981, 27 January and 9 February 1982.

   For the background to the new EEC textile agreement with China, see *Europe*, 20 January, 19–20 and 30 March 1984; *Financial Times*, 2 March 1984.

   For allegations of repercussions on Europe from trade diversion resulting from the US/China agreement, see *International Herald Tribune*, 22 January 1984; *Guardian*, 20 January 1984; *Financial Times*, 5 and 20 January 1984.

   For EEC–US tensions surrounding the price of naphtha, and US oil prices, see *Europe*, 21 February 1981.

2   *Europe*, 7 November 1980.

3   *Europe*, 30–31 March 1981.

4   *Europe*, 9 April 1981.

5   *Europe*, 15 July 1981.

6   G. Merritt, *Financial Times*, 28 October 1981.

7   L. Klinger, *Financial Times,* 28 October 1981.
8   A. Moreton, *Financial Times,* 26 February 1982.
9   R. Chapman, *Guardian,* 8 May 1981.
10 The level of allowable imports has been criticized, however, as being
    too liberal, by the committee of EEC cotton industries, Eurocotton.
    See *Europe,* 18 April 1984.

Chapter 9

1   Under perfect competition, we either assume fixed costs to be absent,
    or else appeal to the notion that marginal cost rises at least above
    some level of output (the cost of squeezing out an additional unit
    from a given plant gets greater, as we reach the limits of plant
    capacity). This allows marginal cost to rise to equal, or exceed,
    average cost.
2   Let us recapitulate the argument for this, which we noted in Chapter
    7 above: perfect competition presupposes a large number of firms,
    each selling an identical product to a large number of well-informed
    buyers. If market price lay above marginal cost, then any firm could
    increase its profits by selling more output at the prevailing price level.
    But, since it sells a product identical to that of its rivals, and since
    buyers are informed as to the prices set by each seller, it requires only
    a negligibly small price cut to attract customers away from rival firms.
    Thus price-cutting would occur up to the point where market price
    coincides with marginal cost. This argument breaks down if firms
    offer differentiated products; for then it is no longer true that any
    price cut, however small, suffices to draw all customers from rival
    suppliers. It also breaks down if there are only a few firms in the
    industry: for the argument depends on the idea that if one firm cuts its
    price, no other firm will respond by changing its price. This is justified
    in the perfect-competition story by appealing to the idea that the firm
    is so small, relative to the market, that a price cut exerts a negligible
    impact on the sales of any particular rival firm.
3   One of the major difficulties in estimation is posed by the fact that
    most tariff changes in the past generation have been very modest.
4   Up to the point at which it coincides with the monopoly price, after
    which further protection has no effect.
5   If the domestic firm's cost schedule is low enough, it will find entry
    profitable; if it is too high, entry will be socially undesirable. In the
    intermediate case, intervention is justified.
6   If a tariff is set at such a level as to induce the entry of a local
    producer, it also thereby gives that producer sufficient protection to
    set a higher price than that which prevailed under *laissez-faire.* The
    net result is a welfare loss (Corden, 1967).
7   The firm's strategy is to choose a pair of output levels, which it
    supplies to the home and foreign markets respectively. Each firm
    takes its rival's output pair as given in choosing its own strategy.

8   A further possibility which is currently considered important by
policy-makers in the UK concerns the idea that efficient foreign firms
might provide a 'demonstration effect' to the domestic counterparts.
9   Technically, the elasticity of demand facing each producer is assumed
to be *unchanged* when the price of rival products rises.

Chapter 10

1   On the motor industry, see for example McMullen and Megna
(1982). A number of recent articles in the *Financial Times* by K.
Gooding (21 September, 20 October and 5 December 1983, 26 March
1984) were particularly helpful in preparing this section. On the
German industry, see also: *The Economist*, 17 September 1983;
Financial Times, 23 and 25 January 1984; J. Davies, *Financial Times*,
17 February 1984. On the French industry, see: *Financial Times*, 26
May 1983; Paul Betts, *Financial Times*, 20 September and 20 October
1983, 9 January and 11 July 1984. On the Italian industry, see: *The
Times*, 15 September 1983; *The Economist*, 19 November 1983;
Financial Times, 23 December 1983. On the UK industry, see:
Investors Chronicle, 7 October 1983; R. Gribben, *Financial Times*, 14
October 1983; K. Gooding, *Financial Times*, 6 February and 21
March 1984; J. Huxley, *Sunday Times*, 12 February 1984; J. Griffiths,
Financial Times, 15 February 1984; J. Huxley, *Sunday Times*, 19
February 1984. On the international industry, see: *Financial Times*,
20 October and 4 November 1983; *The Economist*, 22 and 29 October
1983. On the price-discrimination issue, see: Hindley and Nicolaides
(1983); K. Gooding, *Financial Times*, 24 October 1983. For the
motor-industry view, see *Europe*, 24/25 October 1983. See also C.
Huhne, *Guardian*, 3 November 1983. On the recent price war in the
UK, see *Financial Times*, 6 January 1984.
2   Thus some commentators, for example, argue that Europe will have
to concede assembly operations to the newly industrializing countries
in the medium term, but will retain comparative advantage in engine
manufacture.
3   *The Times*, 24 December 1983.
4   Noelke and Taylor (1981), vol. I, p. 132.
5   *Europe*, 11 November 1983.
6   In November 1983, the differential was 39 per cent (*Europe*, 1 July
1983). These figures are probably biased upwards, in that they do not
take account of list-price discounting, which is quite substantial in the
UK.
7   *Europe*, 27/28 June 1983.
8   *Financial Times*, 24 May 1984; *Guardian*, 5 July and 20 November
1984; *The Times*, 19 October 1984; *Sunday Times*, 21 October 1984.
9   What is claimed (e.g. by Hager) is that an increase in the height of
barriers around the Community will stimulate the relaxation of
barriers within the Community. In other words, if the pressure from

Japanese competition is relieved, then each member state will be more willing to accept greater competiton from firms in other member states. This should be distinguished from the idea that a lack of uniformity in the degree of external protection across member states may induce additional intra-Community barriers designed to hamper third-country imports from entering via other member states. These barriers would of course become irrelevant once member states moved to a uniform degree of external protection.

10 On the Nissan deal, see K. Gooding, *Financial Times*, 2 February 1984.

11 *Observer*, 14 August 1983. See also P. Cheeseright, *Financial Times*, 18 August 1983.

12 K. Gooding, *Financial Times*, 28 September 1983.

13 *New York Times*, 16 April 1983.

Chapter 11

1 The text of the memorandum is reproduced in English in *Europe Documents*, no. 1274, 16 September 1983.

2 That is, the new product generates 'consumer surplus', in the sense that some ('intra-marginal') consumers would be willing to pay *more* than the market price for the new good.

3 Another argument of this kind involves the idea that, for instance, we must continue to produce microchips, in order to maintain capabilities in other parts of the micro-electronics sector. Again, some kind of 'spillover' is implicitly assumed here. This kind of argument is often labelled a 'strategic' argument in the popular literature, but this is a misuse of the term (whose meaning is specified on pp. 147–9).

4 See p. 20 of the Alvey report (Department of Industry, 1982).

5 The legal position regarding such 'infant industry' protection in the case of the compact disc is at best dubious. In May 1984, Japan filed a complaint against the doubling of the EEC duty. The Community defends its action by reference to GATT Article XXVIII. A (slightly opaque) statement of the case was given in *Europe* (2/3 May 1984) as follows:

> According to the Japanese complaint, the measure is unfair and is not covered by GATT article XXVIII because it goes against GATT's fundamental aim: to favour economic growth through expansion of trade. The EEC replies that the measure is temporary: its aim is to give European manufacturers (i.e. for the moment the Dutch Philips company) the possibility of operating on the same plane as the various Japanese makers who, in fact, are using the process developed by Philips.
>
> On the technical plane, Japan contests that art. XXVIII (which in certain circumstances authorizes a contracting party to increase a customs duty) be applicable to *new products,* born of a new

technology. The EEC observes that this article makes no difference between new and old products and that otherwise, Japan itself
used it in the past for a new product (ski shoes made with new
materials); nevertheless, if the contracting parties decide not to
apply art. XXVIII to new products, this decision, the EEC
considers, *would be valid for the future*.

6 For an introductory account, see Shaked and Sutton (1984). For a
formal analysis, see Shaked and Sutton (1983), and the references
cited therein.

7 Strictly: there exists an upper bound, independent of the qualities
offered by rival firms, to the number of firms which can coexist with
price exceeding unit variable cost, at a non-cooperative price
equilibrium.

8 Formally: equilibrium is characterised as a 'perfect equilibrium' in a
three-stage game, in which firms first choose whether to enter, then
choose their product specifications and finally set their respective
prices.

9 Recent press reports documenting the case are: *The Economist* (15
October 1983), *Observer* (16 October 1983), and articles by Victor
Smart, *Observer* (30 October 1983), and Roger Elgin, *Sunday Times*
(9 October 1983 and 20 November 1983). See also *Financial Times*
(18 April 1984) and *Guardian* (17 April 1984).

10 These gaps will be further widened with the introduction, at a later
stage, of the proposed Rolls-Royce/Pratt & Whitney engines, in place
of those initially fitted (General Electric/Snecma).

Chapter 12

1 This account draws on the following sources: J.-M. Quatrepoint, *Le
Monde,* 17 November 1982, 7 February 1983; Guy de Jonquières,
Financial Times, 19 November 1982; *Le Monde,* 10 March and 22
November 1983; *Financial Times,* 10 January and 5 March 1983; E.
le Boucher, *Le Monde,* 10 March 1983; Philippe le Maître, *Le
Monde,* 13/14 March 1983; Walter Ellis, Stewart Fleming and David
Marsh, *Financial Times,* 10 March 1983; J. Crisp, *Financial Times,* 7
April 1984.

2 For a review of these events, see *Le Monde,* 10 and 13/14 March
1983.

3 See: *Financial Times,* 10 March 1983; *Le Monde,* 10 March 1983.

References

Arrow, K.J. (1962), 'Economic welfare and the allocation of resources for inventions', in R.R. Nelson (ed.), *The Rate and Direction of Inventive Activity,* Princeton, Princeton University Press. (Reprinted in N. Rosenberg, *The Economics of Technological Change,* Harmondsworth, Penguin Books, 1971.)

Balassa, B. (1966), 'Tariff reductions and trade in manufactures among the industrialized countries', *American Economic Review,* vol. 56, pp. 466–73.

Balassa, B., *et al.* (1979), *World Trade: Constraints and Opportunities in the 80's,* Paris, The Atlantic Institute for International Affairs. (The Atlantic Papers no. 36.)

Baldwin, R.E. (1979), *The Multilateral Trade Negotiations: Toward Greater Liberalization,* Washington, DC, American Enterprise Institute for Public Policy Research.

Baldwin, R.E. (1982), 'The political economy of protection', in J.N. Bhagwati (ed.), *Import Competition and Response,* Chicago, Chicago University Press.

Batchelor, R., and Minford, A.P.L. (1977), 'Import controls and devaluation as medium term policies', in *On How to Cope with Britain's Economic Problems,* London, Trade Policy Research Centre. (Thames Essays 8.)

Bergsten, C.F., and Cline, W.R. (1982), *Trade Policy in the 1980s,* Washington, DC, Institute for International Economics. (Policy Analyses in International Economics 3.)

Bergsten, C.F., and Williamson, J. (1983), 'Exchange rates and trade policy', in W.R. Cline (ed.), *Trade Policy in the 1980s,* Washington, DC, Institute for International Economics.

Bhagwati, J. (1965), 'On the equivalence of tariffs and quotas', in R.E. Baldwin (ed.), *Trade, Growth and the Balance of Payments,* Amsterdam, North Holland.

Brech, M., and Sharp, M. (1984), *Inward Investment: Policy Options for the United Kingdom,* London, Routledge & Kegan Paul for the Royal Institute of International Affairs. (Chatham House Paper no. 21.)

Brecher, Z.A. (1974), 'Minimum wage rates and the pure theory of international trade', *Quarterly Journal of Economics,* vol. 88, no. 1, pp. 98–116.

Cable, V. (1983), *Protectionism and Industrial Decline,* London, Hodder

& Stoughton in association with the Overseas Development Institute.

Camps, M. and Diebold, W., Jr (1983), *The New Multilateralism: Can the World Trading System be Saved?* New York, Council on Foreign Relations.

Commission of the European Communities (1983a), *Assessment of the Function of the Internal Market*, Brussels, 24 February 1983. (COM (83) 80 final.)

Commission of the European Communities (1983b), *First Annual Report of the Commission of the European Communities on the Community's Anti-Dumping and Anti-Subsidy Activities*, Brussels, 28 September 1983. (COM (83) 519 final/2.)

Corden, W.M. (1967), 'Monopoly, tariffs and subsidies', *Economica*, vol. 34.

Corden, W.M. (1979), *The Theory of Protection*, Oxford, Oxford University Press.

Corden, W.M. (1982), 'Exchange rate protection', in R.N. Cooper, P.B. Kenen, J.B. de Macedo and J. van Ypersele (eds.), *The International Monetary System under Flexible Exchange Rates: Essays in Honour of Robert Triffin*, Cambridge, Mass., Ballinger.

Corden, W.M. (1984), *The Revival of Protectionism*, New York, Group of Thirty. (Occasional Papers no. 14.)

Coutts, K.J., Godley, W.A.H., and Nordhaus, W.D. (1978), *Industrial Pricing in the United Kingdom*, Cambridge, Cambridge University Press.

Dasgupta, P., and Stiglitz, J. (1980), 'Uncertainty, industrial structure, and the speed of R&D', *Bell Journal of Economics*, vol. II, pp. 1–28.

De Grasse, R. (1983), *Military Expansion and Economic Decline: The Impact of Military Expenditure on U.S. Economic Performance*, Armonk, New York, M.E. Sharp Inc.

de Meza, D. (1984), 'The superiority of price controls over export subsidies', London, London School of Economics. (Mimeo.)

Department of Industry (1982), *A Programme for Advanced Information Technology: The Report of the Alvey Committee*, London, HMSO.

Díaz-Alejandro, C.F., and Helleiner, G.K. (1982), *Handmaiden in Distress: World Trade in the 1980s*, Ottawa, North-South Institute; Washington, DC, Overseas Development Council; London, Overseas Development Institute.

Dixit, A. (1984), 'International trade policy for oligopolistic industries', *Economic Journal*, vol. 94. (Conference Papers.)

Dixit, A., and Norman, V. (1980), *Theory of International Trade*, Cambridge, Nisbet and Cambridge University Press.

Dornbusch, R. (1976), 'Expectations and exchange rate dynamics', *Journal of Political Economy*, vol. 84.

Eichengreen, B.J. (1983), 'Protection, real wage resistance and employment', *Weltwirtschaftliches Archiv*, vol. 119, pp. 429–52.

European Communities (1982), 'Council Regulations (EEC) No. 288/82 of 5 January 1982 on Common Rules for Imports', *Official Journal*, 9 February. (25 L35.)

European Communities (1983), *The Customs Union,* Luxembourg, Office for Official Publications of the European Communities.

Fisher, F., McGowan, J., and Greenwood, J. (1983), *Folded, Spindled and Mutilated: Economic Analysis and U.S. vs. IBM,* Cambridge, Mass., MIT Press.

General Agreement on Tariffs and Trade (1982), *GATT: What It is; What It Does,* Geneva.

Ginman, P.J., Pugel, T.A., and Walter, I. (1980), 'Mixed blessings for the Third World in codes on non-tariff measures', *The World Economy,* vol. 3, pp. 217–34. (Reprinted in United Nations Conference on Trade and Development, Geneva, 1982, Reprint Series no. 2.)

Godley, W.A.H., *et al.* (1980), 'Academic criticisms of the CEPG analysis', *Cambridge Economic Policy Review,* vol. 6, pp. 35–42.

Godley, W.A.H., and May, R.M. (1977), 'The macroeconomic implications of devaluation and import restriction', *Economic Policy Review* (Cambridge University Department of Applied Economics), no. 3.

Godley, W.A.H., and Nordhaus, W.D. (1972), 'Pricing in the trade cycle', *Economic Journal,* vol. 82, pp. 853–82.

Greenaway, D., and Milner, C. (1979), *Protectionism Again . . .?* London, Institute of Economic Affairs. (Hobart Paper no. 94.)

Hager, W. (1981), 'Protection in the '80s: the managed coexistence of different countries', in Noelke and Taylor (1981).

Hager, W. (1982), 'Protectionism and autonomy: how to preserve free trade in Europe', *International Affairs,* vol. 58, pp. 413–28.

Harris, R.G., and Cox, D. (1984), *Trade, Industrial Policy and Canadian Manufacturing,* Toronto, Ontario Economic Council.

Henderson, P.D. (1983), 'Trade policies: trends, issues and influences', *Midland Bank Review,* winter, pp. 8–19.

Hindley, B. (1978), 'The economics of an accord on public procurement policies', *The World Economy,* vol. 1, no. 3, pp. 279–88.

Hindley, B. (1983a), 'Protectionism and autonomy: a comment on Hager', *International Affairs,* vol. 59, pp. 77–86.

Hindley, B. (1983b), 'Trade policy, economic preference, and Britain's economic problems', in J. Black and A. Winters (eds.), *Policy and Performance in International Trade,* London, Macmillan.

Hindley, B., and Nicolaides, E. (1983), *Taking the New Protectionism Seriously,* London, Trade Policy Research Centre.

Hodges, M. (1983), 'Industrial policy: hard times or great expectations?', in H. Wallace, W. Wallace and C. Webb (eds.), *Policy-Making in the European Community,* Chichester, Wiley, pp. 265–93.

Holmes, P., and Shepherd, G. (1983), 'Protectionism in the European Community: internal and external aspects', paper presented at the eighth annual conference of the International Economics Study Group. (Mimeo.)

Institute of Directors (1985), *The Common Market: An Agenda for Jobs and Economic Growth,* London.

Jacquemin, A.P. (1979), 'European industrial policies and competition', in P. Coffey (ed.), *Economic Policies of the Common Market,* London,

Macmillan, pp. 22–51.

Jeanneney, J.-M. (1978), *Pour un nouveau protectionnisme,* Paris, Editions du Seuil.

Jones, K. (1983), *Impasse and Crisis in Steel Trade Policy,* London, Trade Policy Research Centre.

Kaldor, N. (1966), *Causes of the Slow Rate of Economic Growth of the United Kingdom,* Cambridge, Cambridge University Press.

Kierzkowski, H. (ed.) (1984), *Monopolistic Competition and International Trade,* Oxford, Oxford University Press.

Krugman, P. (1982), 'The macroeconomics of protection with a floating exchange rate', *Journal of Monetary Economics,* vol. 16, pp. 141–82. (Carnegie-Rochester Conference Series in Public Policy.)

Lal, D. (1981), *Resurrection of the Pauper Labour Argument,* London, Trade Policy Research Centre.

Lamfalussy, A. (1963), 'Contribution à une théorie de la croissance en économie ouverte', *Recherches économiques de Louvain,* vol. 29.

Lapan, H.E. (1976), 'International trade, factor market distortions, and the optimal dynamic subsidy', *American Economic Review,* vol. 66.

Laursen, S., and Metzler, L.A. (1950), 'Flexible exchange rates and the theory of employment', *Review of Economics and Statistics,* vol. 32, pp. 281–99.

Lawson, A. (1981), *Incomes Policy and the Real Wage Resistance Hypothesis: Econometric Evidence for the United Kingdom, 1955–79,* Cambridge. (Cambridge Growth Project Working Paper 509.)

Lyons, B.R. (1983), 'Oligopoly, product differentiation and international trade: theory and evidence', University of Sheffield. (Unpublished PhD thesis.)

McMullen, N., and Megna, L.L. (1982), 'Automobiles', in Turner and McMullen (1982).

Morgan, A. (1984), 'Protection and European trade in manufactures', *National Institute Economic Review,* no. 109, pp. 45–57.

Mundell, R.A. (1961), 'Flexible exchange rates and employment policy', *Canadian Journal of Economics,* vol. 27, pp. 509–17.

Noelke, M., and Taylor, R. (1981), *EEC Protectionism: Present Practice and Future Trends,* vol. I (Section One by W. Hager). Vol. II (by W. Hager and R. Taylor), 1982. Brussels, European Research Associates.

Olechowski, A., and Sampson, G. (1980), 'Current trade restrictions in the EEC, the United States and Japan', *Journal of World Trade Law,* vol. 14, pp. 220–31. (Reprinted in United Nations Conference on Trade and Development, Geneva, Reprint Series no. 34.)

Owen, N. (1983), *Economies of Scale, Competition and Trade Patterns within the European Community,* Oxford, Clarendon Press.

Page, S.A.B. (1981), 'The revival of protectionism and the consequences for Europe', *Journal of Common Market Studies,* vol. XX, pp. 17–40.

Richonnier, M. [rapporteur] (1983), *Quelle stratégie européenne pour la France dans les années 80?* Paris, Commissariat Général du Plan.

Richonnier, M. (1984), 'Europe: Decline is not Irreversible', *Journal of Common Market Studies,* vol. XXII, pp. 227–43.

Rothwell, R. and Zegfeld, W. (1981), *Industrial Innovation and Public Policy,* London, Frances Pinter.

Samuelson, P. (1981), 'To protect manufacturing?', *Zeitschrift für die gesamte Staatswissenschaft,* vol. 137, pp. 407–14.

Shaked, A., and Sutton, J. (1983), 'Natural oligopolies', *Econometrica,* vol. 51, pp. 1469–84.

Shaked, A., and Sutton, J. (1984), 'Natural oligopolies and international trade', in Kierzkowski (1984).

Shepherd, G. (1981), *Textile Industry Adjustment in Developed Countries,* London, Trade Policy Research Centre.

Smith, A. (1983), 'Some doubts on the theory of protection', Sussex University. (Mimeo.)

Spence, M. (1984), 'Cost reduction, competition and industry performance', *Econometrica,* vol. 52, pp. 101–22.

Spencer, B., and Brander, J. (1983), 'International R&D rivalry and industrial strategy', *Review of Economic Studies,* vol. 50, pt 4, no. 163, pp. 707–22.

Steinberger, H. (1984), 'The German approach', in *Extra-territorial Application of Laws and Responses Thereto,* Oxford, International Law Association in association with ESC Publishing Ltd, pp. 77–95.

Turner, L., *et al.* (1980), *Living with the Newly Industrializing Countries,* London, Royal Institute of International Affairs.

Turner, L. (ed.) with McMullen, N. (1982), *The Newly Industrializing Countries: Trade and Adjustment,* London, Allen & Unwin for the Royal Institute of International Affairs.

Venables, A.J. (1982), 'Optimal tariffs for trade in monopolistically competitive commodities', *Journal of International Economics,* vol. 12, pp. 225–41.

Venables, A.J. (1984), *The Theory of International Trade in Monopolistically Competitive Industries,* Oxford, Oxford University (PhD thesis.)

Wolf, M. (1983), 'The European Community's trade policy', in R. Jenkins (ed.), *Britain and the EEC,* London, Macmillan.

Woolcock, S. (1982a), 'Textiles and clothing', in Turner and McMullen (1982).

Woolcock, S. (1982b), 'Adjustment in Western Europe', in Turner and McMullen (1982).

Index